GRAPHOLOGY

GRAPHOLOGY

THE INTERPRETATION OF HANDWRITING

Renna Nezos

RIDER
London Melbourne Auckland Johannesburg

To La and Marie-Thérèse Iatrou

First published in 1986 by
Rider & Company, an imprint of Century Hutchinson Limited,
Brookmount House, 62–65 Chandos Place, Covent Garden,
London WC2N 4NW

Century Hutchinson Publishing Group (Australia) Pty Ltd
16–22 Church Street, Hawthorn, Melbourne, Victoria 3122

Century Hutchinson Group (NZ) Ltd
32–34 View Road, PO Box 40-086, Glenfield, Auckland 10

Century Hutchinson Group (SA) Pty Ltd
PO Box 337, Bergvlei 2012, South Africa

Set by Wyvern Typesetting Ltd, Bristol
Printed in Great Britain by
Butler & Tanner Ltd, Frome and London

British Library Cataloguing in Publication Data
Nezos, Renna
Graphology: the interpretation of handwriting
1. Graphology
I. Title
155.28'2 BF891
ISBN 0 7126 1224 6

parce que, hier soir,
tu as été si gentille
envers mes jasmins . . .

When I read this dedication on the first page of a book, it was one January evening and I had just returned home. I was disenchanted, tired and disorientated; it had just been one of those days.

The book was lying on my desk together with a small bouquet of jasmine, It was Max Pulver's *Le Symbolisme de l'Écriture*.

I stood spellbound, looking at the writing, the layout on the page, the form of the letters, the warmth; and a ray of hope and beauty reached me.

It was not the context; that took quite a while to sink in. It was the atmosphere, the 'aura' of this enchanting writing; full of harmony, rhythm, goodness and courage.

I turned to the first page and read the opening sentence: 'The feeling for and love of handwriting are spontaneous happenings. At a precise moment of our life, their written form falls suddenly under the light of our consciousness.'

How true!

CONTENTS

ACKNOWLEDGEMENTS

My thanks go to Clive Carr to whom I am especially indebted for his encouragement, advice and help. To Roddy Bloomfield for believing in the book. To Rosemary Petitt for her invaluable help and most useful suggestions and to my daughters La and Marie-Thérèse Iatrou for their suggestions, patience and humour.

My thanks also go to all whose writings appear.

GLOSSARY

allocentrism	detachment from the ego (opposed to egocentricity)
emotivity	tendency to be moved by events
filiform	thready (horizontal, elongated, wavy) stroke
Formlevel	six elements which influence the quality of the writing: organization, spontaneity, originality, dynamism, harmony, rhythm
nuancée	slight irregularities which do not affect the harmony of the writing
persona	personal mask adopted to cover the true self
progressive	the overall movement of the writing is directed towards the right with speed and economy
proteiform	many styles of forming one letter
regressive	strokes which should be directed towards the right are directed towards the left

Part I

GRAPHOLOGY

1
INTRODUCTION

Graphology is the study of the psychological structure of the human being through his or her handwriting.

The word 'graphology' is Greek and is a combination of two words: 'graphe' which means writing and 'logos', here represented in one of its nineteen meanings, as 'definition', i.e., stating the precise nature of a word, in this case 'graphe'.

Graphology is a social science and, like all such sciences, depends on research and experimentation – not on intuition or magic. There is nothing magical or mystical about graphology although intuition is extremely useful in the same way that it is useful in other disciplines such as medicine, psychology, physics, history, philosophy, chemistry and law.

Science is an organized and systematic search for knowledge having, as a target, the discovery of truth. There is no science where there is no logic and no constant comparison with reality.

Like all sciences, graphology has its rules and regulations, from which we cannot deviate without running the risk of error.

Finally, like all sciences, graphology's proponents tend to disagree. There has been argument upon argument on various points; whether, for instance, 'harmony' in a writing is a presupposition for positive interpretation of a sign or whether assessing the Formlevel* is restricting or not, and so on. In my mind the majority of the arguments spring from misunderstandings of the initial point.

But, unlike other sciences, graphology has its fierce critics and this reminds me of the words of Herbert Spencer (1820–1903): 'There is a principle which is a buffer against any information, which is proof against all argument and which does not fail to keep every human being in constant ignorance. This principle is to condemn before researching.'

Writing is a personal symbol with a rhythm and Formlevel which is also personal to each individual. It is in accordance with all other means of expression of our personality, movements or speech. It is ruled by the natural laws of expression, according to which every movement expresses an inner tension or reality. It is an outward

* See chapter 4 and Glossary.

index of inner attitudes, clearly and absolutely individualized.

The great difficulty of graphology does not lie in the interpretation of the signs but in the *correct* interpretation.

The symbol exists, it is concrete, we hold it and look at it. The subject exists, he (or she) is concrete, is unique, but we don't see him. The symbol contains the subject in his entirety. There are about 250 signs altogether and each handwriting has no more than forty to sixty. The combinations are many (but not infinite) and they need so to be to explain each person's uniqueness. Every single person who has existed, exists, or will exist in the universe is unique and must be treated as such.

We are all a combination of millions of different factors and no two people can be identical. That is why we all have different writing. Even if we have been taught the same alphabet at the same time and at the same school, the similarities will be many at the beginning but, as the years go by and we grow up, we accumulate experiences and our handwriting evolves with us and takes on a more and more personal style; it develops its own 'aura' which can only be reproduced by one person and nobody else – or almost nobody else.

There are some very rare cases, like Anna Magdalena Bach who, after living with Johan Sebastian Bach for almost thirty years and having great admiration for him, tried to identify with him to the extent of imitating his handwriting. In time her writing became so similar that Bach himself could not tell the difference. Being a musical person herself, even the signs of musicality were present in her handwriting. Cases like this are truly rare.

Let us see first what the 'aura' of a handwriting is – that unique something which is recognizable by everybody, even the non-graphologist.

To start with, it is the way the letters are formed, whether large or small, simple or complicated, joined or apart. Then it is the organization (layout) and spontaneity of the whole writing – be it a page, an envelope or a card – the way it occupies the space, such as the distances between the words or the lines. There is the dynamism of the style – the pressure, strength and speed. Finally, the more sensitive observer will be aware of the harmony and rhythm of a writing.

Whatever the interpretations we give to the various signs, we must always remember that we should never try to give an explanation to a sign on its own, or take a sign out of context. It would be too frivolous and simplistic to say: 'This "n" means egoism, or this "t" means pessimism.' They may not mean that at all. All signs have value only when constant and repetitive. A full explanation of the signs and their significance will be found later in the book.

But when we receive a letter from someone we know, we can tell who it is before we look at the name. Intuitively, we have noticed all the signs mentioned above. If we are not familiar with graphology and are asked how we can tell, we cannot answer. We simply say, 'I recognize the style.'

Handwriting is the smallest movement of the human hand and at the same time the most revealing.

It consists of minute movements flying in all directions: vertical, horizontal, diagonally upwards or downwards, right and left, curved, straight, pressed hard on the paper or lightly, done quickly or slowly.

Since the writing organ – in most cases the hand, right or left – is governed by the central nervous system, the whole process is usually unconscious and therefore very revealing.

The following diagram shows a simplified and bold interpretation of the main written movements and their directions.

Diagram 1 *Main Movements and Their Directions*

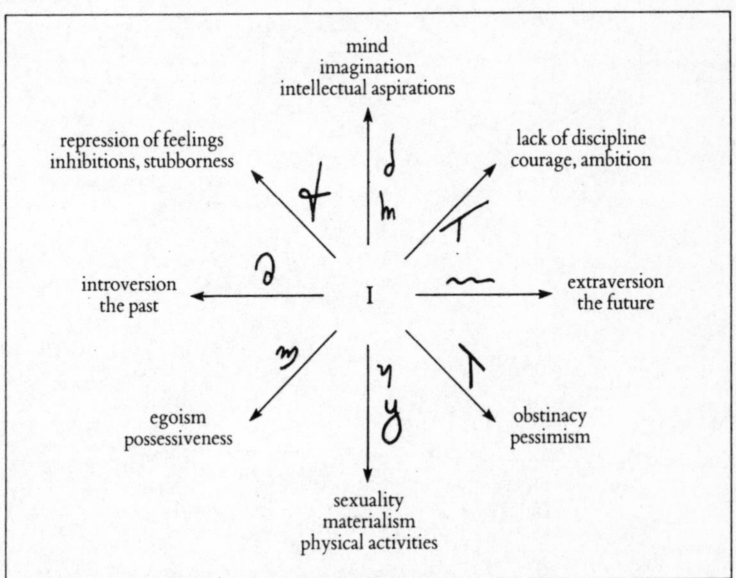

The interpretation of signs is a framework to enable us to make a beginning. The rest depends on the personal knowledge and experience of the interpreter.

The first great obstacle is the correct assessment of the Formlevel.
The second great obstacle is the discovery of harmony.
The third great obstacle is the observation of rhythm.
The fourth great obstacle is the correct classification.
The fifth great obstacle is the correct definition.
The sixth great obstacle is the correct interpretation.

One basic rule of graphology is as follows: the value of a sign is not fixed; its interpretation depends on four factors:

1. The number of times a sign is repeated on the same page;
2. The written zone in which the sign appears (Max Pulver);
3. On the rest of the signs, and
4. The Formlevel of the handwriting (Klages).

2

HISTORY

Graphology has a long and honourable history. We know, for example, that reference to disclosures obtained from handwriting has been attributed to the philosopher Aristotle (384–322 BC), the orator and writer Demetrios Falirefs (309 BC), the poet Menandros Athenaios (born the third year of the 109th Olympiad) and writer Dionysos Alikarnasefs (first century BC) etc. But the first book on the subject only appeared in 1622 in Capri, Italy.

Camillo Baldo, physician, writer and professor of philosophy in the University of Bologna, published a treatise on how to know the nature of a person from his handwriting.*

For a further century graphology remained a hobby for those such as Grohman who, in 1792, published a book on writing in which he says that it is possible to assess even the physique of the body, the voice, the colour of the hair and the eyes from the handwriting alone.

Goethe (1749–1832) was intrigued by some observations he had made and persuaded his friend Lavater to do some research. 'I find an admirable analogy between the speech, the walk and the writing of the majority of people,' Lavater wrote later. He had noticed that the human being constitutes a unity in which everything follows the same pattern. We will never find, for instance, an active man dragging his legs along when walking or speaking or writing in a slow, bored manner; in the same way we never find a non-active man having a swift, light, perky writing.

In 1814 another writer wrote a book under the title, *The Art of Judging the Mind and the Character of Men and Women from Their Handwriting*. It has been suggested that this book was written by Edouard Hocquart (1787–1870), author of another very interesting book, *Physionomie des Hommes Politiques*, which also contains some pages on graphology.

By 1830 in France there was a school of the interpretation of writing, run by Abbé Flandrin who spent most of his life in the research of graphology. But it is not until Abbé Jean-Hippolyte Michon (1806–81) got to work that the ball really started rolling.

* *Trattato come de una Lettera Missiva si Cognoscano La Natura e Qualitá del ó scrittore*, Capri, 1622.

Born in La Roche-Fressange, in France, Michon was a man of culture and great intellectual capacity. For over thirty years he collected thousands of examples of handwriting and signatures, and studied them in the most minute detail. Every single element in the handwriting he named a 'sign', corresponding to a character trait of the writer.

In 1871 he founded the Societé Française de Graphologie in Paris, which celebrated its centenary on 20 March 1971, almost simultaneously with its official recognition of 'utilité publique' by enactment.

In 1872 Michon published his book *Les Mystères de l'Écriture*, and in 1873 he started publishing the periodical, *La Graphologie*, which, in spite of some interruptions over the years, is still being published today by the Société Française de Graphologie as a quarterly journal.

In 1878 he published his second book on the subject: '*La Méthode Pratique de Graphologie*.*

Abbé Michon was not only the godfather of this science but also, despite the criticism he has suffered from our contemporaries, he is indisputably the founder of graphology. He discovered it and laid the foundations of a science. He opened the ground for research to future generations of graphologists.

It is true that his work was based on a 'constant interpretation of signs' (theory of the fixed sign), to the extent that the absence of a sign from a specimen indicated a fault or quality opposite to that which its presence would indicate (theory of negative signs). This is a serious mistake, but let us not forget that graphology in his time was in its infancy.

A few years after Michon's death, his pupil and successor, and often his critic too, Jean Crépieux-Jamin (born in Arras, France, in 1858 and died 24th October 1940), revised the whole of his teacher's work, reclassified and regrouped the system of signs and established new laws on the classification of the signs that are still in use today.

In 1888 Crépieux-Jamin published his famous book *L'Ecriture et le Caractère* which, by 1975, had reached seventeen editions and is included in the works of the Bibliothéque de Philosophie Contemporaine. It has been translated into Spanish, German and English.† He wrote ten books altogether, among them *L'Age et le Sêxe dans l'Écriture, Les Bases Fondamentales de la Graphologie et de*

* Republished by Payot, *Systême de Graphologie*, 1947.

† A copy of this book can be found in the University of Cambridge Library. The copy at the British Museum Library was destroyed in the Blitz.

l'Expertise en Écriture and, finally, in 1929 his masterpiece: *L'ABC de la Graphologie*. In this last book, Crépieux-Jamin consolidates the results of his fifty years of research and gives graphology a sound scientific basis.

Towards the end of the nineteenth century, the Germans began to lead the way in graphological research work.

William Thierry Preyer, a professor of physiology at Jena, was the first to show that handwriting is really brain writing and that it is of no importance which organ directs the instrument with which we write. It can be either the hand (right or left), the foot, the mouth or even the chin and shoulder.

There are numerous examples of writing without the use of a hand, such as Aimé Rapin, the Swiss artist born without arms, who wrote with her foot. Or our contemporary Denise Légrix, the French artist and writer, born without legs or arms, who paints and writes by fixing the brush or pen under her left 'arm' which stops above the elbow.

Crippled people do not have special writing. Training and education eliminate the effects. There are many people who have lost their writing arm and have to learn to write with another limb. At the beginning their writing is very deformed but, little by little, it becomes identical to their previous writing.

Thus the first law of writing is formed: 'The written movement is under the direct influence of the central nervous system. Its form is not modified by the writing organ if the latter functions normally and is sufficiently adapted to its function.' (See p. 13).

Around 1900, Dr Ludwig Klages (1872–1956), physicist, chemist, philosopher, psychologist, characterologist and graphologist, formed his own school. He kept the observations and classifications of Crépieux-Jamin and added his own philosophical ideas on the expressive value of movement, such as the antagonism between *Seele* (soul) and *Geist* (spirit); Apollo and Dionysos; 'polarity', positive and negative, plus (+) and minus (−).

He considered Apollo a negation of life and Dionysos the warmth and plenitude of spontaneity.

He introduced the positive and negative interpretation of signs according to the Formlevel (see p. 21).

Klages introduced an understanding of rhythm in handwriting which, harmoniously developed, defines the Formlevel of the writing: spontaneity, identity, the happy medium between an uneven and a monotonous writing; the succession of movements which, without ever being repeated in exactly the same form, stay harmonious and keep an unconscious order and natural balance. Rhythm is perhaps the most difficult sign to discover, define and evaluate in a handwriting. Rhythm for Klages was an 'indefinite something that can only be understood intuitively'.*

He explains the concept of bipolarity very clearly. In a 'regular' writing, if the Formlevel (FL) is high (+), he interprets regularity as power of will; if the FL is low (−) he stresses the lack of depth of feelings. In an 'irregular' writing, if the FL is high (+), he sees the power of depth of feeling and if the FL is low (−), the lack of will-power.

We do not go as far as that, although this notion of bipolarity is extremely valuable for every psychological interpretation of the signs, and for the build-up of the final portrait.

Another great master of graphology is the Swiss Max Pulver (1890–1953), writer, poet, philosopher and lecturer in graphology at the University of Zurich. He discovered the 'Symbolism of Space' which he elaborated in his book, *Symbolik der Handschrift*, published in 1931 in Zurich. In this study, depth psychology plays a big part.

Pulver was the first to introduce psychoanalysis to graphology. His contribution to handwriting analysis is tremendous. The most important books which he wrote, apart from the one already mentioned, are: *Trieb und Verbrechen in der Handschrift* and his last one, *Intelligenz im Schriftausdruck*.

Pulver pointed out the 'ambivalence' of the human nature which can be a limiting situation if we are unable to achieve a balance between our opposing and compensatory tendencies.

Ambivalence covers the range of human nature. It can be sexual, emotional or spiritual. For Pulver, the fundamental antithesis which characterizes ambivalence plays an indispensable role in personal development through the dynamic activity which it provokes. In the written field ambivalence is shown by the irregularities apparent in all the categories of signs and in all three zones of writing.

Furthermore, Pulver explained 'rhythm'; he introduced the concept of a three-dimensional written field; vertical, horizontal and depth. He also discovered the 'symbolism' of movement, of the various directions and of the stroke layout.

He studied the subject of 'insincerity' (dishonesty) in depth. He considered lying as a symptom of some particular psychological state. He pointed out that, although fast writing, for example, may indicate more sincerity than slow writing, slow writing should not

* *L'Expression du Caractère dans l'Écriture*, first published in German in 1917 (*Handschrift und Charakter*). The twenty-third edition has been translated into French and published by Delachaux-Niêstlé, 1953. See also *Graphologie*, Paris, 1943, and *Les Principes de la Caractèrologie*, Delachaux-Niêstlé, 1950.

necessarily indicate insincerity. He built up an elaborate list of signs indicative of dishonesty under certain conditions.

After the Second World War and for the first time in the history of this science, at least to my knowledge, a seat was given in the medical school of the University of Hamburg to Rudolf Pophal, a German neurologist who opened a new field of inquiry into graphology: the motor-physiological. He taught graphology at the University from 1946 until 1958. He published several books on the subject, one of which was *Die Handschrift als Gehirnschrift* in 1949 and his latest in 1968, *Kinetische Graphologie*. He also published manuals on graphological theory and the interpretation of handwriting for his students who were psychologists and criminologists.

His student and disciple, Heinrich Pfnanne, developed further research for a connection between the brain centres and handwriting. His book *Lehrbuch der Graphologie* is an important manual on graphology.

Unfortunately, none of the above books have as yet been translated into French or English.

Returning to France; in the last fifty years, many great pioneers have done serious work and fruitful research in various fields of graphology, graphometry, graphotherapy and criminological graphology. These pioneers include the following:

Walter Hegar, a German graphologist, fled to France from Nazi Germany in the early 1930s and developed his own system based on the stroke alone. He was the bitterest critic of Klages's system. He called the Formlevel 'fiction', 'theory' and 'scientific sterility'. In his book *Graphologie par le Trait* (Paris, 1938) Hegar develops his methodological study of the stroke. His reasoning is simple: the stroke is measurable and the only direct contact with the object, i.e., the paper. It is an interesting approach, albeit somewhat limited.

Dr Paul Carton, the renovator of Hippocrates's 'naturism', discovered the graphological signs of the four temperaments: Choleric, Melancholic, Sanguine and Phlegmatic. He wrote two excellent books, *Diagnostique et Conduite des Tempéraments* (1947) and *Diagnostique de la Mentalité par l'Écriture* (1967).

René Le Senne who, simultaneously with Professors Heymans and Wiersma of the University of Groningen, studied for many years the differences between the characters of people, developed a system of characterological types which is not only intellectually understandable but can also withstand confrontation, scrutiny or analysis. In his book *Traité de Caractèrologie* (Paris, 1945), he gives a clear definition of character: 'The totality of congenital dispositions which form the mental skeleton of a person.' Le Senne was very interested in the connection between characterology and handwriting.

After his death, in 1954, a manuscript was found on his desk. It was the work of the graphologist Emile Caille who has introduced characterological analysis to graphology. His book, *Caractères et Écritures*, establishes the correlation between handwriting and character.

Ania Teillard was a disciple of Jung's for over thirty years. Under his guidance Teillard developed her system of introducing depth psychology to handwriting analysis. She applied Jung's four main functions: thinking, intuition, sensation and sentiment (feeling) to graphology, together with the two attitudes: extrovert–introvert, the two tendencies: animus–anima and the persona.

Her book *L'Âme et l'Écriture* most recently republished in 1981, is a valuable manual of graphology and indispensable to every serious practitioner.

In the 1950s the Société Française de Graphologie, applied to graphology some of the most recent developments in psychological theories (such as Jung, Freud and Adler). In her book *Apprenez la Graphologie*, Madame Gabrielle Beauchataud incorporated some of these theories. It was the first time that a book on graphology included a number of established psychological approaches such as Characterology, the Temperaments and Jung's typologies.

Hélène Koechlin-St Morand applied the eight mythological (or planetary) types – developed by M. Munzinger and based upon the four elements: water, air, earth, fire – to graphology. Her books: *Graphologie. L'Ecriture et la Typologie Planétaire* and *Les Tempéraments* (1965) are very clear and contain very good examples of writings of the four temperaments.

3

THE LAWS OF WRITING

There are five basic and universal laws upon which graphology depends, as first propounded by W. T. Preyer, Solange Pellat and Gregorio Garavito, German, French and Columbian graphologists respectively.

These laws are essentially independent of the alphabet used. The types of letters are irrelevant. Alphabets are human inventions based on local needs. The laws of writing, on the other hand, are natural phenomena.

However, there are two remarks to be made:

1. Each one of these laws is manifested more frequently or in a more tangible way in a particular alphabet rather than another.
2. To understand them, it helps if we take examples of phenomena appearing in a specific alphabet.

Equally, we must not lose sight of a principle, the ignorance of which has caused much misunderstanding. This principle is: even though the laws of writing are exact and the same cause has the same effect, similar written phenomena may derive from different sources. For instance the following example, though incorrect, makes the point: spots on your nose always cause angular writing, but angular writing may also be caused by spots on your bottom! In this respect, graphology does not differ from other natural sciences.

Let us specify these laws of writing:

The first law is an acknowledgement of source and is of primary importance:

The written movement is under the direct influence of the central nervous system which comprises the brain, the cerebellum and the spinal liquid. The form of the written movement is not modified by the writing organ (hand, foot, mouth, etc.), if this functions normally and is sufficiently adapted to its function.

Fifty years ago there was a difference of opinion about this principle and some thought it to be mistaken.

The misunderstanding came from the fact that the action of the writing organ is seen to be laboured and unnatural when it is not adapted to its function. The writing organ, however – right or left hand or foot, mouth, arm, neck and shoulder – will only act as an imperfect transmitter if it is defective or if it has not yet acquired the necessary training (example 62).

The writing of a right-handed person who lost his or her right arm is very deformed but, little by little and with practice, it will approach the style of the lost right hand and eventually the writing will be identical. Many mutilated people have confirmed this. The same is true for left-handed people.

An easy experiment is to sit comfortably on a flat rock on a beach of fine sand and try to write with the end of your foot, loosening up, relaxing and allowing your natural ability to function. The letters will be very large and the pressure will not be differentiated between the down strokes and up strokes, but you will soon realize that the generating movement of the strokes is the same as that with which you write on paper.

The cerebral influence on writing is also supported by the fact that physiologists have never been able to discover a criterion which will permit them to tell, with certainty, the differences between the brains of the two sexes; neither have graphologists ever discovered any certain differences between the writing of the two sexes. So the conclusion is evident that in all human beings tendencies of the opposite sex exist, more or less unconscious and more or less able to manifest themselves. Handwriting, having its origins in the whole personality, shows these tendencies, even the most unconscious ones. But although we can see a feminine or masculine tendency in a writing, the physical organs that constitute the differences between the sexes are neither animating nor directional, i.e., they, in themselves, do not make their owner behave in a certain fashion. They only construct a part of the personality which may be the most visible, but the underlying tendencies are much more complex and definitely more important.

We all have met men who behave like women and women who behave like men. If sexual differences were as all-important as some psychologists, such as Freud, made them out to be, then all sexually normal men (or all sexually normal women) would have a similar psychological structure and behaviour – which they do not.

Now we come to the second law. This tells us that:

When we write, the 'ego' is active but is not always active to the same degree. Its activity comes and goes, waxes and wanes, being at its highest level when an effort has to be made by the writer (e.g. at the beginning of a word) and at its lowest level when the motion of the writing organ has gained momentum and is driven by it (e.g. at the end of words).

This is a phenomenon that exists in a more or less continuous way in normal people who are aware that they write, when they write.

This ability may disappear in alienated people. If they write at that time, their writing will be a series of words put on paper as if by an automaton.

This law justifies what graphologists have always stated about capital letter which are the start of the writing effort: that under the influence of pride, vanity or arrogance, these initial letters take ample dimensions.

The third law says that:

We cannot voluntarily modify our natural writing at any given time without putting in it the marks of the effort required to obtain the change.

The marks of the effort required to change our writing are many and fall under all eight categories*, e.g. brusque stops, hooks, breakings, deviations, unnatural thinning or thickening of the strokes, etc. They can be confused with signs of distraction or uncertainty, the difference being that an effort to change the writing is voluntary and conscious, whereas distraction and uncertainty are not voluntary or conscious.

Long practice may make fluent an artificial or disguised writing by more or less eliminating the marks of effort; the disguise, however, will always be limited because, if we chase away nature, she will return galloping!

Graphologists will be helped by the study of the 'will' in writing, since it is natural, as we know, for initial attention and effort, stimulated by the will, to diminish in accordance with the degree of intensity of the will.

To detect this attention and effort, there is no better way than to study the written signs of speed and form, especially in the independent elements of the handwriting.

Law number four is about the circumstances under which we write:

The writer who writes under circumstances where the action of writing is particularly difficult, will instinctively use either the forms of letters which are more familiar to him, or forms of letters which are simple and easy to write.

This law is, of course, based on the principle of the 'easiest way out'.

The law covers all manner of situations, such as:

* By 'categories' are meant 'genres' as used by Crépieux-Jamin.

1. People who wish to try to write with their other hand;
2. People who need to add a word or a group of words between the lines of a manuscript;
3. People who write in moving vehicles; and
4. Ill, weakened people who have to write a testament by hand but they are in an uncomfortable position, probably in bed, etc.

The last two laws – three and four – are particularly important for the expert in graphological crime, i.e. anonymous letters, verification of the identity of the writer or suspected fraud (particularly in wills).

The fifth law has the title: *General and fundamental law of individual manifestation.*

The physiological mechanisms which produce the written movement are in correlation with the state of the central nervous system and vary in accordance with it. The written strokes, therefore, are in correspondence with the constitutional varieties of the nervous system and with the momentary modifications of each nervous system.

Briefly, writing varies in accordance with the mental particularities and the temporary dispositions of each one of us.

It has been argued, in connection with this law, that people can imitate its effects. This possibility necessitates education, great care and, particularly, great suppleness of the writing organ, the combination of which, in reality, is the privilege of a very small number of people. Here it must be pointed out, once more, that if we try to voluntarily modify our writing, nature's revenge is instantaneous.

Let us take an example. If we were to try to change our writing, let us say, for reasons of fraud, we would try, if we were clever, to change as many signs of our real writing as we could because, if we didn't, we would risk being found out. So if we had a naturally simple writing we would ornate it. If our writing was small we would make it big, etc., until we ended up with a burlesque, unbalanced concoction.

Just as if we removed the 'make-up' of a clown, however, we would see the real man underneath, so a competent graphologist should be able to wash off the make-up of the writing and see the real person underneath.

But let us take another example nearer to our hearts:

Usually, people who start learning graphology, start changing their writing. They try to shed off the 'bad signs' and imitate the 'good signs'. Unless the 'good signs' are hidden within us, however, we cannot put them on like a frock. We don't become ballerinas by putting on a tutu, we only become ridiculous and foolish. This is what would happen to our writing and, if we insist on wearing a tutu we would soon end up as unbalanced, nervous wrecks.

On the other hand, if we already have the quality represented by the sign we wish to acquire, then the change will only bring it out as it should have been naturally in the first place, and there is nothing wrong with that.

As you will have noticed this last law is a dual one; it deals with the variability of the constitution of the nervous system and with the momentary modifications of each nervous system.

The first part of it was established through observation. The second was established through experimentation.

The elements of observation which allowed the first part to be formed are the following:

1. The observation of the written similarities of individuals of the same psychic particularities;
2. The comparison of written characteristics of different races; and
3. The study of the evolution of the writing of one race through the different stages of its civilization.

The experimental observations underlying the second part of this fifth law are as follows:

1. The direct observation of passing modifications of writing under the influence of circumstances acting on individuals where it was possible to observe sufficiently continuously;
2. Observation of the writing phenomena produced spontaneously in the writing of the observers themselves, whilst under stress or a particular state of mind;
3. The study of the modifications produced in the writings of a subject under the temporary influence of imposed circumstances, e.g. hypnosis; and
4. The study of written tendencies spontaneously manifested in successive writings of a subject under hypnosis or during specific feelings, successively provoked.

The last two observations are experimental. The fourth has raised great interest among many learned people. Drs Ferrari, Hericourt and Charles Richet, nineteenth-century psychiatrists, adopted this method for their own research. They published their results in the *Revue Philosophique*, Vol. XXI, April 1886:

'It was suggested to Mr X that he was, in succession, a veined and crafty peasant, a miser and then a very old man. His face and general appearance changed and was modified to match each suggested personality. When asked to write at the same time, we observed that his writing underwent the same modifications, particular to each new state of consciousness. Briefly, the writing movement was transformed in accordance with the rest of the personality.

Another experiment was made with a woman to whom it was suggested, under hypnosis, that she was, first, Napoleon and then herself at the age of twelve years. Her writing became, once again, typical of these two totally opposed personalities.

The first conclusion to be drawn from these experiments is that the writing follows the variations of the personality.

From this we can establish the principle of the validity of graphology.

These experiments also show that the variations of writing, observed in parallel with the variations of personality, represent at least, in their general traits, the characteristic signs attributed by graphologists to the suggested personalities.

To avoid all misunderstanding', says Solange Pellat, 'I will stress here that the fictitious personality of Napoleon did not make the woman's writing identical to Napoleon's, it showed only the manifestations of the general's character, which was only what was suggested to the woman.

I must also point out that experiments of this kind should not be undertaken by hypnotists who might involuntarily suggest a type of writing at the same time as indicating a type of personality. The graphologist must analyse the writings afterwards and not during the experiment.'

This concludes the five basic and universal laws of writing which we will call the Natural Laws of Writing.

Before we conclude, we must draw your attention to three other laws concerning the science of graphology only, that Crépieux-Jamin himself established. They have been translated from the French by Alex Tulloch, a Scottish graphologist.

First Law:
One must examine the significance of a handwriting trait by considering it as a physiological movement and by comparing the quality, overall size, regularity and consistency of energy with the corresponding psychological movement.

Second Law:
There are no independent signs; there are only general indications which may have different forms. The significance of these general indications can be assessed accurately by tracing them back to their origins and adapting the meaning of the latter to the conditions of the milieu in which the form appears.

Third Law:
One graphological sign does not necessarily represent a single character trait. For example, rising handwriting may indicate ardour, activity, ambition, momentary joy or folly. The value of the sign depends on its cause, its context and its intensity. Handwriting which slopes downwards, for instance, may reveal a passing anxiety, habitual depression or simply bad positioning of the paper.

These, Crépieux-Jamin's own laws, are evidently the golden rules of graphology today. Every serious scientific graphologist abides by them. If he or she does not, he is an artist in fortune telling rather than a graphologist.

4

SYSTEMS OF GRAPHOLOGY

Pulver – Symbolism of Space

As previously indicated (p. 10), Max Pulver introduced the phrase, Symbolism of Space, and applied it to the three zones of writing. The upper extensions indicate matters of the mind, the middle zone indicates emotions and the lower extensions indicate our more materialistic interests.* The connection with the human body is evident.

Diagram 2, 'Symbolism of Space', illustrates the meaning of the three zones.

Perhaps it is appropriate here to mention the conventional size of each zone. All letters without upper or lower extensions (o, i, a, m, etc.) as well as the heads of g, y, p and q, and the base of the letters b, d, h and k, are considered middle zone and should measure between 1½–2½ mm. From 1–1½ mm a writing is called 'small'. Under 1 mm it is called 'very small'. From 2½–4 mm it is called 'large', from 4–6 mm it is called 'very large', and anything over 6–7 mm is called 'exaggerated' writing.

The upper extensions and lower extensions, i.e., l, f, g, etc., in a writing where the middle zone is 2 mm high, should be 4½ mm from the base line, and, in a 3-mm middle zone, 6 mm.

The width of the letters should be approximately equal to the height of the middle-zone letter n or u in each writing. If it is narrower, the writing is called 'squeezed'; if it is wider it is called 'spread out'.

If one zone is more developed than the other two, it means that this writer's interests are more towards the indications of the relevant zone as shown in Diagram 2. That is why the zone in which a sign appears is so important in an interpretation.

* Max Pulver, *Le Symbolisme de l'Écriture*, Stock, Paris, 1953.

Diagram 2 *Symbolism of Space*

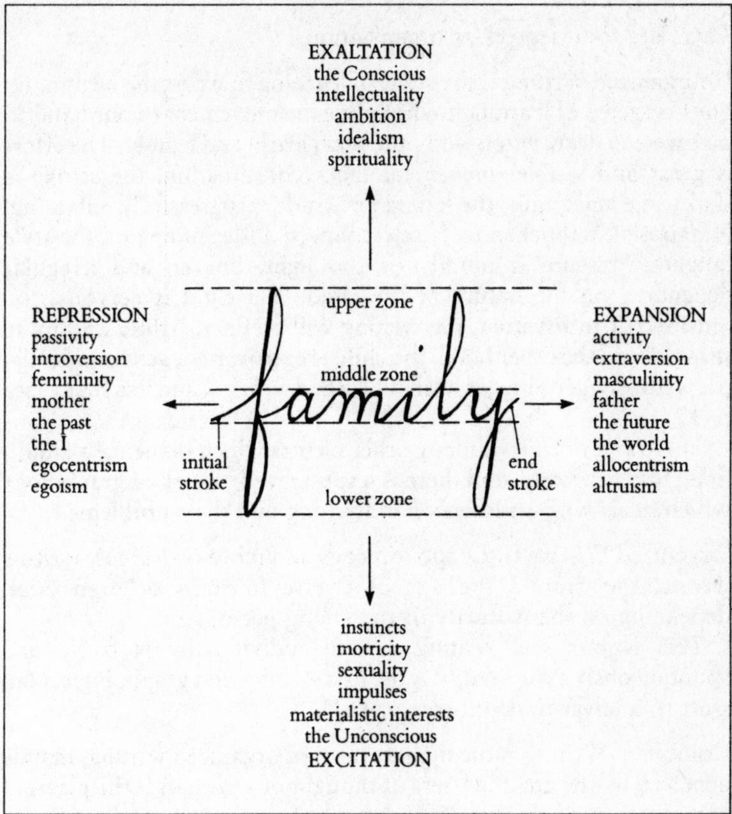

Klages – Formlevel

The Formlevel, as developed by Klages, consists of the combination of six basic elements:

1. The degree of *organization* of the writing;
2. The *spontaneity* of the handwriting;
3. The *originality* of the style;
4. The *dynamism* of the stroke;
5. The *harmony*;
6. The *rhythm*.

Organization

There are four degrees of organization:

Unorganized Writing is the stage of learning to write, the beginning; our first years of learning to discipline the movement of our hand so that we can draw letters and numbers clearly and legibly. The effort is great and visible; movement lacks coordination, the stroke is shaky and uncertain, the letters are crude, progressively enlarging, juxtaposed, retouched or falsely connected (depending on the style taught). Pressure is muddy or too light, uneven and irregular depending on the nature of the child. If a child is nervous, too sensitive or introverted, the writing will be finer, lighter and more shaky. If, on the other hand, the child is extroverted, active and jolly, the writing will be bigger, well nourished with ink and less shaky (see p. 174).

There are, of course, many other factors which influence a child's first efforts to write, and there is a specialized branch of graphology which deals with children's handwriting and their problems.*

Organized Writing is the spontaneous and more-or-less fast writing we achieve around the age of twelve–fourteen or even later, depending on the maturity of the young person.

This is our real writing as our individuality is freely and spontaneously expressed; it is the first writing that graphologists can start to analyse in depth (see p. 161).

Combined Writing is the highest form of organized writing, mainly achieved by the great masters of thought or action. It is the pleasant combination of two or three letters of one word resulting in an elegant and original shape without any unbecoming exaggerations and without losing legibility; although, if any exaggeration occurs yet it is still pleasant, elegant and legible, it does not diminish the standard because it shows an original and creative mind (see p. 149).

This degree of organization is not very common.

Disorganized Writing is usually the result of disease, intoxication, old age, etc., but it still retains the signs of past organization. It is characterized by shakiness, unevenness, fading pressure, thinning of the trail and lack of precision (see p. 153).

* Three of the best books on this subject are: *L'Écriture de l'Enfant* by J. de Ajuriaguerra, *et al.*, published by Delachaux-Niêstlé, Paris; *La Connaissance de l'Enfant par l'Écriture* by Jaqueline Peugeot, published by Privat, Toulouse, and *Votre Enfant: son Écriture* by Marthe Lesourd, Hachette, Paris.

Disorganization can happen at any time in life, it is not confined to old age, and this is one of the reasons why the age of the writer must always be known to the graphologist in order to avoid gross errors of interpretation. The same applies for all four degrees of organization.

Spontaneity

A writing is called 'spontaneous' when the written movement is fluent and free from any signs of effort or constraint (see p. 145).

Spontaneity of writing is often a sign of honesty; the writer feels he has nothing to hide; he has enough confidence in himself and he has better things to do than waste his time writing in an elaborate, laborious fashion. In other words, he cares more about what he writes than how he forms the loops or crosses the t's.

Originality

This writing has spontaneously original forms, far removed from any calligraphic style. The writer has original ideas and the ability to conceive things in a personal manner (see p. 118).

If the original forms are crude, unpleasant and illegible, the writing will be 'crude' and 'illegible', rather than 'original'.

Dynamism

Dynamic writing is vigorous, with good healthy pressure, ample flowing movement, decisiveness and spontaneity (see p. 136).

It shows a dynamic and decisive personality, energetic, active, quick thinking, full of enthusiasm and vigour.

Harmony

Harmony consists of six elements:

1. Proportion: when all proportions of a handwriting are in harmony and there are no striking or shocking exaggerations;
2. Order: the writing is well placed on the page and the layout is harmonious, the paragraphs well kept and the date, signature etc. placed in an aesthetic manner;
3. Clarity: this presupposes no erasings, no scratches, no crossing outs. The writing must be easily legible and clear, the layout orderly and harmonious;
4. Simplicity: a simple writing without mannerisms;

5. Sobriety: the writing is contained within moderate dimensions;
6. Freedom of movement: the writing contains no signs of effort.

A 'harmonious' writing indicates a harmonious character. Harmony is the result of a well-balanced mind and the 'indication of general superiority', according to Crépieux-Jamin.

Rhythm

Rhythm is the periodic reproduction of similar phenomena without monotony. Small inequalities, constantly repeated, similar but never identical, give rhythm to writing.

The rhythm of a writing presupposes good proportion. It is a force which causes no turbulence.

Rhythm indicates a well-balanced character and a brilliant personality; optimism, inspiration, confidence in life, harmonious sensibility, receptivity and a good balance of the four functions: thinking, feeling, sensation and intuition (see p. 218). Rhythm is one of the very few signs that has no negative interpretation.

'Short rhythm' applies to words alone; and 'long rhythm' applies when the writing spreads along a symmetric movement of line or page.

Crépieux-Jamin gives the synonym of rhythm as 'symmetric and cadenced', and the antonym as 'regular'. A. Vels, the contemporary Spanish graphologist, suggests that rhythm is opposed to 'monotonous, automatic or chronometric movement'.

Klages calls rhythm 'the primordial manifestation of life'. It 'embraces all the organic world.' It is 'the beat of the wings of the migrant birds, the trot of wild horses, the undulating gliding of fish.' It is 'as impossible for birds to fly, for horses to trot, for fish to swim in strict time, as it is for humans to breath in tempo with a metronome.'* The combination of the above elements – organization, spontaneity, originality, dynamism, harmony and rhythm – construct the Formlevel (FL) of a handwriting.

Rhythm belongs to the specific group or category of signs called Continuity (p. 168).†

Many causes may influence the rhythm of a writing: anger, hesitation, hastiness, depression, cold, etc. These causes may be physiological as well as pathological of the circulatory or respiratory

* L. Klages, *Expression du Caractère dans l'Écriture* pp. 40–44.

† L. K. Given-Wilson in his translation of Crépieux-Jamin's works under the title, *The Psychology of the Movements of Handwriting*, George Routledge & Sons Ltd, London, 1926.

systems. It is very important to establish that a broken rhythm is not merely accidental – a bad quality pen or paper or difficult circumstances under which the writer was writing, for instance, in a moving train, boat or car, or under the influence of alcohol.

A rhythmic writing is immediately evident to the observer irrespective of context or language.

Note: Rhythm is not necessarily consistent in all rhythmic writings.

The FL corresponds with the real nature of the writer and it is measured in five grades – with divisions – '1', being the highest grade, is extremely rare and '5', being the lowest, is also as rare. Ludwig van Beethoven and Friedrich Nietzsche had writings of the highest FL grade; the average person will range from 2½ to 3½.

However, it is advisable, when evaluating a handwriting, to use the terms 'high', 'medium' or 'low' rather than precise numbers.

The graphologist first examines the FL when he starts to evaluate a handwriting. This assessment is critical because each sign has more than one significance depending on the standard of the FL and the rest of the signs. That is why, on their own, signs mean absolutely nothing.

Qualities which Influence the FL

Education and *culture* play very important roles in the FL. They help the graphologist by making the writing more expressive. The less the education and culture of the individual, the less informative is his handwriting and the lower the FL is likely to be.

There are other factors that can make a writing 'silent' or non-expressive; for instance, when the individuality of a person is hidden, suppressed or so weak that it is almost non-existent. Such writing is called a 'persona' writing, hiding the true self under acquired behaviour.

Conventional, calligraphic, commercial and, indeed, all stylized writings are defined as persona. They all have one common denominator; they are imitative and therefore collective – and, of course, unspontaneous.

The more evolved a person is, the further is his handwriting from calligraphy, since the less need he has to imitate or hide.

Another element of the character of the writer that affects the grade of the FL is *integrity*. Not only as opposed to deceit, but also as regards discipline and justice. Integrity, being a composite element, is one of the most difficult all-round signs to assess in a writing. We are not considering that unconscious, spontaneous honesty which is rare other than in young children. We are talking about the ordinary, commonplace and very conscious honesty in every domain and activity of the individual.

A person can be honest in his dealings with money but dishonest in his attitude towards others or himself. Everybody has the ability to think dishonestly. What matters though is how this affects our feelings, actions and behaviour, as well as other people. Take modesty, for example. This, much praised, so-called virtue affects our honesty as much as pomposity does. It is as dishonest to be modest as it is to be pompous. Only a person with an objective mind can free himself from self-involvement in such emotions, assess his own real value and feel and behave accordingly.

One more element which plays a very important role in the FL is plain simple *niceness*. Positive thinking and kindness of the heart increase the Formlevel even when education has been inadequate, just as meanness of spirit diminishes it in spite of a good education.

The next very important element is *intelligence*; that much discussed, analysed, disputed and variously defined quality of the mind, which has been the subject of great research over the centuries and still is. But no matter how it is defined, in one way or the other, in different fields and in varied degrees, we all have intelligence.

The individual qualities, formed by heredity, the ability to assimilate, effects of education, family background and habits acquired over the years from the environment, play a tremendous part in the volume of intelligence as well as in the way it is manifested.

The proportion of inherited qualities to acquired ones has not yet been satisfactorily assessed. There are many theories but, for our purposes, we will assume that both are equally important.

Lastly, *dynamism*. This is an inner motivation composed of four factors: the excitability of feeling (sentiment), personal abilities (talent), will-power and the ability to exteriorize. All these four factors are inherent to the individual.

Excitability of feeling, which is connected with character, is the ability to feel strongly and deeply. The sentiment then is transformed into energy from within.

Personal ability is talent: music, poetry, architecture, painting or any other talent. This can be developed if it is already present, manifest or latent. It can not be created (at least not in ordinary people).

Will-power is the wish, together with constant, conscious ability, to regulate life according to logical decisions. It directs us towards specific targets.

Ability to exteriorize is the ability to express our feelings and wishes and the need to do so.

Although we may be able to cultivate and develop will-power and the ability to exteriorize, we can do very little about feeling and personal ability.

We have reviewed the elements that affect the FL; education, culture, evolution of the individual, integrity, kindness, intelligence and dynamism. But how do they appear in the handwriting? The answer is not simple. As I have already mentioned, there is no one sign which indicates any one specific thing. What we can say is that a writing which is spontaneous and simplified, original, with happily combined letters, harmonious, rhythmic and containing no exaggeration, is more likely to be of a high FL than otherwise. Exaggerations and disproportions are signs of negative interpretation. Simplification, however, should not work to the detriment of legibility because then the FL also diminishes. Moderation is the golden rule.

To summarize the signs which indicate the Formlevel:

High FL is indicated by rhythm (succession of similar but never strictly identical movements), good distribution of black and white, aesthetic proportion of letters and a consistency and regularity which is pleasing but never too rigid.

Low FL is indicated by emptiness, mechanical movement, lack of expression, a monotonous writing without colour or individuality, messy, muddy or with an exaggerated, lifeless style.

High FL 1–2	*Low FL: 4–5*	
rhythmic – nuancée	monotonous	
	calligraphic	stylized
spontaneous	conventional	stylized
	artificial, etc.	stylized
original	impersonal	
elegant	crude	
harmonious	inharmonious	
well nourished	pale	
dynamic	weak	
supple (slight variations)	rigid	
proportionate	disproportionate	
simplified	ornate	
with relief	flat	
sober – nuancée	exaggerated	
light	heavy	

Note: the FL does not necessarily indicate vitality, physical dynamism or emotivity – it only shows the quality of the soul.

Hegar – the Stroke

Walter Hegar developed his own graphological system which was based on four basic graphological factors: pressure (heavy or light), the quality of the stroke (precise or pasty), movement (straight or curved) and speed (rapid or slow).

He felt that these were the only elements which were not influenced by the writer's directive images but were directly related to his individual temperament.

The combination of heavy, precise, straight and rapid indicate energy in action, whereas the opposite combination of light, pasty, curved and slow, show little reaction.

The combination of these opposites gives sixteen types as shown in the following table.

It must be noted that, for Hegar, pasty writing was 'fluffy borders of the stroke' or 'blurred' because, when he wrote (in the 1930s), there were no ball-point or felt-tip pens and so variations of the stroke were produced only from the way the writer held his pen and not from a choice of writing instrument as is possible today.

Sixteen Types of Stroke

	Active	*Passive*
Pressure	Heavy	Light
Stroke	Precise	Pasty
Movement	Straight	Curved
Speed	Rapid	Slow

Abbreviations:
h = heavy, pr = precise, st = straight, r = rapid, l = light, p = pasty, c = curved, sl = slow

I. Harmonious type indicating pure activity:
h + pr + st + r (1, 3, 6, 13, 16, 22).

II. Harmonious type indicating pure passivity:
l + p + c + sl (8, 10, 11, 18, 19, 23).

III–VI. Types having three active elements and one passive:
- III. h + pr + st + sl (1, 4, 6, 14, 16, 24).
- IV. h + pr + c + r (2, 3, 6, 17, 20, 22).
- V. a + p + st + r (1, 3, 5, 13, 15, 21).
- VI. l + pr + st + r (7, 9, 12, 13, 16, 22).

VII–XII. Types having two active elements and two passive:
- VII. h + pr + c + sl (2, 4, 6, 18, 20, 24).
- VIII. h + p + c + r (2, 3, 5, 17, 19, 21).
- IX. h + p + st + sl (1, 4, 5, 14, 15, 23).
- X. l + p + st + r (7, 9, 11, 13, 15, 21).
- XI. l + pr + st + sl (7, 10, 12, 14, 16, 24).
- XII. l + pr + c + r (8, 9, 12, 17, 20, 22).

XIII–XVI. Types having one element active and three passive:
- XIII. h + p + c + sl (2, 4, 5, 18, 19, 23).
- XIV. l + p + c + r (8, 9, 11, 17, 19, 21).
- XV. l + pr + c + sl (8, 10, 12, 18, 20, 24).
- XVI. l + p + st + sl (7, 10, 11, 14, 15, 23).

Each type is a combination of four graphological signs (in groups of two). Each pair represents a personality trait (see below). It should be remembered that no writing is totally 'pure' and the interpretation will vary accordingly, e.g. see type I and type III where speed only may vary.

1.	h + st	Energy and decision. Energy applied in pursuit of goals.
2.	h + c	Energy guided by imagination. Imagination is constant with the need to achieve goals and make ideas concrete.
3.	h + r	Energy stimulated by activity and vice versa.
4.	h + sl	Intense inner activity. In some cases grave inhibitions. Inner nervous tension.
5.	h + p	Practical energy in touch with senses and feelings. Superego: conflict between energy and enjoyment. Possible pleasure from brutality.
6.	h + pr	Energy guided by individual's laws of morality or principles. Incorruptible energy not easily sidetracked, e.g. by tiredness.
7.	l + st	Glib decision-making. Emotionally affected by having to make a decision when faced by reality.
8.	l + c	Imagination and sensitivity. Perceptions and emotions excite each other. Imagination influenced by the emotions. The greater the curve the greater the possibility of false perceptions. Possible mythomania.
9.	l + r	Easily motivated activity.
10.	l + sl	Depending on degree of slowness, either assimilation and observation or hesitation, timidity and emotional exhaustion.
11.	l + p	Hunger for sensual impressions, ranging from sensitivity to colour to total gratification of the senses. Delicacy of feelings.
12.	l + pr	Intellectual and cerebral sensitivity. Cold-heartedness.
13.	st + r	Extreme decisiveness. Sometimes lack of imagination.
14.	st + sl	Lack of assurance. Decisiveness despite fear of obstacles.

15.	p + st	Decisions in the service of heart and senses. Decisions tend to accord with needs (sadness springing from resignation). Can be sidetracked.
16.	pr + st	Incorruptible decisiveness based on firm principles. Cold decisiveness unaffected by feelings or emotions.
17.	c + r	Imagination and activity closely connected to complex ideas.
18.	c + sl	Imagination influenced by an awareness of obstacles. Sense of form and ceremony. Anxiety, worry, agony.
19.	p + c	Imagination both nourishes and/or sublimates the feelings. Imagination may be carried away by the senses. Appreciation of forms.
20.	pr + c	Imagination nourished by moral, social or religious ideas and by principles. Mystical imagination, utopian illusions and fantastic ideas.
21.	p + r	Activity in the service of feelings or senses. Can be sidetracked.
22.	pr + r	Activity inspired by ideas of personal morality or rigorous principles. Cold and insensitive activity, ignoring feelings and senses.
23.	p + sl	Awareness of obstacles through feelings. Tendency to exaggerate obstacles and be ground down by them. Passivity plus a need for contact with reality. Inactivity or laziness with physical malaise. General low-spiritedness.
24.	pr + sl	Inner obstacles opposed to freedom of emotional life. Repression of feelings and sensual needs.

5

THE SIGNS

Eye training means learning to look at a handwriting, exercising the brain to observe the slightest movements of pen on paper and noticing all the different ways the letters are formed.

In graphology no sign is insignificant. Every little thing counts. The smallest hook or irregularity can be significant and indicative of a mood or trait of character, a good quality or a fault.

Some signs may look similar to the untrained eye. Experience and devoted study will clarify the confusion.

As we saw in the Introduction and in the laws of writing, no one sign indicates one trait of the writer's personality. The same trait of character in different people may appear under a different combination of signs. That is why we can never take a sign out of context and also why we can never have a complete list of signs as such.

In the pages that follow you will find only an incomplete indication of the interpretation of each sign. Combinations of signs are infinite, like people.

There are two ways of listing the signs: either by category or alphabetically. They should never be listed in order of importance since no sign out of context is more important than the next; the dominants vary from writing to writing. Some signs belong to more than one category, such as irregularity, for instance, which may apply to all seven categories.

The order of the categories is unimportant, although it is advisable to start with layout and to finish with the particular signs. This makes sense since the first thing we notice in a writing is usually the layout, and the last, more often than not, the i dots, the punctuation, etc.

After we have learned how to look at each writing and to see the various signs and write them down in their order of dominance (and before we start with their interpretation), it would be wise to repeat Crépieux-Jamin's advice:

1. When we seek to interpret the graphic signs we must consider them as a physiological movement corresponding to a psychological particularity in quality, extent, consistence and strength;

2. The value of the graphic signs is relative because the same movement could be produced by different causes in different people;
3. The skill of the graphologist lies in distinguishing, among many possible interpretations, the one which applies to the overall condition of the writing, is the most logical and the most necessary psychologically.

Also, we must always remember that:

1. No sign should ever be interpreted alone. All signs are invalid when taken out of context;
2. All signs can be contradictory, complementary, predominant, confirmatory or compensatory (Teillard);
3. All signs have value only when they are constant and repetitive;
4. The FL must always be considered in order to interpret a sign correctly.

The Anatomy of Writing

Letters are written symbols and are constituted of nine elements:

1. Traits – any stroke made by the pen in one move;
2. Down strokes – any vertical stroke drawn downwards;
3. Up strokes – any vertical stroke drawn upwards;
4. Ovals – the 'eyes' of the letters in the middle zone, e.g. a, o, g, d, etc.;
5. Upper extensions – all the down strokes of the letters l, k, t, b, h, d and f to the baseline, also of the capital letters;
6. Lower extensions – all down strokes of the letters g, j, y, p, q and f from the baseline down;
7. Loops – all upwards strokes of the upper and lower extensions which curve and cross the upper or lower extension, forming loops;
8. The essential parts – the skeleton of the letter which is indispensable to its structure;
9. The secondary parts (or accessories) – ornamentions or parts which are not essential to the structure of the letter.

The letters have five different zones:

1. Initial zone – the point where the letter starts;
2. Final zone – the point where the letter ends;
3. Upper zone – all upper extensions, i dots, t bars, accents and a part of the capital letters;

4. Middle zone – all letters or parts of letters which occupy the space between the baseline and the top of the letters a, o, etc.;
5. Lower zone – the lower extensions of the letters g, y, f, etc., the lower extensions of capital letters and all that extends below the baseline.

Writing has three dimensions:

1. vertical; 2. horizontal, and 3. depth.

The Categories and Their Signs

The following list of signs is amplified under their respective categories (pp. 38–206).

Layout

Layout covers the distribution and organization of the text on the page. It indicates the adaptability of the writer to his environment, the method and sense of organization, time, activities, space, etc.

The sheet of paper represents the world, the space within which we evolve. The 'guiding images' (ideas which disect thought) are also represented by layout.

Layout contains eighteen signs. These are: aerated, chimneys, clear, compact, confused, disorderly, envelopes, invasive, irregular (see Continuity), margins, messy, neat, orderly, spaced out, spacing, tangled lines, underlined, unnecessary dots.

Dimension

Dimension deals with the size of the letters. It indicates the writer's opinion of himself and, consequently, the way he affirms his personality. It also shows the adaptability of the writer. Dimension covers variability in height, amplitude or spread (width or breadth). The Symbolism of Space (pp. 20–21) is also applicable to the evaluation of dimension: upwards symbolizes mind, imagination, intellectual aspirations; downwards symbolizes sexuality, materialism or physical activities.

Dimension contains twenty-four signs: compensatory, diminishing, disproportionate, enlarged, enlarging, exaggerated, expanded, extensive movements, full, irregular (see Continuity), large, low, prolonged downwards and upwards, prolonged downwards, prolonged upwards, proportionate, reduced, small, sober, squeezed, superelevated, tall, very large, wide.

Pressure

Pressure includes the study of the pressure of the writing instrument on the paper and the quality of the stroke.

It indicates the intensity and originality of the personality, the vitality, the importance of instinct and material values, the state of health and gives an indication of the influence of psychic health upon physical health.

The choice and handling of the writing instrument are determined by the totality of the personality, with very few exceptions.

Pressure contains thirty signs altogether, eighteen refer to the weight of the stroke as follows: clubbed, deviated, flat, heavy, irregular (see Continuity), light, medium, notched, pale, in relief, robust, sharp-pointed, spasmodic, spindle-shaped, superficial, trenchant, weak, well nourished.

Twelve signs refer to the quality of the stroke: blurred, congested, dry, fine, firm, medium, tension, pasty, precise, runny, smeary, thick, thin.

In order to assess pressure correctly we need the original document rather than a photocopy.

The signs which are not apparent in a photocopied document are as follows: *flat*, *heavy*, *light*, *medium tension*, *pale*, *robust*, *superficial*, *trenchant*, *weak*, *well nourished*, *congested* (sometimes photocopying fills in the little ovals), *pastose* (this can easily be confused with *trenchant*, *well nourished*, *thick* or *heavy* if photocopied), and *thick*.

It is also advisable to use a magnifying glass; the naked eye is not always adequate.

Form

Form is one of the most important categories. It has two parts – it deals with the way the letters are formed and with the way they are connected. It indicates the character, personality, memory (to some degree), attention, tastes, ideals, virtues, attitudes, aptitudes and originality of the writer. The formation of the letters tells us whether the writer is rich or poor in imagination, whether he is close to, or far from, his unconscious with its eternal images or archetypes. It also tells us whether a person is endowed as an artist, has latent artistic possibilities, an imposing personality or otherwise, and is dependent or independent.

It is important, when considering form, to know the style of writing taught in each particular country as this will affect an individual's form.

Form contains sixty-three signs: ample, angular, animated, arabesques, arcades, artificial, bizarre, bow ties or loops, closed, complicated, confused (see Layout), conventional, copy-book, covering strokes, cramped, disguised, distinguished, double curves, double joins, elegant, filiform (see Glossary), formless, garlands, graceful, gross (see Particular Signs), harmonious, illegible, impersonal, inharmonious, irregular (see Continuity), lassos, limpid, looped garlands, lower extensions, mannered, mirror writing, mixed (semi-engular, semi-garlanded), narrow letters, natural, negligent, open, original, ornate, proteiform (see Glossary), regular, round, rounded, shark's tooth, simple, simplified, soaring, spelling, spirals, square, stylized, supported, swords (see Particular Signs), triangles (see Particular Signs), typographic, ungraceful, upper extensions, vulgar, whips.

There are eight forms of connection of the stroke:

Angles –
Garlands –
Arcades –
Loops –
Filiform –
Double curves –
Supported –
Square –

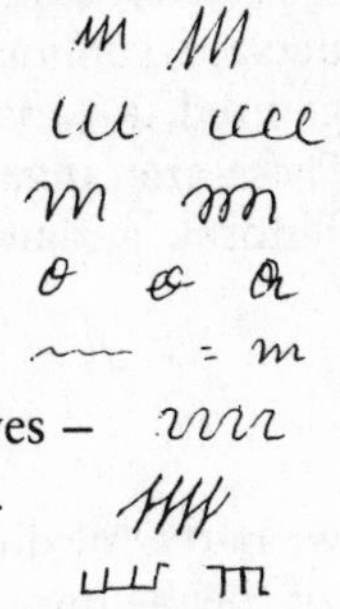

See also Continuity when considering connections.

Speed

Speed indicates the ways of reacting, manifested or not, the speed of thought and response of the writer, the degree of intelligence (see Form and Continuity), natural vivacity, creativity and nervous tension.

In a general way, a fast writing is more favourably considered than a slow one. Two kinds of speed can be differentiated: *absolute* speed which indicates a writer's intelligence and culture and *relative* speed, i.e. that at a given time in one specimen of writing. Slowing down of speed reveals hesitation, sometimes inhibition, complexes and the tendency to conceal something.

Speed contains eighteen signs: abbreviated, accelerated, carried away, constrained, controlled, dynamic, effervescent, flying strokes, illegible (see Form), irregular (see Continuity), poised, precipitated, rapid, resolute, slack, slow, slowed down, spontaneous.

Continuity

Continuity indicates the continuity of reasoning and action of the writer, logic, perseverance and capacity to achieve or otherwise. It indicates independence or lack of it and spontaneity of feeling.

The activity of the unconscious, which is often opposed to the writer's conscious ideals and ideas, may momentarily influence the writing trail. Retouches and corrections of all kinds interrupt the spontaneous flow of the writing by an intervention of the unconscious.

Continuity contains forty-two signs: agitated, amended, automatic, broken, calm, combined, comfortable, connected, constant, disconnected, discordant, disorganized, false connections, faltering, fragmented, free, grouped, hesitant, homogeneous, hopping, inhibited, irregular, jerky, lapses of continuity, mingling letters, monotonous, nuancée (see Glossary), organized, overconnected, resting dots, rhythmic, shaky, stable, sticks, structured, sublimated, suspended, unfinished, unnecessary lines, unorganized, unvarying, variable.

There are ten forms of continuity. These are: angular, arcades, combined, connected, double curves, filiform, garlands, grouped, looped, supported.

Direction

Direction, like Form and Pressure, has two parts: the direction of the *lines*, which indicates the stability of behaviour, orientation, fluctuation of mood and state of mind (moral and intellectual) of the writer, and the *slant* of the stroke, which shows the degree of impetuosity and ardour in action, the impulsiveness or restraint of the emotions and the moods.

The *Symbolism* of Space contributes towards an evaluation of direction: rightwards is the 'you', the outside world, the future, masculinity, action, goals; leftwards symbolizes the 'I', introspection and the past.

Direction contains twenty-five signs altogether; thirteen refer to the direction of the lines: concave, convex, descending, diving, galloping downwards, galloping upwards, horizontal, irregular (see Continuity), rigid, rising, stable baseline, undulating words, wavy lines.

Twelve refer to the direction of the stroke and the slant: centrifugal, centripetal, irregular (see Continuity), leftward, progressive, regressive, reverse, rightward, rigid, twisted, vertical, very slanted to the right.

Particular Signs

These include all the small particularities which do not fit into any of the above categories, such as figures, punctuation marks, diacritics and the signature. Each sign is studied individually. If a sign is not constant and repetitive it must be considered a particular sign and not as belonging to any of the other categories. For example, if, in writing, the majority of the lower extensions (or the t bars) are in the shape of triangles, then this sign belongs to form; if, however, there is only one or two (for instance in the signature) then it is a particular sign.

Some of the most common particular signs are: accents, capital letters in the middle of words, final strokes, hooks, lassos, lyrical d, shark's tooth (see Form), signature, spirals (see Form), starting strokes, strong regressive strokes, swords, triangles, wavy strokes.

The first two categories: Layout and Dimension, show the adaptability of the writer and his respect for others.

The third and fourth, Pressure and Form, reveal character, temperament, personality, will and vitality.

The fifth and sixth, Speed and Continuity, indicate the rhythm of activity and intellectual abilities.

The seventh, Direction, expresses, stability, sensibility, mental health and the ability to express feelings.

In addition, there are short sections on signs of insincerity (p. 205) and pathological signs (pp. 205–6).

Layout

Aerated

Category: layout
Synonym: moderately spaced out
Antonym: compact, concentrated

Description

The spacing between words is wider than the width of the letter m of the middle zone of the same writing, and there is enough space left between the lines so that the lower extensions of the line above do not touch the upper extensions of the line below.

The white (space) and the black (writing) are evenly spaced out and air can circulate freely between words and lines.

Interpretation:

General Clarity of thought. Ability to face up to the problems of everyday life. Need for space. Autonomy.

Favourable Independence. Objectivity. Clear judgement. The writer will not easily be influenced by other people's opinions. His intelligence is clear and to the point. Talks little (function is thinking). He is usually the 'director' or 'chairman'.

It is also a sign of a cultured mind. Ability to embrace a situation in its essential structure without bothering much about the details.

If the writing is large: generosity.

Unfavourable In a low Formlevel (inharmonious or artificial writing) it will show dilettantism, or emotional difficulty in communicating his or her inner feelings.

Aerated writing is illustrated in examples 5, 8 and 44 (pp. 263, 264 and 284).

Chimneys

Category: layout

Description

When the two eyes see differently there is a visual separation of the written page into two vertical halves. This partition consists of a wider gap between two words, in the course of the lines, thus forming a 'chimney' separating the right from the left and running from top to bottom. This chimney is not necessarily in the middle, nor is it necessarily straight from the top to the bottom of the page. It may undulate from right to left but will always reveal distinct differences in the fluency of writing – sometimes corrections are concentrated on one half of the page more than on the other. Raymond Trillat, the contemporary French graphologist, who highlighted the chimneys, believes that the side corresponding to the weaker eye (right for right, and left for left eye) will have more corrections, less fluency.

The place of the chimney shows the point where the text passes from the visual field of one eye into the visual field of the other.

Here, too, Symbolism of Space (pp. 20–21) may give us an explanation. When the written anomalies appear on the right of the chimney the writer is in conflict with the 'father' image or society. When the written anomalies appear on the left of the chimney, the conflict is with the 'mother' image and the self.

Chimneys are illustrated in examples 7 and 43 (pp. 264 and 284).

Clear

Category: layout
Synonym: orderly, legible
Antonym: confused, illegible

Description

A clear writing is legible, simple and regular. The letters, the words and the lines do not mingle and are kept within the normal dimensions, matching the size of the whole.

Interpretation

General A distinct notion of differences between things; between what is 'mine' and what is 'yours', what is 'correct' and what is 'incorrect'. When the margins are also respected and the layout is clear, it will show a cultivated mind.

Favourable Conscious activity. Clarity of thinking. Good reasoning. Reason rules the imagination. The writer is sincere and, if the lines are straight, the letters precise and the pressure 'in relief', then it shows nobility and purity of character and a high level of intelligence. The person is loyal, truthful, intelligent and in harmony with the Universe. If the rest of the signs show an introvert person, then this person will organize matters to suit his inner harmony. If he is an extrovert, he will tend to organize himself to adapt his own life to the social scene he moves in.

Unfavourable Conventional and mediocre intelligence. The writer has learned to follow the disciplines of order and organization. The poverty of his character does not stop him from being the 'good pupil' who learns his lessons, but he can only repeat what he reads. 'Insignificant people are poor, not necessarily deprived of resources,' says Crépieux-Jamin. 'The clarity of their handwriting safeguards their good sense and their honesty. If they are deprived of this sustenance, their mental balance, becomes perilous.' Clear writing in its negative meaning often coincides with Jung's persona type.

Clear writing is illustrated in example 1 (p. 260).

Compact

Category: layout
Synonym: compact, condensed
Antonym: expanded

Description

A writing is called compact when the letters, the words and the lines are close together without necessarily losing legibility. As a whole, the text dominates the white spaces.

Interpretation

General Compact writing shows attention and concentration of thought. Compactness may also occur when writing on a small piece of paper or a postcard; this shows adaptability and suppleness of character.

Under certain conditions (hunger, cold, tiredness, fear, depression) the writing will become compact, particularly if the writer is of a nervous disposition.

Favourable It indicates the ability to direct the attention to the problem in hand, a well-disciplined mind, prudence, economy, order, reserve, discretion, introversion (with a closed and sober writing).

Unfavourable Avarice, narrowness of the field of consciousness. Tendency to accumulate goods, to safeguard possessions. Inhibitions, selfishness, distrust, lack of self-confidence.

When the writing is also angular, dry and squeezed (narrow letters) then it shows a limited vision, touchiness, meanness, pettiness, lack of social sense and confusion of thought. Also, when the lower extensions of one line mingle (tangle) with the upper extensions of the line below and the pressure is smeary, it indicates a tendency to immorality, lack of repulsion for dirt and easy contact with the world of crime.

Compact writing is illustrated in examples 9 and 21 (pp. 265 and 269).

Confused

Category: layout
Synonym: illegible
Antonym: clear, legible

Description

A confused writing is one in which the distribution of spacing is insufficient and the legibility is compromised. The letters, words and lines overlap. Forms are complicated or imprecise, with many abbreviations. The whole makes the text equivocal and obstructs and slows down the reading.

This writing may be associated with the animated, disproportionate, disorderly, vulgar, inharmonious and dashing writing (flying strokes).

Interpretation

General Confusion of the three spheres: intellectual, emotional and instinctive. The functions are mingled. There is no differentiation between predominant and auxiliary, the four functions of thinking, sentiment, intuition and sensation as propounded by Jung.

Persistent, confused writing in children should be considered as an indication of mental retardation.

With signs of disorganization (p. 153) confused writing shows only a pathological origin caused by illness.

Favourable If the writing is fast, irregular, uneven and animated it shows an excessive imagination which may lead to exaggeration and illusion, but also to a pronounced sense of humour and wit. The writer's judgement will be insufficient; he will be ingenious, impulsive, confident, suggestible and spontaneous.

If the movement is concentrated more in the lower extensions, the person manifests a taste for change, variation and a tendency to bite off more than he can chew.

Unfavourable If the cause of confused writing is not external, i.e. haste, a moving support, etc., then it is indicative of lack of restraint and prudence, mental confusion and instability, excessive nervous tension. Tendency to associate with immoral people. Disorganization of distribution of work, time and expenses. Lack of consideration for others. Disorderly habits. Negligence, laziness, incorrect behaviour, gross attitudes.

Confused writing is illustrated in example 9 (p. 265).

Disorderly

Category: layout
Synonym: confused, unruly
Antonym: harmonious, clear, regular

Description

There are two kinds of disorderly writing: active when the writing is animated, eager and fervent and passive when it is is negligent, slow and flabby. In both cases the writing is inharmonious since it is discordant, confusing, complicated and exaggerated. It is wise to ask for a second, even a third, sample of writing before it is classified as disorderly writing. It may be accidental.

Interpretation:

General With a lively movement it shows impulsiveness, excessive activity, disorder caused by lack of time.

With a slow, negligent writing: lack of interest and caring, amorality, ignorance, excessive emotionalism, anxiety, inadaptability, improvidence.

In disorderly writing much depends on the rest of the signs.

Disorderly writing is illustrated in example 9 (p. 265).

Envelopes

Category: layout

The writer's social behaviour and his inner reality are also expressed in the way he writes the address on the envelope.

The Symbolism of Space pp. 20–21 applies here.

If the name and address are placed near the top of the envelope this shows idealistic and intellectual tendencies. Also lack of objectivity.

If they are placed near the bottom this shows practicality, sense of reality, materialistic tendencies, egocentricity, but also courtesy.

If they are placed near the left side this shows introversion, timidity, self-effacing attitudes, retrospection, traditionalism, pessimism.

If they are near the right half of the envelope this shows extroversion, self-confidence, worry about the future.

If they are in the centre of the envelope this shows order, precision, aestheticism.

If the address on the envelope is illegible, the writer is negligent, thoughtless and lacks foresight.

If the writing on the envelope is the same as the text's, then the writer is in harmony with himself and at ease with society and the world.

If the writing on the envelope is different, the writer puts on a mask for society.

If the writing on the envelope is calligraphic or in any way ornate, the writer is ostentatious, he values honours and formalities, he tends towards megalomania.

Invasive

Category: layout
Synonym: overrun
Antonym: orderly, contained

Description

The writing overflows, it leaves no margins and the text covers the whole page. It can be small or large, fast or slow.

Interpretation:

General Extroversion. The writer is generally ebullient. He likes to talk about himself, to narrate stories, to fill up the space around him as far as possible with his voice, his manifestations, his presence, he likes to communicate, to exchange his ideas, feelings, etc.

A large writing with expansive movements shows a generous nature which makes contact easily with other people, is at home everywhere, and will put others quickly at their ease. He or she likes luxuries and all the nice things of the material world.

If, however, the writing is more or less concentrated and leaves very little or no space between words and lines, the writer, although still extrovert and expansive, is generally more of an opportunist, ready to profit from every situation. Taking financial risks becomes an obsession here rather than a necessity.

In any case, this type of writing indicates an 'invasive' attitude; the writer is inquisitive. He, or she, will nose around in other people's affairs. He lacks discretion and tact.

Invasive writing is illustrated in example 23 (p. 270) also in 'Margins' Ex. No. 2 (opposite page).

Irregular

See Continuity, p. 146.

Margins

Category: Layout

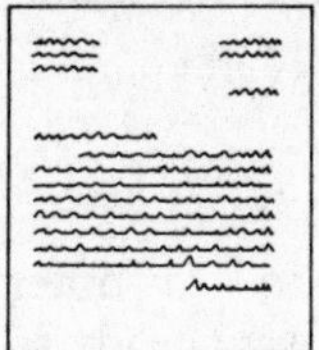

Typographic layout:

The text is framed by margins as in books.

Favourable Need for privacy. Introversion. Sense of one's own value.

Unfavourable Desire to be original, to be different. Uncertainty of one's own value (particularly if the margins are kept too rigorously and with great care and attention).

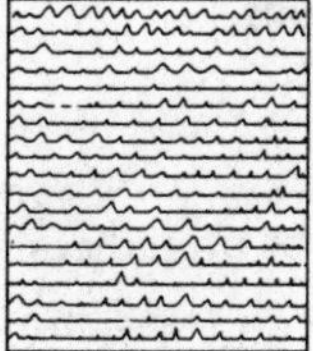

Absence of margins:

Favourable Need to communicate. The writer feels that he or she has a lot to say and never enough time or space to do so.

Generosity of feelings. Manifestation of affection.

Unfavourable Lack of organization of life. Brash. A spendthrift. Lack of respect and consideration. Weak memory. Laziness. Talkativeness.

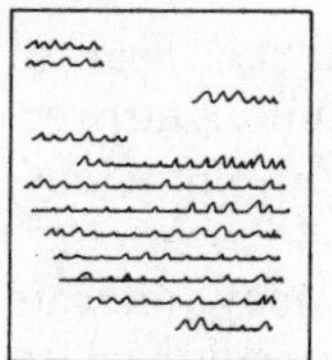

Left margin progressively enlarging:

Favourable Extroversion. Need for independence. Zeal. Optimism. Ambition (especially when the lines climb upwards).

Unfavourable Tendency to overspend. Obsequiousness. Vanity. Lack of organization of time and activities. Dislike of discipline imposed by parents (in certain cases, Oedipus complex). Exhibitionism (particularly with a large writing, spread out or expanded, distended or swollen).

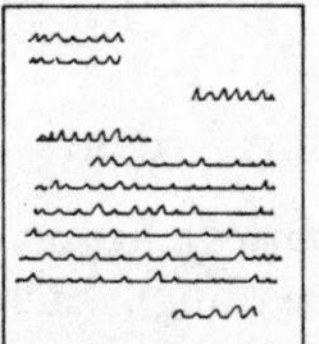

Left margin progressively decreasing:

Favourable Introversion. When the decreasing of the margin is used in order to fit in a very long text, a lack of planning and a discourtesy to the reader are indicated; the writer pays more attention to what has to be said than to the reader.

Unfavourable Egocentricity. Fixation on the past. Attachment to mother. Difficulty in accepting blame and a tendency to blame others for one's own failures. Fatigue. Depression. Pessimism. Loss of self-confidence.

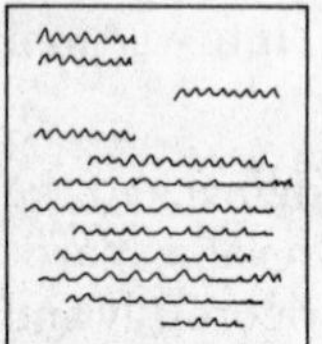

Irregular margins:

Favourable Versatility. Sensitivity to other people's feelings. The writer is always ready to help.

Unfavourable Lack of order and discipline. Inadaptability. Changing ideas, tastes, decisions. Instability. Versatile emotions.

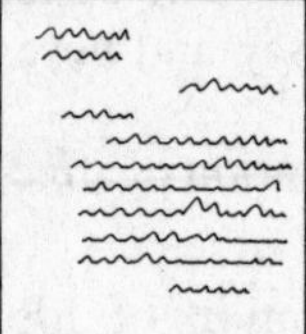

Left margin wide:

Favourable Extroversion. Lack of prejudices.

Unfavourable Wasting of time and activity. Disregard of duties. Prodigality. With a small writing it indicates excessive respect for the receiver of the letter. Timidity.

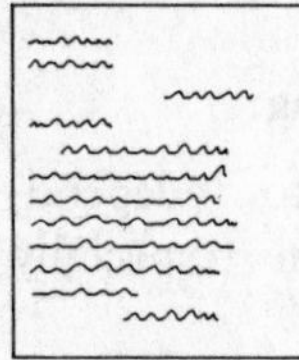

Right margin wide:

General Timidity. Hypersensitivity. Fear of contact with others. Fear of the future. Introversion. Need for self-protection. Self-consciousness.

A very wide right margin may indicate fixation on mother, strong influence of the past, Oedipus complex or pessimism.

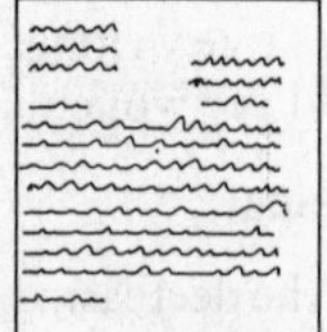

Narrow or no left margin:

In the USA it is the common way of writing; a habit which springs from the use of automatic or electric typewriters.

Favourable Practicality. Economy. Activity.

Unfavourable Indifference to courtesy. Regression (if supported by regressive writing). Lack of taste. Distrustfulness. Lack of confidence. Avarice. Egoism. Selfishness.

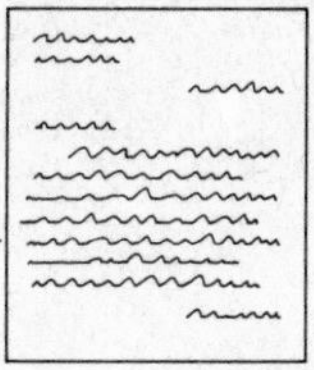

Right margin irregular:

General 'The writer cannot adopt a decisive and firm attitude towards people and situations.' (Daim and Bousquet).

Irresponsible attitudes. Lack of organization and foresight.

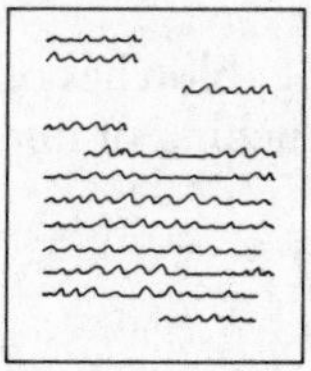

Left margin regular:

General Order. Good ability to organize. Self-control. Regularity. Success. Strong and sustained will-power.

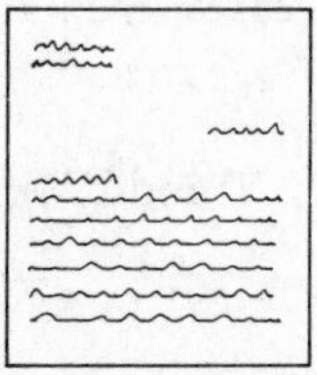

Top margin large:

General Courtesy, respect for the reader. Distinction. Good education and social culture. With a small writing it may be lack of confidence or inadaptability.

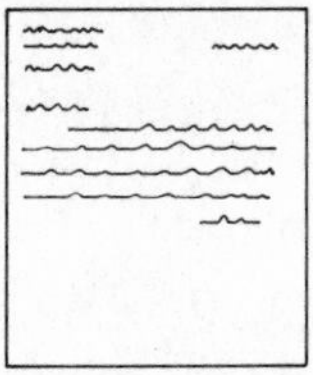

Bottom margin large:

General Aestheticism. Lack of worry, if the text is well balanced in the middle of the page. If the text is concentrated at the top of the page: bad taste, lack of organization and foresight.

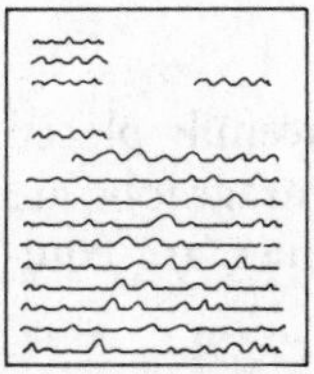

Bottom margin small:

General Lack of ability to organize. Lack of aestheticism. Economy. If the writing is fast and of good FL the writer did not want to interrupt his thoughts to turn the page.

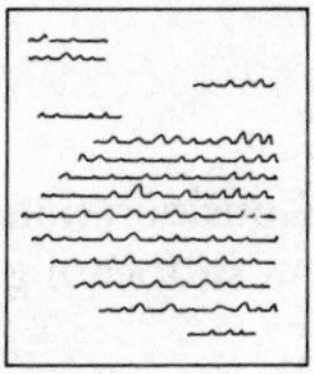

Convex margin:

General A constant effort for self-control without success. The writer makes resolutions which only last a short time and then he falls back into his old self and old habits.

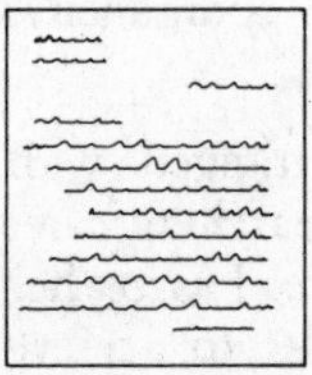

Concave margin:

General This is the opposite of the previous one; the attitudes, naturally more relaxed, are successfully controlled by a sense of economy, often hidden behind liberal spending habits.

Messy

Category: layout
Synonym: dirty, grubby, untidy
Antonym: clean, tidy

Description

Children in primary school tend to have messy writing; blotches of ink on the paper or dirty finger marks, repeated retouching of one correction, untidy crossing out of words or lines etc.

Interpretation:

General Lack of education, coarseness. In certain cases, mental debility when accompanied by supporting signs.

Messy writing is illustrated in examples 23 and 32 (pp. 270 and 276).

Neat

Category: layout
Synonym: studious, diligent
Antonym: negligent

Description

The margins are large and neat, the headings are gracefully placed and in aesthetic harmony with the rest of the text. Paragraphs are clearly indicated and with the same indentation; lines are equidistant.

Interpretation:

General Courtesy, good taste.

Favourable Good judgement. Good imagination. Consideration for other people. The writer can live with others without suffocating either his or their tendencies.

Firmness of attitudes and behaviour. Attractive spontaneity. Sympathy. Order. Method. Prudence.

Unfavourable When the text is set out and arranged with conscious, effortful attention, rigorously and with searching care, the writer lives under his own constant surveillance. His or her spontaneous tendencies are being suffocated in order to achieve self-control and good behaviour. This shows a lack of sincerity. Affectation. Lack of suppleness.

This writing reflects the adaptability of Jung's persona type.

Neat writing is illustrated in examples 10 and 36 (pp. 265, 278 and 279).

Orderly

Category: layout
Synonym: well presented
Antonym: disorderly, confused

Description

The layout is clear, the writing is proportionate, legible and margins and paragraphs are correctly kept.

Interpretation:

General Good organization. Clear mind. Respect for the reader.

Favourable With a spontaneous writing: good reasoning, logic, conscientiousness, modesty, objectivity, good judgement, clear thinking.

Unfavourable When the writing is artificial, calligraphic (copybook), stylized, rigid, etc., an obsession with order.

Orderly writing is illustrated in examples 1, 2, 5, 10, 12 and 46 (pp. 260, 261, 263, 265, 266 and 286).

Spaced Out

Category: layout
Synonym: extended, separated
Antonym: squeezed, compact

Description

The intervals between words and lines dominate the written space.

Interpretation:

General In a squeezed writing (angular and narrow letters) it shows a need for privacy and isolation. With a widely spread writing it shows lack of reflection and lack of ability to embrace a multitude or a variety of subjects. In both cases, however, it is a need for freedom and breathing space.

Favourable Clarity of thinking. Orderly thoughts and ideas, if the distances are not too excessive. The writer desires (or lacks) more personal freedom, an easier life, likes space and air. He needs light and colour. With a spread out writing, it shows generosity, natural kindness and need of contact with others, together with sociability (if the writing is also progressive, fast, rounded and the letters wide).

Unfavourable Lack of judgement. If the distances between words and lines are excessive then it shows lack of ability to follow up logical sequence of ideas, lack of reflection, impulsiveness, impressionability. Tendency to talk and act without prudence. Superficiality. A spendthrift (with an inharmonious, ample and fast writing).

If the words are formed with small angular letters squeezed together it is an indication of the writer's well-developed ability to judge critically but also his difficulty in making logical connections.

If excessive, this combination of signs will indicate schizoid and/ or schizothymic tendencies. If it is also coupled with diagonal strokes (t bars and final strokes) it shows a systematic rebelliousness.

When the writing is crude, imprecise, confused, disorderly, then it shows prodigality, lack of discipline, a slack character.

Spaced out writing is illustrated in examples 6 and 7 (pp. 263 and 264).

Spacing Between Lines

Very wide Isolation. Timidity. Need to keep a distance. Introversion. The writer feels flooded by intrusions. With narrow word spacing: lack of spontaneity. Difficult contact with people. Fear of contact. Coldness (see example 7, p. 264).

Very narrow Narrow concept of life. Lack of expansion. See Tangled Lines (p. 51) (see example 21, p. 269).

Irregular Disorderliness. Lack of judgement, or false judgement. Ambivalence. Superficiality. Lack of cohesive thinking. Inner conflicts (see example 17, p. 268).

Spacing Between Words

Very wide Need of freedom, space and air. Clarity of thoughts (with supporting signs). Order. Good judgement. See also Aerated (p. 38). (See example 17, p. 268.)

Very narrow Need for social contact or fear of loneliness. Inefficient judgement. Narrow field of consciousness. Stinginess. Pettiness (see example 21, p. 269).

Irregular Lack of freedom of feeling. Inner conflicts. Inconsistency of will-power and action (energy). Lack of expansion of the psyche (psychological barriers). Scattered imagination. Lack of emotional equilibrium. Lack of inner harmony and peace (see example 26, p. 273).

Spacing Between Letters

Very wide Spontaneity of affections. Naivety. Talkativeness. Spreading of self. Thoughtlessness. Superficiality. Lack of depth. Prodigality. Lack of orderly feelings. Selfishness. Weak emotivity. Shallowness (see example 64, p. 298).

Very narrow (Not mingling, but less than the letter 'o' of the same writing.) Stinginess. Self-importance. Preoccupation with self. Jealousy, Inferiority complex. Insecurity. Parsimonious personality. Introversion. Mingling letters: (see example 30, p. 275).

Irregular Sensitivity. Worry. Uncertainty. Problematic emotivity. Ambivalence. 'Tug of war' between expansion and suppression. Possible lack of inner harmony. (See examples 14, 36, 53 and 60 (pp. 267, 278, 279, 290 and 294.)

Spaced out writing is illustrated in examples 6 and 7 (pp. 263 and 264).

Tangled Lines

Category: layout
Synonym: mingled
Antonym: clear

Description

The confusion of upper extensions with the line above or of the lower extensions with the line below. A secondary form of 'confused' writing.

Interpretation:

General Intellectual exaltation. Exaggerated inner motivation. General disorder. Confusion of thoughts.

Tangled lines are illustrated in example 22 (p. 270).

Underlined

Category: layout

Description

Underlining is used to emphasize, to attract the reader's attention to one particular part, or word, of the text. It can be a straight or an undulating line drawn underneath a word or a group of words, once or many times. It can be a change of slant, i.e. italic writing in books, or an increase in size of the letters in an out-of-context manner. Repeated quotations, exclamation or question marks, the use of different coloured ink etc. all comprise underlined writings which are not necessarily in good taste.

Interpretation:

General Excitability. Vehemence. If the underlining is hazardous with no reference to the meaning of the text, it is an indication of a mania.

When a signature is much larger and broader than the text (twice its size or more) it is the same as drawing a line under it. It shows that the writer is confident and likes to put himself in evidence.

Underlined writing is illustrated in example 22 (p. 270).

Unnecessary Dots

Category: layout
Synonym: unnecessarily punctuated

Description

Accents, dots and dashes (hyphens), colons, full stops, etc. placed out of context.

Interpretation:

General When there is a full stop at the beginning of a word it shows hesitation or reflection before action. In small children a full stop at the end of a word expresses the need to rest to regain concentration. If this persists into puberty it is a sign of mental retardation, when supported by other signs.

This is a sign of oppression. It expresses physical illness, mainly cardiac deficiency or respiratory trouble.

Unnecessary dots are illustrated in example 15 (p. 267).

Dimension

Compensatory

Category: dimension
Synonym: disproportionate
Antonym: proportionate

Description

The overdevelopment of one zone in order to compensate the underdevelopment of another zone.

Interpretation:

General The readjustment of energy from one field of action to another. This presupposes that the manifestation of the libido moves from one specific field to another without affecting the consciousness of the writer.

This change is usually caused by external physical or emotional circumstances, e.g. accidents resulting in some form of handicap, the loss of a beloved one, etc.

Favourable The writer has adapted to a new situation in his life, social or physical, in a socially useful, positive and more or less constructive way. The developed zone will indicate the field of new activity which compensates for the old.

Unfavourable Tendency to neurosis, psychosis, demonstration of fictitious suffering, sexual perversions (depending on the particular zone of development).

Subjective overcompensations varying from extreme self-esteem to self-destructiveness; from excessive imagination to hallucinations; from indolence to criminality and, generally, activities indicating diminished responsibility.

Compensatory writing is illustrated in examples 7 and 10 (pp. 264 and 265).

Diminishing

Category: dimension
Synonym: relaxing, tapering
Antonym: enlarging

Description

The size of the letters in one word diminishes progressively, as may also lines, and pages, and individual letters e.g.

Interpretation:

General Desire to penetrate in depth and understand matters. Tiredness. Finesse. Sensitivity. Old age. Depression. Inhibition.

Favourable Self-supporting character. Intellectual ability and finesse. Diplomacy. Prudence. Impenetrability. Subtlety and evolution of the mind. Perspicacity. Culture. Ability to penetrate other people's minds. Sensitivity. Emotivity.

'The writer understands other people and can put himself in their position, but, in so doing, he risks losing his own point of view.' (Pulver)

Curiosity. Ability to convince others.

Unfavourable Precipitate action. Laziness. Flabbiness. Superficiality. Effort which does not last. Self-indulgence. Timidity. Insecurity. Depression. Lack of confidence. In some cases and with supporting signs, it shows moral weakness, hypocrisy. Dissimulation, lying (if diminishing becomes filiform).

With light pressure, thin strokes, small to medium size, rather fast and mostly grouped it indicates selfishness, egocentricity, narrowness of the field of consciousness (narrow-mindedness), opportunism. If also pale, aerated, with small irregularities mainly in the middle zone it shows extreme sensibility directed towards the self, lack of inner harmony, emotional suffering. General negativity.

Diminishing writing is illustrated in examples 3 and 8 (pp. 262 and 264).

Disproportionate

Category: dimension
Synonym: immoderate
Antonym: proportionate

Description

The rules of handwriting are discarded. There is no symmetry. The irregularities are shocking. The writing is discordant.

Interpretation:

General All disproportions are indicative of exaggerated tendencies, of an imbalance of the personality, of lack of taste, judgement and an intellectual inferiority.

Favourable (Only when the disproportions are not shocking or exaggerated.) Impulsive dynamism. Fancy ways of expression. Optimism. Imagination (with disproportions mainly in the upper zone). Strong sentimentality (when disproportions appear mainly in the middle zone). Pronounced instinctive tendencies (with disproportions mainly in the lower zone).

Unfavourable Intellectual inferiority. Weak moral judgements. Vulgarity. Impulsiveness. Tendency to exaggerate. Arrogance. Exaggerated disproportions will indicate a lack of psychic equilibrium (madness).

Disproportionate writing is illustrated in examples 22 and 56 (pp. 270 and 292).

Enlarged

Category: dimension
Synonym: dilated, expanded
Antonym: shrunk, shortened, miniatured

Description

This is a circumstantial sign. It can only be assessed after comparison of many samples by the same writer and, if it is comparatively larger than his usual writing, we can call this particular sample enlarged.

Interpretation:

General The reasons for enlarged writing may be many and varied. The most common are enthusiasm, joy, anger, fear or excitement.

Other reasons can be lack of adequate light or bad eyesight.

Sometimes in the same manuscript there may be words or lines larger than the rest. This effect, when it is conscious, means that the writer wished to emphasize the meaning of these special words or lines. When it is unconscious (the enlargement – in this case mainly of words – is not so pronounced, but still quite evident) it is called 'affective word', and it simply shows a stronger feeling by the writer concerning the particular word e.g., 'money', 'peace', 'love' or the name of a person.

The signature also may be enlarged. This shows self-confidence and is another aspect of 'underlined' writing. The writer values himself.

Enlarged writing is illustrated in example 23 (p. 270).

Enlarging

Category: dimension
Synonym: amplified
Antonym: diminishing

Description

When the size of the letters in one word enlarges progressively, as may also lines, and pages, and individual letters.

Interpretation:

General Sanguine temperament. Credulity. Imprudent eagerness. Extroversion. Naivety. Predominance of 'magic thinking' over 'logic thinking'; the thinking process is more or less infantile, childish, motivated by sentimentality, admiration, other people's thoughts, etc.

The writer likes to complicate things, to hide; he likes to surround matters with mystery. His attitude is open, frank, naive.

Favourable Honesty. Confidence. Joyous and expansive character. Spontaneity. Freedom of expression. Enthusiasm.

Unfavourable Lack of consideration, tact and finesse. Tendency to exaggerate. Childishness. Lack of serious, objective judgement. Sterile discussions. Possible rudeness. Brusqueness. Hurtfulness. Tendency to lie. Silliness. Stupidity.

Enlarging writing is illustrated in example 14 (p. 267).

Exaggerated

Category: dimension
Synonym: excessive, extreme, without measure
Antonym: simple, harmonious

Description

When the proportions of the forms and the dimensions exceed, in one way or another, the normal as established by the rules of writing.

Very big or very small writing, very heavy or very light, very spaced out or very squeezed, very slanted to the right or to the left, very fast or very slow etc. are all called exaggerated writing.

When capital letters are used in place of small ones and there is an excessive use of underlining, punctuation, exclamation marks etc., exaggerated climbing lines and an increasing size of writing – these are also called exaggerated writing.

Interpretation:

General The interpretation of exaggerated writing depends on the type of exaggeration as well as on other signs. As a general rule it shows dash, energy, zeal, eagerness, excitability, exaltation, pride, impulsiveness (if the writing is fast), versatility, exaggeration, vindictiveness, combativeness, clumsiness, tendency to lie, nastiness, instability, creativity. imagination, ambition, enthusiasm, spiritedness.

Any exaggeration may indicate the opposite to what its initial sign means. For example, whereas a prolonged upwards writing may show intellectual ability, exaggerated upward extensions may indicate stupidity.

Exaggerated writing is illustrated in example 14 (p. 267), and 55 (p. 291).

Expanded

Category: dimension
Synonym: enlarged, amplified
Antonym: compressed, cramped, squeezed

Description

General amplification of the writing with a progressive direction (see p. 186). It is a form of centrifugal writing. The distance between letters will be not less than 2½–3 mm at its smallest; forms will be rounded, ample and the layout aerated.

Interpretation:

General Libido in progression (see p. 217). Extroversion. General expansion of the individual. Euphoria, plenitude. Function of sentiment.

Favourable Easy, communicative nature. Honesty. Sentimentality. Joy. With original forms: artistic tendencies. Aestheticism. Creativity. Ability. Agility. Frankness. Generosity.

Unfavourable Dilapidation. Excessive talkativeness and euphoria. Dissipation.

Expanded writing is illustrated in example 14 (p. 267).

Extensive Movements

Category: dimension
Synonym: greatly developed
Antonym: small, narrow, cramped

Description

The writing surpasses the normal movements. Dimensions are exaggerated, especially in capital letters and final strokes.

Interpretation:

General Extroversion. Sanguine temperament.

Favourable When the movements are harmonious (see p. 107), it indicates imagination, pride, aestheticism, creativity, sense of beauty, an imposing personality. Many great artists have extensive movements in their handwriting.

Unfavourable When the movements are inharmonious* (see p. 109) it shows mediocrity. The writer wishes to stamp his personality on others; he wants to be remembered.

Impulsiveness. Inhibitions overcompensated by exhibitionism. Extreme talkativeness. Exaggerated imagination. Over hearty. Complicated nature.

Extensive movements are illustrated in example 14 (p. 267).

Full

Category: dimension
Synonym: distended, inflated
Antonym: narrow

Description

The curves, ovals and loops (upper and lower) are exaggeratedly inflated.

Interpretation:

General Self-satisfaction. 'Exuberant vitality, need to gesticulate, circulate, talk about themselves, attract attention, exhibit their physique, express their ideas.' (Carton)

Sanguine temperament. Imagination. Joy. Enthusiasm. Illusions.

Favourable Extroversion. Vitality. Plenitude. Imagination. Optimism. Ambition. Creativity.

Unfavourable Exhibitionism. Presumption. Vanity. Affectation. Megalomania. Hysteria. Tendency to exaggeration. Self-satisfaction. Overexcitedness. Mythomania. Overcompensation of complexes. Escapism.

If this sign is more dominant in the lower zone it shows overexcited sensuality and a strong subconscious.

Full writing is illustrated in examples 23 and 27 (pp. 270 and 274).

Irregular

See Continuity, p. 160.

Large

Category: dimension
Synonym: ample, extensive
Antonym: small

Description

The small letters are between 2½–4 mm (when they are between 4–6 mm the writing is called very large; anything more than 6 mm is called exaggerated). The proportional height of the upper and lower extensions and of the capital letters is 4½ mm with a 2 mm middle zone and 6 mm with a middle zone of 3 mm.

Interpretation:

General Extroversion. Main function is Sentiment or Sensation. Sanguine temperament. Expansion. Plenitude. Dynamism. Exuberance. Vigour.

Favourable Good ability to express feelings and thoughts. Largeness of the field of consciousness and of mind. Sociability. Generosity. Loyalty. Moral values. Pride and dignity. Authority, Independence. Activity. Enthusiasm. Initiative. Distinction. With combined writing: imagination, intuition (Teillard), strong libido.

Unfavourable Exaltation. Vanity. Exhibitionism. Need to play a part in society. Megalomania. Dictatorial attitudes. Overestimation of self. Authoritarianism. Despotism. Arrogance. Lack of objectivity. Pretentiousness.

Often a large writing is a manifestation of an overcompensated inferiority complex. Other signs in the writing may support this possibility.

Large writing is illustrated in examples 13, 23 and 27 (pp. 266, 270 and 274).

Low

Category: dimension
Synonym: short
Antonym: prolonged

Description

The upper and/or lower extensions do not reach the length of 1½ times the middle zone. In very low writing there is no noticeable difference between the middle zone and the upper or lower extensions. When capital letters are as short this writing is also called low.

Interpretation:

General This kind of writing is often seen in people who, through some form of suffering, have renounced any ambition or expectations. It is sometimes also seen in 'simple but great men'

(Crépieux-Jamin). It has never as yet, however, been found in very energetic people.

Favourable Humbleness. Predominance of inner life. Level-headedness. Judgement. Possible asceticism.

Unfavourable Depression. Feebleness of character. Submission. Passivity. With a vulgar writing: fatalistic attitude. Routine-loving character. Lack of dignity. Dissimulation. Hypocrisy.

Low writing is illustrated in example 11 and 44 (pp. 266 and 284).

Prolonged Downwards and Upwards

Category: dimension
Synonym: extended upwards and downwards
Antonym: low

Description

The upper and lower extensions are longer than the normal average proportion as set for each particular style of writing.

Interpretation:

General Extroversion. Need for change. Sanguine temperament. Possibly overactive (with supporting signs such as speed, angularity, tension, etc.). Lack of organization of energy and activities.

Emotional and/or mental imbalance. False judgement. Subjectivity (always with supporting signs).

Prolonged downwards and upwards writing is illustrated in examples 23 and 42 (pp. 270 and 283).

Prolonged Downwards

Category: dimension
Synonym: extended downwards, prolonged lower extensions
Antonym: low, contained in the middle zone

Description

Two-and-a-half times the size of the middle zone. The abnormally prolonged lower zone is also one of the two reasons for tangled lines. See also Lower Extensions (p. 111).

Interpretation:

General Very long lower extensions are indicative of the condition of people who cannot stay for long in one place (dromomania). Overactivity. Great sportsmen and sportswomen.

Ballet dancers and all those who manifest a great physical activity and movement have this sign in their handwriting.

Favourable The writer does not lose contact with reality. His thinking is concrete, objective and practical. A down-to-earth character. Sensible with money. Good organizational capacity.

Unfavourable Materialism. Excessive sensuality, sexual needs (if the writing is also broad with well-nourished pressure). Overactivity.

Prolonged downwards writing is illustrated in examples 10 and 22 (pp. 265 and 270).

Prolonged Upwards

Category: dimension
Synonym: tall, prolonged upper extensions
Antonym: low

Description

The first part of an initial letter or the first letter of a word or the capital letters are disproportionately elevated upwards or downwards (without loops). High t bars also belong to this category.

For downwards extension with loops see Prolonged Downwards (p. 61).

Interpretation:

General Pride. Excessive sense of dignity. Despotism. Inferiority complex.

Favourable Authority. Decisiveness. Courage. Patriotism. Ambition. Independence. Pride. Genuine general superiority (if the rest of the writing is clear, legible, nuancée, combined and other signs of high Formlevel). Idealism. Sensitivity. Broad understanding of spiritual matters and matters of the mind (with supporting signs). Strong intellectualism. Intuition, if the extensions are firm and simplified (aerial). Imagination. Mysticism.

Unfavourable Inferiority complex overrcompensated by arrogance (Teillard). Fear of demotion. Suffocating authoritarianism. Rigidity towards inferiors, submission to superiors (Vels). With narrow and tall capital letters: susceptibility (Beauchataud). Constant feeling of dissatisfaction. Envy. Need to dominate, to stand higher than other people.

Often people holding a high office either by birth or by achievement, i.e. qualifications, work, marriage, etc., have this sign in their writing.

With supporting signs it is often (more often than one expects) a sign of paranoia (overestimation of self, social inadaptability, defective judgement and distrust). Possibly stupidity.

Prolonged upwards writing is illustrated in examples 26 and 31 (pp. 273 and 275). See also 'Upper Extensions' p. 130.

Proportionate

Category: dimension
Synonym: balanced
Antonym: discordant, incongruous

Description

Proportionality is the principle condition for harmony, says Crépieux-Jamin. The letters will have small differences and no disproportion.

Interpretation:

General Good equilibrium. Moral superiority. Ability to evaluate situations after prudent observation. Controlled imagination. Tendency to look for clarity, to search for the essential and aesthetic. Scientific mind. Speculative ability. Order. Morality. Level-headedness. Sense of justice. Will-power. Sense of duty. Self-control.

Unfavourable When proportionate and regular, lack of imagination and creativity. Lack of intuition. Tendency to imitation, duplicity.

Proportionate writing is illustrated in examples 1, 8 and 46 (pp. 260, 264 and 286).

Reduced

Category: dimension
Synonym: smaller
Antonym: enlarged, dilated

Description

The normal dimension of a writing is suddenly reduced.

Interpretation:

General The need for speed can reduce the dimension of a writing considerably. In addition, a small postcard will usually force the writer to reduce the size of his or her writing. Cold, depression, illness, grief, old age, are also causes which reduce the size of writing.

Favourable Adaptability, suppleness of mind and, with supporting signs (clarity, simplicity, spontaneity, etc.), sincerity of character, depth, consideration.

Unfavourable Alienated people often reduce their normal size of writing to any extent. Insufficient mental development. Occasionally, it may indicate dissimulation – with other supporting signs.

Reduced writing is illustrated in examples 16 and 33a (pp. 267 and 276).

Small

Category: dimension
Synonym: little
Antonym: large

Description

The size of the middle zone letters is lower than 2 mm high (see also Large, p. 59). The capital letters and upper and lower extensions may be longer or shorter than the normal average.

Interpretation:

General The significance of small writing varies. For instance, it can be bad eyesight, cold, tiredness, grief, depression, also old age.

Introversion. Function Thinking (if small and simplified). Modesty. Reduction of expansive ability. Difficulty in communicating feelings.

Favourable With a good Formlevel: ability to concentrate. Intellectual discipline. Great capacity for intellectual work. Objectivity. Reflection. Prudence. Sense of reality. Predominance of inner life (with a fine limpid stroke). Erudition. Attention to detail. Meticulous character. Specialization.

Unfavourable If the small size of the writing is not caused by mental debility and if the Formlevel is low this will show a mixed personality. Lack of ability to undertake big tasks. Inferiority complex. Cunning (the weapon of the weak). Inability to fully understand what goes on. Fear. Timidity. Doubt. Insecurity. Lack of capacity to create big or complicated things. Narrowness of the field of consciousness. Fatigue. Distrustfulness. Dissimulation. Disappointment. Anxiety.

If the writing is smaller than 1 mm and lacks sobriety, this shows neurosis and a feeble vitality. Susceptibility. Pendantry. Lack of enthusiasm. Mental debility (with supporting signs). Limited intelligence. Nervous character (Adler).

Small writing in women shows strong animus (Jung) – especially when it is also simplified, combined and fast.

If the stroke is thick, pressure deep and the writing complicated, the writer will be an introvert with a Sensation function.

Small writing is illustrated in examples 1, 8, 16 and 49 (pp. 260, 264, 267 and 284).

Sober

Category: dimension
Synonym: moderate, contained
Antonym: animated, amplified

Description

The scriptural movement is contained within moderate dimensions. The writing is spontaneous with no striking exaggerations.

Interpretation:

General Moderation. Circumspection. Objectivity. Firmness of character. Introversion. Function Thinking.

Favourable Self-control. Discipline. Attention. Reflection. Sagacity. Prudence. Positive thinking. Orderly, methodical mind. Intellectual abilities. Integrity, discretion, intelligence are the typical qualities of this type. The writer functions through his mind and his reason overpowers his feelings. His judgement is clear and impartial.

Unfavourable Timidity. Lack of expansion through lack of courage. Lack of panache and flair, of imagination and intuition (Klages). If the writing is also angular, rigid and regular (monotonous) it shows austerity, severity, coldness, uncompromising attitudes and fanaticism.

Sober writing is illustrated in examples 1, 16, 43, 44 and 46 (pp. 260, 267, 284 and 286).

Squeezed

Category: dimension
Synonym: consolidated
Antonym: wide, expanded

Description

The letters are very close together, whilst the distances between the words and the lines may, or may not, be normal or even wider.

Interpretation:

General Inhibition, lack of expansion, introversion. Tendency or ability to compartmentalize.

Favourable Ability to concentrate one's forces to produce successful results. Attention. Order. Circumspection. In a good Formlevel: prudence, sense of order. Ability for 'fiddly' work. With supporting signs, good memory, abilty to systematize, 'filing' mind.

Unfavourable Egoism. Meanness. Pettiness. Laziness. Narrowness of conception; inability to expand emotionally.

The interpretation of this type depends much on speed, pressure and Formlevel.

See also Narrow (p. 115) if the letters are narrow, and Wide (p. 69) if the letters are wide and tall (p. 67).

Squeezed writing is illustrated in example 30 (p. 275).

Superelevated

Category: dimension
Synonym: extended upwards, raised
Antonym: low, contained in the middle zone

Description

Small letters or parts thereof extend upwards in disproportion to the rest of the writing.

Interpretation:

Favourable Excessive activity – more mental than physical. Tendency to exaggeration of self; a feeling of superiority, ambition, independence, pride. Honesty.

In a simplified writing, and if the superelevations are not exaggerated (good Formlevel), it indicates intelligence and creativity. 'Tall' projects to achieve.

Unfavourable Imbalance of the mind. Exaltation. Impressionability. Inflated 'self', egoism, susceptibility. Dishonesty.

See also Prolonged Upwards (p. 62).

Superelevated writing is illustrated in examples 25 and 54 (pp. 272 and 296).

Tall

Category: dimension
Synonym: high
Antonym: small, wide

Description

The middle zone letters are disproportionately taller than wide. Not to be confused with Prolonged Upwards or Superelevated where only certain letters extend upwards. See these signs.

Interpretation:

General Social consciousness. The writer is proud of his or her social status, inherited or acquired. Independence.

Vanity. Sensitivity concerning other people's opinions about themselves. Particularly common in women and artists who are well known in society.

Also opportunism and (with supporting signs) unscrupulous ambition. The writer may be a 'thruster'; he will have little or no scruples which inhibit him or her from climbing up, either in business or in society.

Tall writing is illustrated in examples 30 and 34 (pp. 275 and 277).

Very Large

Category: dimension
Synonym: very big
Antonym: very small

Description

The main body of the writing is very large, (approximately between 4 mm and 6–7 mm or over).

Interpretation:

General A sure sign of extrovert behaviour, often with tendencies to hysteria.

The writer likes to impress people, to be noticed, to be admired for whatever reason. He or she may use any means for this purpose.

Priests and primadonnas often write very large.

Excessive pride – possibly covering deeply rooted inferiority complex. Superficial sentimentality. Excessive confidence in self, family or position. Pomposity. Emptiness. Inner void.

Partially sighted people, also, may have a very large writing for obvious reasons. In this case the above comments may or may not apply. The rest of the signs (whether the stroke is firm, resolute and robust or hesitant, shaky, faltering or broken), the speed and the Formlevel will guide us.

Very large writing is illustrated in examples 34 and 37 (pp. 277 and 280).

Wide

Category: dimension
Synonym: letters spread-out, broad
Antonym: narrow

Description

The middle zone letters are wider than high and more developed in width at their base than at their top. Also, the space between the letters (within the words) is wider than the letters a, o, etc. Capital letters are often also wide.

Interpretation:

General Self-satisfaction. Good health. Extroversion. Need for social contacts. The function is Sentiment.

Favourable Confidence. Brilliance. Rich imagination. Good memory. Generosity. Happiness. An easy-going and charitable character. Expansion. Openness. Euphoria. Joy. Satisfaction. Frankness. Spontaneity of behaviour. Nonchalance. Ability to act dynamically. Lateral thinking.

Unfavourable Pride. Imprudence. Tendency to indiscretion. Laziness. Self-indulgence. Vanity. Coquetry. A waster of time, money and activities. Impatience. Superficiality. Talkativeness. Brashness. Lack of inner richness. Lack of reflection. Lack of inhibition. The writer enjoys public celebrations and is not put off by the presence of others. Desire to attract attention to himself. Tendency to extravagances. Exaggerated extroversion.

As always, all interpretations depend on the rest of the signs and on the Formlevel.

Wide writing is illustrated in examples 13, 14, 27 and 61 (pp. 266, 267, 274 and 295).

Pressure

Pressure is divided into two sections: weight and stroke.

Clubbed

Category: pressure (weight)
Synonym: thickening, spasmodic
Antonym: needle-like, sharp-pointed

Description

The progressive thickening of any end stroke, abruptly stopping to form a club ending. This is a braking of the writing rhythm. It belongs to the spasmodic group of signs (p. 78).

Interpretation:

General Inhibition. The constant accumulation of energy from strong emotions and passions which may have more than one outlet. Inferiority complex.

Favourable If this energy is directed consciously into action it will be expressed as productive activity, courage, dynamism, decision, etc., albeit aggressively and brusquely.

Unfavourable Explosiveness. Violent tendencies. Perversity. Need to impose his or her own ideas and wishes at any cost. Self-affirmation, intransigence, inflexibility (if the clubs are in the vertical strokes). Predominance of instinct, brutality, bestiality, possible criminal tendencies (if the clubs appear vertically in the lower zone, in a low Formlevel and with supporting signs). Inadaptability. Alcoholism.

Clubbed writing is illustrated in example 21 (p. 269).

Deviated

Category: pressure (weight)
Synonym: displaced, lateral
Antonym: flat

Description

The pressure, instead of being on the vertical down stroke, is either on the up stroke or on the horizontal stroke.

Interpretation:

General Transference of psychic energy. Depending on the rest of the signs and, of course, on the Formlevel, this sign will indicate a deviation of the writer's tendencies, energies, interests and tastes, from the conventional, socially acceptable route to more original (if the FL's good) or unorthodox (with a medium FL) or even antisocial activities. The range is large and varies from transvestism to homosexuality, from systematic rebelliousness to terrorism, etc.

Deviated writing is illustrated in examples 11 and 27 (pp. 266 and 274).

Flat

Category: pressure (weight)
Synonym: even
Antonym: in relief, distinct

Description

When there is no distinction in pressure between the up and down strokes. This type is similar to Pale (p. 75), only here the pressure of the stroke is also light.

Interpretation:

General If it is not caused by faded ink or a very soft pen, and if the writing is slow, it indicates laziness, or writing debility usually caused by mental debility (depending on supporting signs).

If the writing is fast, accelerated or precipitated, with well-formed letters or combined, it shows an agile and supple mind. (Speed usually lightens the pressure.)

In all cases, the libido is weak, the writer may be depressed and/or resigned, 'in low ebb'.

Flat writing is illustrated in example 19 (p. 268).

Heavy

Category: pressure (weight)
Synonym: pressed, thick, weighted
Antonym: light

Description

The pen weighs heavily on the paper. The weight is proportionate with the length of the down stroke on which it is measured, i.e. in a 6 mm down stroke the weight gets heavy before it reaches the halfway mark. In a 2 mm (or less) writing, this weight will not be possible, therefore it will only appear in extensions and capital letters. Any disproportion between the weight and height of small letters is significant. This sign often results in club, spindle and artificial writing.

The weight affects speed.

Interpretation:

General The interpretation of this sign must be appropriate to the pen used, particularly if the writer has not chosen it himself. It would be advisable to get more than one example of the same writing; a good quality biro will produce a different heavy writing to that written with a fountain pen, and so on.

In any case, heavy writing shows materialism, sensuality, a heavy disposition of the mind and, generally, a predominance of instinct.

Favourable If the writing is easy flowing, spontaneous, large enough to be clear, simplified, connected, rounded and well spaced, it shows good vitality, harmony between the instinctive and the intellectual life and a realistic approach to life.

Unfavourable Heaviness of thought. Lack of sensibility and finesse. Oportunism. Brutality (with supporting signs). Laziness.

If the writing gets progressively heavy it may show hypertension or circulatory trouble. A general check-up would be advisable.

Heavy writing is illustrated in examples 21 and 26 (pp. 269 and 273).

Irregular

See Continuity, p. 160.

Light

Category: pressure (weight)
Synonym: ethereal
Antonym: heavy, weighty

Description

The pressure on the paper is light. The writing occurs more through the agility of the hand than through a guiding contact with the paper. If the writing is also small in dimension then it is called Fine (p. 83).

Interpretation:

General The function is Thinking (auxiliary Intuition), or vice versa.

Weak vitality. Delicate nature. Feeble instincts.

Favourable If the writing is harmonious, progressive, combined, simplified and of a good Formlevel: wisdom, sagacity, creative and subtle mind, spirituality, elegance of character (a light writing does not have to be without relief [distinct pressure]).

Finesse. Respect. Adaptability. Suppleness. Idealism. Intuition. Receptivity. Sensitivity.

Unfavourable The writer lacks stamina, gets easily tired, he or she is fragile. Lack of productivity. With supporting signs: debilitating sensitivity, lack of practical sense and sense of reality. Lightness of character. Inconsistency. Superficiality. Evasiveness (with filiform).

Light writing is illustrated in examples 2, 29 and 40 (pp. 261, 275 and 282).

Medium

Category: pressure (weight)
Synonym: normal pressure
Antonym: heavy, light

Description

The pressure of the pen on paper is neither too heavy nor too light. The stroke is of medium firmness (neither taut, wavy nor slack), and the contour is neither too blurred nor too precise.

Interpretation:

General The writer is usually neither too dynamic, forceful or weak. His creative abilities are average.

He will undertake normal tasks and see them through.

Depending on other signs, as always, the writer will have an average understanding of life and of self.

A small, limpid, progressive writing, vertical or slightly slanted to the right, poised or rapid and connected or grouped, will indicate a person who has more understanding but less achieving capacity.

Medium pressure is illustrated in examples 3, 5 and 28 (pp. 262, 263 and 275)

Notched

Category: pressure (weight)

Description

Excessive pressure of pen on paper, mainly at the start of the down strokes; this forces the nib of the pen to separate, thus forming a double stroke: ' ɼ '.

Interpretation:

General Strong discharge of energy – often hardness of attitudes. Decisiveness, with little consideration of other people's positions or feelings (if the writing is also angular). It is generally the sign of a strong character, not always and not necessarily favourable.

Note: Notched writing does not appear in writings executed with a simple nib pen, like biros, felt-tips, etc. This writing may also be caused by worn-out or rusted pen nibs.

Notched writing is illustrated in example 37 (p. 280).

Pale

Category: pressure (weight)
Synonym: unobtrusive, without relief, dull, colourless
Antonym: coloured, nuancée

Description

The forms of the letters are correct but dull, without relief. The writing is regular, clear, simple, uniform and tranquil, without life and without intensity in any category. There is no distinction in pressure between the up and down strokes.

Interpretation:

General It is an impersonal writing which shows exactly that: lack of intensity of personality. Lack of energy. Lack of experience.

Favourable Moral principles. 'Proper' education. Gentleness. Modesty and all seductive but precarious qualities. The writer has plenty of unused virtues. If he or she is young then this writing may be called 'waiting writing'. The person is waiting to grow up when she or he (this kind of writing is more common in young women than in young men) will be able to put into action all their marvellous qualities; they will then grow out of this writing.

Unfavourable Depending on the form and the slant it will show a feeble character, silly or superficial, without great penetration of thought or judgement. It often shows mental debility.

Pale writing is illustrated in example 20 (p. 269).

In Relief

Category: pressure (weight)
Synonym: distinct, shaded
Antonym: pale, flat

Description

Contrast of pressure between the down and up stroke with well-defined contours. The writing looks as if it is embossed.

Interpretation:

General Good mental equilibrium and inner harmony if the change of pressure is achieved smoothly and not spasmodically.

Favourable Imposing, radiant personality. Stability. Will-power. Self-control. Energy. Vitality. Resistance to influences, without rigidity. Stamina. If the writing is original and combined: originality, creativity. This writing is produced mainly by people who practise a profession requiring powers of observation, imagination and good visual ability, e.g. medical practitioners, architects, sculptors, graphologists, etc.

Unfavourable If the writing is very animated, exaggerated, particularly in the lower zone, then it shows a predominant, excessive sensuality, passionate sentimentality and materialism.

In relief writing is illustrated in examples 2, 7, 10, 12 and 69 (pp. 261, 264, 265, 266 and 303).

Robust

Category: pressure (weight)
Synonym: strong
Antonym: weak

Description

The writing is pressed down, rapid, decisive, constant, spontaneous and taut. The stroke should be wide and well sustained throughout.

Interpretation:

General Dynamism, firmness. Predominance of nervous energy. Strength of character. Decisiveness.

Favourable Productivity. Strong activity and energy. Assurance. Self-confidence. Ability to impose oneself. Strong and imposing personality.

Unfavourable Egoism. Materialism. Lack of consideration and compassion. Dogmatism. Despotism. Ostentatious character. Brusqueness, violence, brutality (Vels).

Robust writing is illustrated in examples 10, 27 and 67 (pp. 265, 274 and 301).

Sharp-Pointed

Category: pressure (weight)
Synonym: needle-like final strokes, needle-like endings
Antonym: clubbed writing or club endings

Description

The final stroke of a letter is pointed like the point of a sewing needle (the sign may also appear in the initial stroke, though rarely).

Interpretation:

General The sharp-pointed ending of a stroke is a discharge of nervous tension. Generally, it shows inefficient self-control over the writer's instincts, desires and needs. It is an aggressive impulse manifesting a combative tendency.

Favourable If the aggression is sublimated or directed towards matters of the mind then there is acuteness of intelligence, a penetrating and vivid mind, inventiveness and ability to untangle complicated problems. Also curiosity, quick wittedness, ability to criticize and analyse.

Sharp-pointed writing is often found in people who use sharp-pointed instruments in their profession, such as surgeons, sculptors, engravers, butchers, toreadors, etc., or in people who need to penetrate with their brain such as researchers, critics, psychologists.

Unfavourable Impatience, irony, offensiveness. With prolonged final strokes ending in a needle-like point it shows anger, fury, rage and 'bad character' if the sign is persistent.

If the Formlevel of the writing is very low it shows nastiness, irritability, violence, the need to dominate, hurtfulness, sadistic or masochistic tendencies (depending on the rest of the signs such as clubs, angular writing, etc.), hardness, even cruelty (see the writing of criminals, murderers).

Suicidal tendencies are sometimes manifested by this sign when supported by signs of self-destruction, manic depression, etc.

In a weak writing with light pressure it will show nervousness, anxiety, jealousy, sensitivity, susceptibility, particularly in female writing.

When the pressure is strong, digging into the paper, sometimes even tearing it, then it may be a sign of a criminal tendency.

Sharp-pointed writing is illustrated in examples 5, 31 and 60 (pp. 263, 275 and 294).

Spasmodic

Category: pressure (weight)
Synonym: spindle shaped, dotted
Antonym: even

Description

This is a sister sign to spindle-shaped and clubbed (pp. 78 and 70).

In a writing of medium or light pressure there is a sudden thickening of the down stroke or of the paraph (flourish after the signature or underlining of the signature).

Interpretation:

General Predominance of instinct. Unconscious reflexes. Sexual overexcitability. Nervous twitching. Contractions due to unconscious reflexes of the nervous system. Warped and strayed eroticism. Perversion, viciousness. Regressed sexuality causing nervous explosions. Excessive avidity taking the form of gluttony. Hysteria. If the writing is discordant and sharp-pointed it shows strong aggression.

Lack of self-control. Paroxysmal tendencies. Violence. If this sudden pressure appears occasionally in the upper zone with a small, lower zone and a clear, aerated and light middle zone, it indicates a tendency to mysticism.

Medically, it might indicate an irregularity, either of the endocrinal glands (at puberty, menopause, etc.), or visceral spasms (of the heart, liver, intestines, etc). (Vels).

With filiform strokes and large capital letters it indicates a dominant, overcompensated inferiority complex. Lack of stability. Neurosis.

Spasmodic writing is illustrated in example 21 (p. 269).

Spindle-Shaped

Category: pressure (weight)
Synonym: spasmodic
Antonym: even

Description

The down strokes thicken in the middle like a spindle. It is a variation of the spasmodic group of signs (p. 267).

Interpretation

General A sign of materialistic orientation, sensuality, greediness, eroticism, etc. With supporting signs, it will also show coquetry, affectation, lack of spontaneity and superficiality.

Lack of modesty, shamelessness. Lack of reserve. Exhibitionism. The writer is 'more voluptuous than really sensual. He likes to attract attention . . . likes compliments, mannerisms, presents, congratulations and all the little superficial frivolities which please women . . . that is why, when there are spindle-shaped strokes in men's writing, it shows feminine tastes.' (Vels)

In a clear, aerated and generally light writing, if the spindles appear in the upper zone with a shortened and simplified lower zone, it will indicate mystical tendencies (sublimation of desires). This writing is often seen in monks, nuns, etc (Vels).

In a calligraphic writing, and if the spindle is not constant, it will show a taste for routine, slow or difficult adaptability, clumsiness.

Spindle shapes also appear in the writing of people who suffer from glandular problems, from heart, liver or intestinal ailments, and from addiction to intoxicants such as alcohol. Also in epilepsy. It results from a nervous discharge of energy.

Spindle-shaped writing is ilustrated in example 14 (p. 267).

Superficial

Category: pressure (weight)
Synonym: apparent pressure
Antonym: heavy, pressed down

Description

The writing looks heavier on the paper than it really is. Under a magnifying glass the down strokes will appear granulated and sinuous. Also the colour of the writing is not evenly distributed and varies in intensity.

Interpretation:

General The writer desires to be more productive and creative than he believes himself to be; he therefore tries to appear as such.

Inauthentic behaviour and lack of depth of personality; the writer fools himself about his abilities and his own importance; he wishes to fool others and adopts narcissistic attitudes (Vels).

Lack of inner resources. Feeling of inferiority. Susceptibility (when also irregular), but also receptivity and sensitivity (with supporting signs).

Superficial writing is illustrated in example 18 (p. 268).

Trenchant

Category: pressure (weight)
Synonym: sharp
Antonym: light, firm

Description

The pen scars the paper irregularly and without control.

Interpretation:

General Indicates violent tendencies. The writer is impulsive and instinctive. He lacks self-control, he is egoistic and inconsiderate. His instincts are overwhelming and obvious. He imposes his will brusquely; his orders must be obeyed. He has no respect for other people's wishes and no scruples. He has strength of execution. He will reach his goal despite difficulties. He is a brutal careerist. But also an achiever.

Trenchant writing is illustrated in examples 21 and 63 (pp. 269 and 297).

Weak

Category: pressure (weight)
Synonym: inconsistent, lax
Antonym: robust, firm, rapid

Description

The writing is slow, curved and monotonous. The pressure will be light and/or blurred. The general state of the writing is inconsistent, without firmness or decisiveness.

Interpretation:

General Phlegmatic temperament. Feeble libido. Reduced physical needs. Tiredness. Inactivity.

Favourable With a spontaneous, progressive writing it will show loyalty, patience, sociability, kindness of heart, tolerance and calm.

Unfavourable Lack of initiative, indifference, laziness. Feeble energy. Fatigue. The writer's greatest strength will be manifested in a refusal to commit him or herself to any task requiring activity, physical or mental – when occasional angles appear in the writing (Crépieux-Jamin). Mediocre intelligence. Stubbornness. Weak will. Inactivity. Apathy. Diminished needs. Lack of clarity of judgement.

Weak writing is illustrated in examples 19 and 40 (pp. 269 and 282).

Well-Nourished

Category: pressure (weight)
Synonym: coloured, rich (in ink), velvety
Antonym: thin, light

Description

Halfway between heavy and light writing. The depth of well-nourished writing is normal. Pressure is well sustained. Movements are big and sure.

Interpretation:

General Dynamism. Sense of values. Activity. Good vitality. Creative imagination. Practical sense. Productivity. Sustained energy. Sensuality. Sense of shapes and forms (written) and architectural). Good psychic and physiological equilibrium. The function is Sensation (auxiliary sensation).

Well-nourished writing is illustrated in examples 1, 4, 6, 11 and 43 (pp. 260, 262, 263, 266 and 284).

Blurred

Category: pressure (stroke)
Synonym: moist, runny, out of focus, fluffy
Antonym: distinct, precise

Description

The opposite of precise pressure: the borders of the strokes are not sharp; they look as if they are out of focus or runny.

Interpretation:

General It is usually a sign of fatigue or depression. The energy is diminished, the writer cares little about things around him. His conduct is becoming lax, he is incapable of paying attention, he is imprecise and unstable.

This condition may be temporary.

One must be wary of the texture of the paper. If it is absorbent, this sign may mean nothing.

Blurred writing is illustrated in examples 6, 28 and 53 (pp. 263, 275 and 290).

Congested

Category: pressure (stroke)
Synonym: clogged, ink-filled
Antonym: clear

Description

The ovals of the small letters, or the loops of the upper and lower zones, are filled with ink.

It appears often in muddy and pasty writings when the stroke is blurred; in these cases the interpretation of the writing is reinforced by the congested ovals or loops.

Congested writing may also be caused by a bad quality or very soft pen (felt-tip pen), or by old, evaporated (thickened) ink. Also, a lazy hand or very small writing may produce the same sign.

Because of the nature of its meaning the graphologist must verify the cause of the congested writing before proceeding to interpret it. It will help if he asks for more samples of the same person's writing to make sure that it is not accidental.

Interpretation:

General When this sign appears in a blurred, thick writing it supports the interpretation of the writing.

When it appears in a writing with light pressure, thin, weak, with signs of hesitation, it shows general ill health such as tuberculosis or cardiovascular disorder.

It may be caused by extreme tiredness or anaemia, old age, intoxication of all kinds, arteriosclerosis, neurasthenia or depression, or hypertension.

In less common cases it may be a sign of excessive sexuality.

In any case, the writer should be advised to have a general medical check-up.

Congested writing is illustrated in examples 10, 26 and 41 (pp. 265, 273 and 283).

Dry

Category: pressure (stroke)

Description

Similar to thin (light and without relief). In dry writing the letters are taller and narrow. The writing is light, angular and squeezed, but the stroke is not necessarily always thin. The dryness should be seen in the movement and not in the width of the stroke alone. Usually, dry writings are quite regular.

Interpretation:

General Predominance of thinking, reserve. Laconic personality.

Favourable The writer is 'serious'. His thinking is precise, cautious, academic, objective and analytical. Tendency to solitude. Independence.

Unfavourable Hardness of feelings. Coldness of attitude. Lack of imagination and aridity of conscience. Intransigence. Inflexibility. Distrustfulness. Stinginess. Calculated attitudes (with supporting signs). A sombre personality with a heart of stone.

Dry writing is illustrated in examples 22, 35, and 69 (pp. 270, 277 and 303).

Fine

Category: pressure (stroke)
Synonym: delicate, thin
Antonym: pasty, thick

Description

The writing is thin and rather small; therefore, a large writing can never be fine. (Crépieux-Jamin).

Interpretation:

General Modesty. Timidity. Lack of breadth. Finicky and anxious. Feebleness of libido. The function is Thinking (auxiliary Intuition). Introversion.

Favourable Delicacy of disposition. Modesty. Sensibility. Tact. Intellectualism. Asceticism. Mysticism. This type, particularly when it is aerated, connected, progressive and combined is the writing of erudite, scholarly people (Teillard).

Unfavourable Lack of practical sense. Physical weakness. Inactivity. Anxiety. Inhibitions. Mental debility. Narrowness of mind. Old age.

Fine writing is illustrated in examples 8 and 66 (pp. 264 and 300).

Firm

Category: pressure (stroke)
Synonym: steady, consistent
Antonym: hesitant, shaky, faltering

Description

The written movement is more or less angular, firm, sure, constant and precise. Down strokes are neat, resolute and robust without breakages or shakiness.

Interpretation:

General Energetic and powerful character. Activity. Good health. Strong libido, in progression (p. 217). Vitality. Passion.

Favourable Self-composure. Stability, maturity and strength of character. Firmness. Action. Energy. Virility (see animus, p. 221). Maturity. Self-control. Psychic dynamism. Resistance. Decisiveness. Resolution. Brilliance of personality. Resistance to influence.

Unfavourable Extreme sensitivity creating tension which could provoke violent, brusque and aggressive reactions. On occasions, even brutality (with supporting signs).

Firm writing is illustrated in examples 4, 46, 62 and 69 (pp. 262, 286, 296 and 303).

Medium Tension

Category: pressure (stroke)
Synonym: moderate pressure
Antonym: heavy, light, weak, flabby

Description

The tension of the stroke is neither taut nor slack and the strokes keep their firmness without being either hard, flabby or weak.

Interpretation:

General It is a happy medium. The writer is adaptable without losing anything of his own personality. His attitudes are firm but not rigid, supple without being weak, tolerant but not passive, decisive and active but not intolerant, resilient but not inflexible, etc. The interpretation of this type, like all the others, depends very much on the rest of the signs and on the level of the Formlevel.

Medium tension is illustrated in examples 1 and 43 (pp. 260 and 284).

Pasty

Category: pressure (stroke)
Synonym: rich, heavy
Antonym: light, thin

Description

A well-nourished stroke with very little or no distinction between the up and down strokes; thick, slow and soft. If pasty writing is also pressed down and is heavy, then it is not called pasty but heavy.

Interpretation:

General The function is sensation.

Favourable With malleable and aesthetic forms, original and rhythmic, it shows the artistic talent of the writer; sense of colour and form. Taste for visual and tactile sensations. Sensuality. Warmth of personality.

Unfavourable Acute sensuality. The writer follows his instincts without reasoning. Tendency to flabbiness. Self-indulgence. Lack of constraint. Greediness.

In some pathological cases: bad health (circulatory or cardiac deficiencies), alcoholism.

The pathological interpretation of this writing should not be mentioned to the writer himself because he is likely to develop psychosomatic symptoms or become obsessed with his health.

Pasty writing is illustrated in examples 18 and 61 (pp. 268 and 295).

Precise

Category: pressure (stroke)
Synonym: in focus
Antonym: blurred, out of focus, fluffy

Description

The borders of the stroke are precise, neatly sharp and without fluff or blurr. The writing appears firm and 'in focus'. Consistency in direction helps precise writing, whereas hesitation does not.

Interpretation:

Favourable Good self-control. Clarity and order of mind and thought. Good mental equilibrium. Will-power. Tendency to precision. Perseverance. Orderliness. Objectivity. Ability to concentrate. Discipline. Moderate energy. Sensitivity.

If the writing is angular: stability.

If the writing is small: ability to concentrate on small details. The function is Intuition (auxiliary Thinking), or vice versa.

Unfavourable With angularity and other supporting signs: puritanism, austerity, coldness.

Precise writing is illustrated in examples 9, 14, 62, and 68 (pp. 265, 267, 296 and 302).

Runny

Category: pressure (stroke)
Synonym: dripping
Antonym: precise

Description

The top side of the stroke is precise (in focus) and the bottom side blurred, like a fringe. Particularly common in a writing with flying strokes (Beachataud).

Interpretation:

General Strong vitality. Strong will-power. Strong instincts. Impulsiveness. Aggression. Authoritarianism. Rage. Violence. Snarling, cantankerous, nagging person (with supporting signs). Also, ill-tempered, vicious, unpleasant, wicked, evil, mischievous, spiteful, nasty.

Depending on the Formlevel and on the supporting signs the graphologist will choose the ones which apply to each writing.

Runny writing is illustrated in example 27 (p. 274).

Smeary

Category: pressure (stroke)
Synonym: smudgy, muddy
Antonym: light

Description

The writing is thick in every way; the strokes are full of ink to the extent of filling up the ovals of the small letters, particularly when writing with a fountain pen. The graphologist must carefully examine this sign in case it is accidental, for instance, done by a piece of fluff stuck on the nib of the pen; in this case it will appear on one or two lines only and should be discarded. Modern felt-tip pens also may produce this sign but not the ballpoint pen.

Interpretation:

General Greediness. Sensuality. Disorder. A smeary writing, when it is not accidental, is a sign of coarseness, roughness and vulgarity.

If there are also signs of depression it will show neurasthenia, tiredness and feebleness; in these cases there is not enough energy to lift the hand from the paper and this produces this kind of writing.

Hypertension and/or circulatory difficulties also will produce this sign.

Hysteria is often expressed with a smeary pressure in a filiform writing with abrupt variations in size and other signs of imbalance.

Other psychoses which show an increase of sensuality can also be expressed with a smeary writing. The conscious gets inundated with instinctive impulses and images from the unconscious (Pulver).

Smeary writing is illustrated in examples 26 and 32 (pp. 273 and 276).

Thick

Category: pressure (stroke)
Synonym: wide, heavy
Antonym: thin, taut

Description

The stroke is pasty, wide and indistinct without depth; the movement is slow, without tension. The writing is curved, round, slack and weak.

Interpretation:

General Sensuality. The writer succumbs easily to all materialistic pleasures. His will is weak. He is slow and lazy. He lacks finesse and tact.

He can have good memory, particularly a visual memory (if the writing is heavily coloured, not pale) and, although he lacks creativity, he can be a good executor (Vels).

Thick Writing is illustrated in example 18 (p. 268).

Thin

Category: pressure (stroke)
Synonym: slim, slender, dry
Antonym: nourished, thick, dilated

Description

The writing is long (middle zone), light, narrow and 'dry', without depth, tension or dynamism in the stroke.

Interpretation:

General Introversion. The writer is physically frail and delicate. Nervous temperament, grumpy, insecure, anxious. Impressionable and weak, he is very likely to let himself be influenced in any direction. Timid. Inconsistent. He adapts with difficulty to the world. Touchy. Lacks imagination. If the writing is also angular and of a monotonous slant his behaviour is antisocial and rigid.

With a fine irregular writing widely spaced: isolation, asceticism, strong intellectuality but still clumsy and 'dry' when associating with others.

Thin writing is illustrated in examples 29 and 38 (pp. 275 and 281).

Form

Ample

Category: form
Synonym: generous
Antonym: dry

Description

The whole writing is ample, graceful and in relief, the movement is flowing, original and full without being dilated. Curves are predominant and the forms of the letters are generous and harmonious. There are no exaggerations. This writing is often combined.

Interpretation:

General Good vitality. Libido in progression. Intuition. Imagination. Extroversion.

Favourable Large field of consciousness. Open mindedness. The writer possesses the art of living; he is creative, enthusiastic, intuitive and aesthetic. He communicates with ease; he can express his thoughts and feelings with ease and fluency. He is imaginative and resourceful.

Unfavourable Lack of objective judgement; the writer finds it difficult to detach himself emotionally and make an objective evaluation of a situation. Tendency to exaggeration. Possible confusion of imagination with reality.

Ample writing is illustrated in examples 4, 13 and 14 (pp. 262, 266 and 267).

Angular

Category: form
Synonym: spiky, jagged
Antonym: rounded, in garlands

Description

Predominance of angular movement, replacing curves with angles within the letters or in the connections between letters.

Interpretation:

General In the old days it was often used by women (the French Sacré Coeur style). Its interpretation varied enormously according to its position, its direction, its intensity, the rest of the signs and the Formlevel. We can, however, say that its principal, general meaning is resistance; from intransigence and stubbornness to independence and firmness, from anger and violence to decisiveness and honesty, etc.

Favourable In a rapid writing with good firm pressure and a vertical or gentle right slant it shows firmness of character, decisiveness and a tendency to impose one's own decisions. Great capacity for work, stamina. Febrile activity, self-discipline, independence, power of logic and reason. The more regular the writing the more it shows strength, will-power and control over the writer's own sentimentality. A virile nature.

Straightforwardness, severity, austerity, discipline, perseverance, consistency, integrity, well-developed professional attitudes.

Unfavourable If the writing is narrow (squeezed) as a whole, and slow, it will indicate extreme emotivity, inhibition, prejudice, indifference towards other people's feelings. Narrowness of mind. Pendantry. Excessive sensitivity. Mistrustfulness. Egocentricity. Schizoid tendencies. Inferiority complex. Envy. Aggression. Obsessive tendencies. With regressive forms of writing it will show an entrenched and negative attitude: a stubborn, peevish, ill-tempered and vicious character.

Men with angular writing in a good Formlevel have good, commanding qualities. They are intelligent, combative, albeit obstinate. 'They are more valuable in society than in the family.' (Crépieux-Jamin)

In women, angular writing indicates a need to disguise their natural personality. If the writing has good tension and firmness in both movement and pressure and the angles are acute it shows a wish to manipulate others towards the writer's own desires and interests.

If the angles are supple and the writing is nuancée, rapid and harmonious then it shows a supple intelligence of the highest quality. The writer has achieved an inner balance. He has reduced his needs to the minimum and has solved any conflict within himself. He or she has reached a state of serenity.

Angular writing is illustrated in examples 3, 21, 22, 65 and 69 (pp. 262, 269, 270, 299 and 303).

Animated

Category: form
Synonym: lively, eventful
Antonym: contained, prudent, modest, sober

Description

An agitated writing, vivacious, rapid with ample movement, mobile and with exaggeration of the stroke in all directions.

Interpretation:

General Activity, imagination, extroversion, gaiety.

Favourable Dynamism, ambition, richness of imagination and intensity of life. Well-organized activity if, despite the agitations, there is order and rhythm in the writing. With a combined connection it also shows social adaptability.

Unfavourable Vanity, overexuberance. Nervous tension. Exaggerated reactions. Lack of self-control. Behaviour is impulsive and instinctive needs are made quite evident by the writer. Immature character and mentality. Impetuosity.

Animated writing is illustrated in examples 14 and 23 (pp. 267 and 270).

Arabesques

Category: form

Description

Flying curves usually starting from the initial letter (capital letter), covering or underlining the word that follows. Smaller arabesques occur in the middle of words.

Interpretation:

General Inspiration. Ceremoniousness.

If the arabesque is in the upper zone it indicates an imposing protectiveness, arrogance or patronizing attitudes. The writer is only too happy to demonstrate and prove his superiority.

If the arabesque is underneath the word, the writer is obliging, graceful, amiable (if the writing is also in garlands), polite and ceremonious (with copy-book writing).

Arabesque writing is illustrated in examples 3, 45, 51 and 55 (pp. 262, 285, 289 and 291).

Arcades

Category: form
Synonym: cambered, arched
Antonym: in garlands

Description

The connections and/or the letters m and n are shaped in the form of an arch; arches can also appear as an initial stroke, in the upper zone and in the middle zone.

Interpretation:

General Beauchataud gives three general interpretations for the arcade: 'Show off; construct; protect.' In any case the arcade is a covering, enclosing shape; its interpretation revolves around the significance of this, both positive and negative.

Favourable Prudence, reflection and reserve. Lack of spontaneity. Individualism. The writer has good manners, pride, poise. He is polite, ceremonious and courteous. He has good taste, originality of conceptions and ideas. He is creative and constructive. His sense of form is developed.

In the upper zone: constructive and creative imagination. Many writers and artists have arches in the upper zone. Arcades may, however, show vanity, narcissism, pride and a need to stay apart. They are also a sign of introversion and introspection.

Unfavourable Arrogance, disdain, pretension, vanity, coldness. Tendency to hide, to dissimulate one's natural inclinations. Lack of trust in people generally. Egoism, hypocrisy (with angles, filiforms, etc.). With a banal writing: conformity. The arch is one of the signs of dishonesty (see p. 205).

When the chain of arcades regresses slightly, thus forming a little loop (eye) as it progresses rightwards, e.g. the forms are large, wide and the stroke is thick, pasty and rather blurred, it is a sign of narcissistic tendencies, exhibitionism and often amorality and dissimulation with supporting signs.

Arcades are illustrated in examples 3, 4 and 19 (pp. 262 and 269).

Artificial

Category: form
Synonym: affected, disguised, systematic, conventional
Antonym: spontaneous

Description

Pretentious forms. Systematic and stereotyped writing done with evidently conscious and voluntary effort.

The principal elements of artificial writing are exaggeration: inharmonious, too regular, too large, too small, too thick, too light, etc. Constraint: angular, automatic, low, pale, calligraphic, imprecise, inhibited, slow, monotonous, typographic (script), regular, suspended (letters), constrained, retouched, etc. Complication: confused, tangled, disorderly, ornate, etc. Fancy: bizarre, *baroque*, *eccentric*, *extravagant*, mannered, etc. (Crépieux-Jamin).

Interpretation:

General The function is Sensation. Introversion. Artificial writing is generally used to dissimulate weakness of character. Insincerity of character if this style is constant and systematic.

Favourable Need for originality. If the writing is also rapid and combined, as well as original and harmonious, it shows creativity, independence and aesthetic sense. Imagination. Taste for beauty.

Unfavourable Snobbery, Narcissism. Coquetry. Exhibitionism. Extravagance, Arrogance. Lack of spontaneity. Lack of sincerity. Feeling or complex of inferiority (depending on the rest of the signs). With big exaggerations it will indicate various kinds of mental imbalance. Compensatory overestimation of self. Neurosis. Superficiality. Egoism. Silliness.

Artificial writing is illustrated in examples 19, 20, 30, 51 and 52 (pp. 269, 275, 289 and 290).

Bizarre

Category: form
Synonym: affected, extravagant
Antonym: simple, correct

Description

An intentionally ornate writing, and therefore artificial, with bizarre strokes, often baroque and grotesque, designed to draw attention. It is a mannered writing, strange and exaggerated, affected, slow and extravagant.

Interpretation:

General Snobbery. Desire to attract attention, excessive vanity. Lack of sense of the ridiculous. Exaltation. Extravagance. Narcissism. Coquetry.

Favourable Depending on the overall state of the writing it shows an originality of behaviour in opposition to the conventional. An inventive mind and renovating abilities, if there are no unbalanced exaggerations.

Unfavourable Intellectual exaltation. Mental debility. Ostentation. Disorder of the imagination. A bizarre character; a whimsical, odd person.

Bizarre writing is illustrated in examples 14 and 55 (pp. 267 and 291).

Bow Ties or Loops

Category: form
Synonym: little lassos
Antonym: simple

Description

The ovals o, a, d, g, etc. are connected with a small regressive movement forming a bow (not necessarily closed), usually at the top of the oval.

Interpretation:

Egocentricity. Diplomacy. Dissimulation. Mistrust. Ulterior motives. Hypocrisy. Calculation.

With light, feeble writing this sign shows inhibition, lack of courage. Egoism.

See also Double Joins (p. 102).

Bow ties or loops are illustrated in examples 26, 35, 48, 62 and 67 (pp. 273, 277, 287, 296 and 301).

Closed

Category: form
Synonym: shut
Antonym: open

Description

The ovals are firmly closed. The writing gives the impression of being hermetically sealed.

Interpretation:

General Egocentricity. Need to captivate others. In a good Formlevel: introversion, discretion, prudence, reserve, inhibition. With a weak, slow writing: dissimulation, egoism, distrustfulness, anxiety, ambivalence. Hesitation (with supporting signs). Exhibitionism and narcissism (with a pasty, round, large, mannered and spread-out writing); the writer insists on being noticed.

See also Double Joins (p. 102) and Bow Ties (see above).

Closed writing is illustrated in examples 20 and 50 (pp. 269 and 289).

Complicated

Category: form
Synonym: unnecessary strokes
Antonym: simple

Description

Containing strokes that are unnecessary to the formation of the letters. This sign has infinite variations.

Interpretation:

General Exaggerated self-importance. Tendency to complicate things unnecessarily. The writer tends to attribute importance to things of no importance. Hesitation.

Favourable Ability to present things in a more interesting manner. Strong imagination. Rhetorical talent. Poise. Meticulous person.

Unfavourable Inhibitions, Indecision. Lack of simplicity. The imagination rules the reason. Incoherence. Desire to attract attention to onself, to impress, to influence others.

The writer may be frivolous, coquettish, mannered, affected. Lack of simplicity and of honesty. Narcissism; extravagance. Neuropsis. Mythomania. Mental delirium. Amoral tendencies. Confusion. Lies. Intrigue. Dishonesty. Fraud.

Complicated writing is illustrated in examples 14, 22, 50, 51 and 55 (pp. 267, 270, 289 and 291).

Confused

See Layout, p. 41.

Conventional

Category: form
Synonym: conformist
Antonym: original

Description

The description of this writing varies not only from decade to decade but also from country to country. It usually shows a regularity in most or all of the categories, a stability of movement, a cadence of speed (when sufficient fluency has been acquired). It follows the fashion from generation to generation. It can be angular or in garlands, usually slightly slanted to the right, and it can be connected or typographical (print style) and vertical, for example, the 'sergeant-major' style, written above a ruler.

Interpretation:

General Conformity. Conventionalism.

Favourable If harmonious and rhythmic, it shows attachment to principles, courage, moral and emotional stamina, and stability of character. Resistance to hardship, politeness, courtesy, adaptability and reliability.

Unfavourable Lack of originality, lack of personality, lack of spontaneity. Overestimation of self (with supporting signs). Snobbery. Hypocrisy. Superficial concern or compassion.

In all cases it indicates the writer's suppressed feelings.

Conventional writing is illustrated in examples 12, 25, 35, 38, 47 and 48 (pp. 266, 270, 272, 277, 281 and 287).

Copy-Book

Category: form
Synonym: ceremonious
Antonym: negligent

Description

The reproduction of forms, movements, dimensions and proportions of a set style taught at school e.g., copper-plate italic, Sacré Coeur, etc. without any modification. 'Persona' writing. Not necessarily slow.

Interpretation:

General Lack of dynamism and originality. Taste for regularity and routine. Conventionalism. Identification with the social or professional role in life. The writer's 'dignity' is the one attributed to him by his profession or work. This welding of the personality with his or her work or social role deforms the character at a risk of it becoming rigid, mechanized, hard. It loses flexibility and adaptability. The writer wears a mask (persona), behind which all naturalness and spontaneity are strangled.

When this identification becomes a second nature it is pointless to try to look behind the mask, says Jung, because we shall only find a little, miserable creature. Consequently, the copy-book writing often indicates hidden, regressed feelings and neuroses of all kinds.

The stronger the personality of the writer the more the writer breaks away from the model taught at school.

Unfavourable Lack of inventiveness and initiative. Lack of creative imagination. Conformity. Egoism. Impenetrability. Limited intelligence. The intelligent person knows how to put to use his or her psychic forces, to channel them.

In copy-book writing we cannot tell whether there is a 'blockage' or a 'camouflage' of the creative forces of the writer.

Note: Every stage of the evolution of an individual is expressed by an evolution of the forms in his or her writing.

Copy-book writing is illustrated in examples 16, 22, 30, 48 and 52 (pp. 267, 270, 275, 287 and 290).

Covering Strokes

Category: form
Synonym: regressive
Antonym: progressive

Description

Covering strokes are produced by a retrograde movement of the pen returning on the same stroke, preceded by an abrupt change of direction.

They can appear in the upper or in the lower extensions, as well as in the middle zone, particularly in the a, c, e, i, m, n, o, r, u, w and z. They can be vertical, slanted in any direction, horizontal or curved.

The supported connections, the shark's tooth and the double-joined signs, are part of the covering-strokes group of signs (see pp. 128, 122 and 102).

Interpretation:

General In a garlanded writing they show timidity, embarrassment, inhibition and self-deception. The writer is embarrassed, possibly by the failure of his original ambitions, and he tries to hide it, manipulating the truth in every possible way.

It is always a sign of profound inhibition affecting freedom of expression. The result is deceit.

In an arcaded writing they show a particularly closed and unnatural character. With supporting signs a calculated and reserved attitude. Insincerity is evident through the writer's inability to penetrate matters in depth and his tendency to dissimilate his lack of understanding.

In an angular writing they show a strict and conventional education and upbringing (Sacré Coeur).

If the covering strokes are mainly in the upper zone the interpretation is of inhibitions in the intellectual sphere. Insincerity here is only a result of disappointment.

Max Pulver stresses that the dissimulation of intention takes the written shape of rounded accents, initial and final strokes and upper extensions where vanity and dementia (insanity) are closely connected.

If the covering strokes appear mainly in the middle zone they show sentimental illusion and hence cunning and hypocrisy of behaviour in public and in private.

If they appear in the lower zone they show dissimulation in the instinctive sphere. With heavy pressure, particularly, they are the indication of sexual and erotic dissimulation. With light pressure they are simply dissimulation of material things.

Curved covering strokes, being the most difficult to produce, show a form of dissimulation and insincerity which is most agile and refined.

Covering strokes are illustrated in examples 19, 24 and 38 (pp. 269, 271 and 281).

Cramped

Category: form
Synonym: retracted, withdrawn
Antonym: expanded, free-flowing, comfortable

Description

The letters are uneven, incomplete and inefficiently developed. Cramped writing shows hesitation and difficulty in the formation of the letters. It is slow, diminished in size and the forms are deprived of movement and expansion.

Interpretation:

General Fatigue. Old age. Senility. Ill health. Worry. Hesitation, indecisiveness and confusion caused by physical weakness or illness. With supporting signs it indicates a niggling character, finicky nature, narrowness of mind, meanness and pettiness.

Cramped writing is illustrated in examples 19, 20 and 41 (pp. 269 and 283).

Disguised

Category: form
Synonym: artificial
Antonym: spontaneous

Description

The habitual forms of a writing have been intentionally changed, disguised. When the writer tries to change his normal writing he will use the opposite signs to his usual ones. For instance, he will change the slant and the size, being the most obvious and easy to alter.

Interpretation:

General The motives for changing one's writing vary from humorous to criminal. It is always a dissimulation, and shows ill faith and cowardice.

Anonymous letters motivated by different causes, from marital jealousy to treason, are a good example of this type of writing.

Disguised writing falls into the field of criminological graphology and a graphologist should not try to tackle it without the assistance of an expert in this field.

The only possible statement we can make at this stage is that there is no such thing as a totally successfully *disguised* writing.

Disguised writing is illustrated in examples 16 and 36a (pp. 267 and 278).

Distinguished

Category: form
Synonym: noble
Antonym: gross, crude

Description

The forms are simple, harmonious, proportionate and pleasing to the eye. Freedom of movement (comfort) and clarity are imperative in order to call a writing distinguished.

Interpretation:

General Nobility of character and attitudes. Good education. Good manners. Consideration of other people's opinions and feelings. Courtesy. Good taste.

The family circle plays no part here. It is only a matter of individual character and personality.

Distinguished writing can be found at all social levels, as can crude and gross writing. Men and women of great charm are in a class of their own which may or may not have any connection with their family background.

Distinguished writing is illustrated in examples 1, 2, 3, 5 and 66 (pp. 260, 261, 262, 263 and 300).

Double curves

Category: form

Description

The connections between the down strokes (mainly in the middle zone) alternate between garlands and arcades in the same letter, e.g. .

Interpretation:

General Weakness. Lack of will-power, of backbone. Sweetness of character and of behaviour. Conciliating attitudes. Inoffensive personality. Lack of firmness. The writer avoids situations where he or she will have to take decisions. He dislikes obligations and everything attached to them.

In a low Formlevel writing and with other supporting signs, (muddy pressure, etc.) it will indicate cowardly behaviour, insincerity and dissimulation.

Double-curved writing is illustrated in example 19 (p. 269).

Double Joined

Category: form
Synonym: closed
Antonym: open

Description

The ovals 'o' and 'a' are firmly closed; the stroke forms first a 'u' and then goes around again to finish the letter

Interpretation:

General Egoism. Dissimulation. Mistrust. Calculation. Hypocrisy. Simple-mindedness. Unevolved character. Tendency to neurotic or hysterical behaviour.

It is a regressive movement; a more complicated form of 'closed' writing.

Secretiveness is more conscious and, with supporting signs such as bow-ties, looped garlands etc., more deliberate or calculated than in simple closed ovals.

Social amiability may also be expressed if the writing is curved, velvety, wide, etc.

See also Bow Ties (p. 95) and Closed (p. 95).

Double joined writing is illustrated in examples 27 and 47 (pp. 274 and 287).

Elegant

Category: form
Synonym: pleasant, graceful, distinguished
Antonym: heavy, uncouth, gross

Description

Elegant writing is orderly and constructed with curves and small flying movements towards the right. The letters are mainly of typographic origin, simplified and combined. This writing is usually small.

Interpretation:

Favourable Distinction. Good taste. Good manners. Charm. Graceful attitudes.

Unfavourable The slightest exaggeration of any of the elements which construct this writing will make it lose its elegance and delicate charm. It will show coquetry, affectation, conceit, self-complacency, with an obvious need to appear attractive.

Elegant writing is illustrated in examples 29, 45 and 66 (pp. 275, 285 and 300).

Filiform

Category: form
Synonym: thready
Antonym: clear

Description

The middle zone letters, particularly the m and the n, become like a wavy thread. Threadiness can also appear at the end of words, as well as a connection between letters and words. It is a form of Diminishing writing, p. 54.

Interpretation:

General Adaptability. Evasive attitude. Variability. Phlegmatic temperament. Filiformity is often caused by haste; the writer needs to jot something down very quickly. It is a need to simplify the writing for reasons of speed, economy of movement and time. Ill or lazy people may also have this sign arising from economy of effort.

Favourable Creative and original thinking. Ability to improvise solutions and also to see opportunities. Mental activity (with combined writing, original and fast) (Vels). Great physical activity. Adaptability. Diplomacy. Simplification. Inventiveness. The function is intuition.

Unfavourable Laziness. Nervousness. Tiredness. Indecision. Easily impressed. Physical weakness. Impatience. Running away from responsibilities. Often irresponsible behaviour. Instability. Filiformity is also one of the signs of dishonesty (p. 205), deceit, defiance, equivocal behaviour, dissimulation, intrigue. Instability. Inferiority complex. If there is also disproportion between capital letters and the small ones it shows overcompensation of an inferiority complex (Teillard).

Filiform writing is illustrated in examples 11, 17, 49, 58 and 64 (pp. 266, 268, 288, 293 and 298).

Formless

Category: form
Synonym: shapeless, unstructured
Antonym: correct

Description

The writing becomes disfigured from imprecise forms. It is illegible, tormented and ugly, crude or gross, depending on the cause.

Often, a writing may become formless from excessive speed, another expression of the writer's personality.

Interpretation:

General This writing is found at all social levels. Writers often have shapeless writing caused by speed. Pascal and Napoleon had very rapid and formless writing.

In a low Formlevel it shows clumsiness, coarseness, rudeness, vulgarity, roughness, offensive attitudes, lack of social culture, mental confusion. In a less low Formlevel it will indicate excessive activity, uncontrollable, impulsive vitality and/or profound sensitivity (depending on supporting signs, for instance, in combinations, pressure, etc.).

In any case, it shows gaucherie, clumsiness and lack of consideration for the reader.

Some nervous illnesses also produce this kind of writing.

Formless writing is illustrated in examples 23, 53 and 56 (pp. 270, 290 and 292).

Garlands

Category: form
Synonym: rolled up, in festoons
Antonym: angular

Description

The bottom of the letters on the baseline is curved like a cup, substituting all angles or arcades with open curves, for instance, when the word *mama* becomes *uauua*. The garland is also found as an initial or final stroke.

Interpretation:

General Sociability. Benevolence. Kindness. Extroversion. The function is Sentiment. Openness. Adaptability. Easy, relaxed behaviour. The more spread-out the garlands the more sociable is the person; also, the more chance of superficiality, sensuality and lack of scruples.

To interpret this type of writing it is helpful to establish function and attitude first. For instance, if the writing is small the main function would be Thinking; in this case the adaptability etc. will be mental rather than sentimental and so on.

Favourable Receptivity. Amiability. Suppleness. Sensitivity. Devotion. Ability to recognize the value of other people's work (Klages). Spontaneity. Sympathy. Compassion. Altruism. Self-sacrifice. Hospitality. Rich emotional world.

Unfavourable When the writing lacks tension and stability it shows indecision, someone who is easily influenced, hesitation, lack of independence. 'Lack of initiative' (Klages). If the pressure is heavy on the baseline it shows selfishness and materialistic interests. Sensuality. Lack of modesty in sensual pleasures. Negligence, nonchalance, lack of activity, coldness, if the pressure is light and flabby. Triviality. Indolence. Laziness.

Some psychologists consider the garland to be a feminine trait and, when it appears in men's writing, they attribute a feeble character; this is not far from the truth under the right circumstances, i.e. with supporting signs. If the garland, however, coincides with a good firm pressure in men's writing it shows productive activity, practical sense and adaptability.

Garlanded writing is often found in artists, psychologists, writers, diplomats and people who deal with children.

If the garlands are deep and the writing is descending and light in pressure it may also indicate melancholia, lack of energy, feebleness, the causes of which can vary from physical to psychological.

When the chain of garlands regresses slightly every time, thus forming a little eye (looped garlands) as it progresses towards the right, it is generally an indication of egocentricity, sociability and calculated amiability. If the garlands are also deep, speed is slow and pressure is pasty, blurred, muddy or runny, it shows amoral tendencies.

Garlands are illustrated in examples 4, 10, 11, 26, 27 and others (pp. 262, 265, 266, 273 and 274).

Graceful

Category: form
Synonym: agreeable, harmonious
Antonym: ungraceful, unpleasing

Description

With pleasing curves, clear, harmonious, simplified, limpid, rounded and poised or accelerated. Angular writing is rare in this category, and harmony and rhythm are almost always present.

Interpretation:

General It is mainly an indication of kind-heartedness and charm. Softness of attitude, sweetness of nature. All amiable and positive qualities are attributed to this type. Grace, good manners, progressive thinking, sociability, aesthetic talents (art), inner harmony, good equilibrium of functions, modesty, discretion, clarity of thoughts, impartial judgement, distinction, simplicity and resolution.

Graceful writing is illustrated in examples 3, 4, 5, 47 and 62 (pp. 262, 263, 287 and 296).

Gross

Category: form
Synonym: crude
Antonym: elegant, graceful, distinguished

Description

Heavy and slow writing, often with various exaggerations. Formless and ungraceful.

Interpretation:

General Lack of manners, mainly through lack of education. Disorderly behaviour and attitudes. Tendency to exaggeration. Confusion. Rudeness. Gross people, however, are not necessarily bad and although it is very difficult, if not impossible, to shed their rudeness after the age of puberty, it does not necessarily follow that they are negative; they can be honest and useful to society in their own way, particularly if they are energetic and have a sense of humour.

Gross writing is illustrated in examples 23, 50 and 53 (pp. 270, 289 and 290).

Harmonious

Category: form

Description

Good proportions and order of general layout, clarity, simplicity and sobriety of stroke and fluency or freedom of movement are the six basic elements of harmonious writing.

Interpretation:

Favourable Harmony of writing corresponds to harmony of the writer's character. It is the 'great mark of superiority' says Crépieux-Jamin. It indicates all things good: positive thinking, good equilibrium of tendencies, functions and attitudes (Jung), well-developed aestheticism, a cultivated mind, sociability, self-control, distinction of character, sensitivity, imagination, clarity of thinking. Nothing disturbs the writing's aesthetic look and nothing disturbs the writer's solid equilibrium (Trillat).

Harmonious writing is illustrated in examples 1, 2, 3, 13, 46, 49 and 66 (pp. 260, 261, 262, 266, 286, 288 and 300).

Illegible

Category: form
Synonym: confused, imprecise
Antonym: legible, clear, limpid

Description

Illegibility in a writing can be caused by excessive speed ('precipitated' writing); bizarre forms (deformed writing); the absence of some letters in the words ('unfinished' writing); lack of order in the layout ('confused' writing); and disorganization ('disorganized' writing).

Interpretation:

General To interpret illegibility we must always look for its association with other signs. Generally, it shows neurosis, febrile activity, intrigue. A tendency to imprecision, mystery, secrecy and dissimulation. A need to be 'different'. Avoidance of responsibilities, instability. Fatigue or lack of morality. Dishonesty.

When it is caused by excessive speed it shows lack of order and precision in action. Carelessness. Thoughtlessness. Lack of foresight. Equivocal tendencies.

When it is caused by jerkiness it shows great nervous tension. The writer has difficulty in relaxing or calming down.

When it is caused by an extremely diminished size of middle zone, it may indicate depression, crippling inhibition.

In all cases it will indicate unresolved personal problems. Often creative people have illegible writing; they wish to be different, unconventional and original. They have a taste for abstract thought and for art.

Illegible writing is illustrated in examples 9, 17, 26, 33a and 40 (pp. 265, 268, 273, 276 and 282).

Impersonal

Category: form
Synonym: insignificant, banal
Antonym: original, individual

Description

Very close to a conventional model. It looks as if it does not fit anyone. It is totally, or almost totally, lacking in individual movement.

'But let us not forget that no character is like any other and let us not imitate the graphologists who, when faced with a writing whose secrets are beyond their grasp, think themselves clever at solving their problem by classifying the writing as banal and thus saving themselves the trouble of studying it. The people who they dismiss only too easily as banal hold all sorts of surprises for them.' (Crépieux-Jamin)

Interpretation:

General Conformity. Banality. When written by young people in adolescence it is not yet grounds for despair. But when it is produced by adults it shows a sterility of character and personality. Teachers, nuns, army people often have impersonal writing. It is a form of professional deformation. It is a very rare writing and in any case is mainly used by a non-emotive person (emotivity will always insert its typical irregularities in anyone's writing). As Crépieux-Jamin says, 'On barren ground the harvest is always meagre.'

Impersonal writing is illustrated in examples 24, 35 and 38 (pp. 271, 277 and 281).

Inharmonious

Category: form

Description

Disproportions, complications, exaggerations, confusion, vulgarities, etc. constitute inharmonious writing.

Inharmonious writing, like all other signs, depends for its interpretation on the other signs, both favourable and unfavourable.

Inharmonious writing should not dispose the graphologist negatively towards the writing. Prejudice is the cause of many misjudgements. Many inharmonious writings have other qualities.

Harmony is one of the six components which constitute the Formlevel. The others are organization, spontaneity, originality, dynamism and rhythm (see p. 21).

Inharmonious writing is illustrated in examples 22, 23, 24, 50, 53, 56 and 63 (pp. 270 and 271).

Irregular

See Continuity, p. 160.

Lassos

See Particular Signs, p. 195.

Limpid

Category: form
Synonym: clear
Antonym: confused, crude, formless, shapeless

Description

Good layout, great clarity, aerated spacing, harmonious, progressive, distinct pressure (in relief), neat strokes, simplified; these are the presuppositions for a limpid writing.

Interpretation:

General It is usually the sign of a 'luminous mind' and a 'noble character'. It indicates clarity of thinking, simplicity, sincerity, morality. If it is also aesthetically combined, proportionate and rapid, it will show high intellectual abilities, simplicity of character, distinction and serenity.

Sometimes, i.e. with infantile forms, slow or poised writing, excessive spacing and with some discreet disproportions, it can be the writing of an insignificant mind, albeit highly moral, sincere and simplistic, with a very modest but honest intelligence.

Limpid writing is illustrated in examples 44 and 66 (pp. 284 and 300).

Looped Garlands

Category: form
Synonym: regressive garlands
Antonym: progressive garlands

Description

The garlands, as they progress, form a little loop, resulting from a small regressive movement of the hand, the result is like a line of 'e's.

Interpretation:

General It is usually a sign of selfishness because of the leftward movement necessary to form the little loop.

If the writing is slow, regular, heavy, with a pasty pressure, and the garlands are deep and trailing on the baseline, this sign will indicate strong sensuality, amorality, materialism and passivity.

If the writing is also inhibited it shows withdrawal and timidity.

If the writing is generally weak, slow, with a vertical or leftward slant and the garlands are deep, the writer is calm, melancholic, passive, inactive, but also loyal and devoted.

If the writing is rapid, with sharp pressure, but rather without character (somewhat artificial), it shows superficiality, easy adaptability, calculated amiability, lack of depth and emotivity.

Looped garlands are illustrated in examples 26 and 62 (pp. 273 and 296).

Lower Extensions

Category: form

Description

These can be straight or curved, rightwards or leftwards leaning, long or short, heavy or light (etc.), and will be interpreted here according to the Symbolism of Space (pp. 20–21 and below).

Interpretation:

General Generally, all lower extensions are the expression of primitive forces, particularly when the pressure is strong. They represent 'unconscious images' (Pulver). In favourable interpretations they will show, therefore, the richness of imaginative life and, in unfavourable, exaggerated tendencies, pretensions, etc.

The lower extension in the form of sticks (simplified) generally express the ability to concentrate and show objectivity and intensity of thinking. They may show narrowness of the field of consciousness, depending on the rest of the signs and categories. If they are also connected to the next letter with a straight line, see Narrow Letters (p. 115).

If the lower extensions are disproportionately short (atrophied) this is usually an indication of a sterile imagination, or concentration of interest in matters of the heart or of the mind, depending on the body of the writing, or withdrawal from materialistic interests, or (depending on pressure and the rest of the signs) a feeling of unfulfilled sensuality or impotence.

Richly formed lower extensions: prolonged, looped, ample (example 7, p. 264) etc. may be interpreted on a wide scale, from creativity and the need for perfectionism to vanity, from rich imagination to degeneration (sexual or otherwise), coquetry to folly, from negligence to mental confusion.

Max Pulver divides the forms into four categories:

1. scriptural plenitude shows, generally, a high degree of aestheticism and feeling, clarity and maturity of the personality;
2. narrowness shows, generally, an intellectual exclusivity with all its advantages and disadvantages;
3. simplified forms show objectivity and the ability to separate the essential from the superfluous;
4. richness of forms (spirals etc.) show, generally, a social agility, varying from diplomatic talents to plain lying, a rich imagination, pedantic or complicated attitudes, etc.

If the lower loops are closed high (in the middle zone and, depending on the particular letter, on the rest of its formation and the rest of the signs), it may indicate loyalty, repletion or selfishness.

If they are closed low (atrophied loop) there is a desire to be appreciated or a feeling of impotence of some kind.

If the lower loops are broken but still closing, it is a sign of worry, or of difficult contact with people or of an inferiority complex, or of cardiac deficiency or overwork. The rest of the signs will guide us to the right interpretation.

If the lower loops are in the form of triangles, see Triangles (p. 203).

If the lower loops turn towards the left and do not close (if the writing is not stylized) this generally represents a return to the past. It is what the psychiatrists call a 'complex of deprivation' (premature weaning). It is an egocentric and infantile form of movement which cannot 'give', it can only 'take'.

If the lower extensions are turned towards the right when they are meant to turn towards the left, it indicates a need for independence, probably (depending on the rest of the signs) motivated by the lack of it (fear, deprivation, disappointment, etc.).

If they turn towards the left, and if they are systematic, they can be an affectionate sign, albeit egotistical.

If they form a figure of eight, a little lasso of coquetry (with supporting signs), it indicates a need to please (often lesbians form the letter 'f' in 8). If, however, they also form a triangle ( ) it shows self-control and the writer does not give up or lose courage easily. Interpretations can vary from dynamism to paranoia, from opposition to violence, etc. (example 22, p. 270).

If the lower extensions turn sharply leftwards and upwards without returning to the right, it shows spite, malice and resentment. It is generally a sign of past dissatisfaction which can be transferred to action and success or stay inactive and festering.

If this last form continues curving downwards ( ) it indicates a need for secrecy in the domain of the instincts.

If the lower extensions curve towards the left, forming a huge balloon and curling rightwards without closing, it shows vanity, imagination, coquetry, lack of activity (see Spirals, p. 126), poetic tendencies (with supporting signs).

If the lower extensions end in a hook, turning rightwards or leftwards, see Hooks (p. 194).

As no one sign can ever be interpreted on its own, so the lower extensions can only be interpreted in conjunction with the rest of the writing, pressure, speed, continuity, Formlevel, etc.

See also 'Prolonged Downwards' p. 61.

Mannered

Category: form
Synonym: affected, fancy
Antonym: simple

Description

A pretentious, fancy, theatrical writing. It is another form of embellished, ornate writing and bizarre writing (pp. 119 and 94).

Interpretation:

General Bad taste. Self-admiration. Narcissism. Triviality.

Mediocrity. Affected manners. Ceremonious politeness. Exalted vanity. Pretentious and fancy personality.

Mannered writing is illustrated in examples 14, 51, 55 and 56 (pp. 267, 289, 291 and 292).

Mirror Writing

Category: form
Synonym: reversed, from right to left
Antonym: from left to right

Description

The writing is written in reverse flow to normal, as in lithography. It has been established that this is the normal writing of left handers.* Convention and tradition teach the contrary (at least in the Western world), probably because the majority of people are right handers and it is easier to watch the writing progress on the paper without the hand obstructing the view.

Some right-handed children, at a very early age, have an ability to write in mirror style. It has been said that, in such cases, there is a history of physical or mental ill health in the family.† More recently it is thought that these children may simply have greater mental ability than average.

Note: if single letters are written in mirror fashion it is also 'mirror writing', e.g. q = p.

Mixed

Category: form

Description

The mixing of angles and curves in the same writing.

Interpretation:

General Generally used by individuals who are assessed differently by the various people who meet them.

* Karl Vogt, University of Geneva, 1880; Dr Martial Durand, Bordeaux, 1881.
† Andrée Lecerf.

Adaptability and suppleness of mind in a good Formlevel. Creative abilities. A good balance between spontaneous attitudes and reserve.

If there is a slight predominance of angular movement the writer is more 'firm' than 'sweet'. If there is a slight predominance of curved movement the writer is more 'sweet' than 'firm'.

The interpretation of this writing should be shaped and coloured in accordance with the Formlevel and the rest of the signs.

Mixed writing is illustrated in examples 7, 8, 13 and 24 (pp. 264, 266 and 271).

Narrow Letters

Category: form
Synonym: squeezed letters
Antonym: wide

Description

The letters of the middle zone are taller than wide. The ovals are narrow and the distance between the letters of the same word is very small. Also, when the lower extensions are in form of sticks and connect to the next letter with a straight line.

Interpretation:

General Inhibition. Libido in regression (p. 218). Prudence. Introversion.

Favourable Modesty. Gentleness. Reflection. Ability to concentrate the thoughts on one subject. If the writing is also simple and graceful: sensitivity and prudence.

Unfavourable Mistrustfulness. Mockery. Egoism. Jealousy. Envy. Avarice. Inferiority complex. Bitter and disdainful character. Scornful. Provoking. Parsimonious.

Narrow letters are illustrated in examples 20, 30 and 70 (pp. 269, 275 and 304).

Natural

Category: form
Synonym: not artificial
Antonym: artificial, disguised

Description

Natural writing is universal. It is any writing which is not forced, artificial or disguised. The writer has chosen the forms which suit him and has rejected whatever he dislikes and does not suit him, thus establishing an accord between his tastes and potential and their natural expression.

As children at school, we are taught a certain style of writing. This style is different from one country to another. In some countries where there is no style, government-recommended, the styles taught differ from school to school.

At the beginning all writing is difficult, effortful and disguised. With practice the child gets accustomed to tracing the same strokes and the art of writing becomes less and less strenuous, less and less conscious. The writing starts to take an individual style, although, at the same time, it keeps the fundamental style taught in the primary school. At this stage the writing starts being called natural.

Interpretation:

General A natural writing is not necessarily good, just as a totally natural person is not necessarily a good person. Civilization corrects faults, disciplines instincts and teaches people how to live in society with respect and harmony. Education, culture and civilization modify writing but do not make it unnatural or artificial.

In a similar way, natural writing could be more the indication of a gross and crude character than otherwise.

Spontaneous and comfortable writing expresses better the harmony or an evolved character. (See pp. 145 and 150.)

Natural writing is illustrated in examples 3, 5, 6, 9, 17 and others (pp. 262, 263, 265 and 268).

Negligent

Category: form
Synonym: slack
Antonym: neat, studious

Description

Lack of precision in the formation of letters. Incomplete letters. Omission of accents and/or t bars and i dots or of whatever facilitates the reading of the writing. The writing may be weak, lifeless, limp, slack or smeary.

Interpretation:

General Oversimplification. Preoccupation with expressing thoughts rather than respecting the rules of good writing.

Favourable With a dynamic, animated, decisive writing, fast, simplified and semi-angular it is indicative of activity, intuition, ability to take quick decisions, even of genius (Napoleon and the famous French mathematician Pierre de Fermat).

Unfavourable Indifference, negligence, laziness, lack of ability to concentrate, precipitate action.

With half-formed letters (incomplete), imprecise and ambiguous forms, slow speed, leftward slant and/or a generally low Formlevel it may indicate insincerity, dissimulation or lying.

Negligence may also be caused by illness or old age (disorganized writing).

Negligent writing is illustrated in examples 17, 33, 40, 58 and 60 (pp. 268, 276, 282, 293 and 294).

Open

Category: form
Synonym: open ovals, crenellated
Antonym: closed, double joined

Description

The ovals o, a, q, g, etc. are open at the top or to the right. If they are open on the left or at the bottom it may be a sign of insincerity.

Interpretation:

General This sign is more often found in women's writing. It shows receptivity, the need to talk, to express oneself. Spontaneity. Generosity. Confidence.

With a calm and homogeneous writing, rather small, low and/or proportionate it indicates melancholia and a sense of loneliness.

Favourable Sincerity of sentiments. Devotion. Altruism. The writer is ready to sacrifice his own needs for the sake of others. Self-denial. He will give himself spontaneously and with confidence (this may be imprudent). His generosity is genuine and without ulterior motive.

Kindness. Charitability. Natural sweetness.

If the writing is also slanted to the right and in garlands, the writer demonstrates his or her affections without inhibition. He expresses his emotions quickly and without disguise. (Primary response, p. 226).

Unfavourable If the writing is weak, slack or with flying strokes, it indicates talkativeness, lack of perspicacity, unreliability and lack of self-discipline. A dispersed expansion.

Lack of tact. Indiscretion. Weakness of character. The writer has difficulty in keeping things to himself; he is 'lightweight' and 'silly', too emotional. Disorderly, inconsequent and absent-minded. Imprudent. Lack of control in action.

Open writing is illustrated in example 19 (p. 269).

Original

Category: form
Synonym: inventive
Antonym: stylized, conventional

Description

The forms produced are far removed from calligraphy or any other taught style of writing; they are personal to the writer. However, the writing stays clear, legible, simplified and aesthetic. No vulgarity, exaggeration or ornamentation can be called original, no matter how 'original' it might be.

Originality is one of the six elements of the Formlevel, the others being organization, spontaneity, dynamism, harmony and rhythm.

Interpretation:

General Creativity. Originality of conceptions and ideas. Prolific and productive imagination. Occasionally, creative genius, e.g. César Franck; great capacity for creative work if the writing is also dynamic. Klages compares originality with rhythm. It is, he says, originality seen 'spatially'. He explains that the differences between the leaves of the same tree and between the children and their parents are original. Therefore, originality could not exist without organic life and life is rhythm itself, differences which are constantly repeated but never identical (see p. 9).

Original writing is illustrated in examples 3, 4, 5, 9, 45 and 68 (pp. 262, 263, 265, 285 and 302).

Ornate

Category: form
Synonym: embellished, decorated
Antonym: simple

Description

Unnecessary flourishes which complicate the writing. Ornamentations appear mainly in capital letters, the lower zone and the signature. The 'snail shells' and 'spirals' present in the middle zone are also embellishments.

The writing belongs to the category of exaggerated writing.

Interpretation:

General Vanity, Pretention. Imagination.

Favourable A sense of form will produce ornamentation. Fertile imagination. Seductive tendencies. Aestheticism and art – if the ornamentations are pleasing to the eye and harmonious. A taste for formalities. Need for expression. Sanguine temperament.

Unfavourable Pretentious and ostentatious nature. Coquetry. Frivolity. Superficiality. Bad taste. Flamboyance with supporting signs. Emptiness. Excessive exuberance. Search for effect. Overcompensated inferiority complex. Arrogance. Lack of judgement, measure and critical sense. Egocentricity.

Ornate writing is illustrated in examples 14, 22, 31, 51 and 55 (pp. 267, 270, 275, 289 and 291).

Protoform

Category: form
Synonym: unstable
Antonym: constant

Description

The writer uses many different ways of forming the same letters. This is an exaggerated form of unstable writing.

Interpretation:

General The interpretation here differs from children to adults. Children and retarded adults are hesitant when trying to choose a suitable form; this hesitancy is not in itself equivocal.

Depending on the Formlevel and associated signs this writing shows, first of all, instability and inconsistency. The writer varies in his emotions, tastes and tendencies.

Favourable Ability to vary according to the needs of the moment. Adaptability. Inventiveness.

Unfavourable Infidelity. Hypocrisy. Dissipation. Squandering. Inattentiveness. Frivolity. Deceit. An impostor.

Protoform writing is illustrated in example 13 (p. 266).

Regular

Category: form
Synonym: stable, orderly, uniform
Antonym: irregular, agitated, uneven, discordant

Description

Consistency in dimension, slant, spacing, form and pressure.

Interpretation (not valid if the writing is artificial, automatic, stylized, monotonous or 'persona'):

General Strong libido. Stability, regularity in action.

Favourable Discipline. Order. Good equilibrium of emotions and actions. Strong, constant will-power over instincts.

If the writing is angular: energy, vitality, psychic force (Teillard).

Sense of duty and sense of responsibility. Moral conscience. Puritanism.

Unfavourable With a rigid, angular writing: inflexibility. Routine. Lack of finesse. Dissimulation. Hypocrisy. Negative attitude towards others. Weak intellectually. Insincerity. Rigidity. Mediocre intelligence. Shallowness of feelings. Indifference.

Regular writing is illustrated in examples 2, 10, 19, 20, 48 and 52 (pp. 261, 265, 269, 287 and 290).

Round

Category: form
Synonym: circling, very curved
Antonym: angular

Description

Ovals formed like circles. This shape affects the letters o, a, g, etc. as well as the m and n. Not to be confused with rounded writing in which the ovals are elliptical.

Interpretation:

General This writing is more common in children; it is an easy form to understand and imitate. It shows calm, passive adaptability and general apathy.

Favourable Sociability. Adaptability. Niceness. If the pressure is coloured or well-nourished it shows hospitality and cordiality.

Unfavourable Insecurity; the writer will adapt and accept out of weakness and egoism (the round movement is forcibly regressive, p. 187). He or she needs peace. Laziness. The writer is incapable of independence and initiative.

Lack of sensitivity. Passivity. Indolence, Docility.

Apathetic and amorphous characters usually have round forms in their writing. With signs of calculated amiability (looped garlands, little loops in the middle zone, large writing etc.) the writer has a well-developed, self-interested activity, decisiveness, excessive selfishness and a very low level of sensitivity.

Round writing is illustrated in examples 16, 26 and 59 (pp. 267, 273 and 294).

Rounded

Category: form
Synonym: curved
Antonym: angular

Description

Replacing the angles with curves and accentuating the existing curves. Garlands and arcades derive from this sign. Not to be confused with round writing. Here the letters a, o, g etc. are elliptical not round.

Interpretation:

General Rounded writing does not exclude either firmness or flabbiness and that is why it can only be interpreted in accordance with other signs.

Favourable With arabesques it shows sociability, complaisance; in a typographic writing: grace (Crépieux-Jamin); in a large writing: imagination, extroversion (Jung's function of Sentiment); with a progressive writing: kindness of heart, niceness (Crépieux-Jamin); in a small writing : suppleness of attitude (Jung's function of Thinking).

Unfavourable With a slow writing: laziness, flabbiness, negligence, indifference (Crépieux-Jamin); with a regressive writing: selfishness (Crépieux-Jamin); with strong pressure at the base of the letters: selfish sensuality (Vels); with flabby writing: passivity, indolence, feebleness, lack of initiative (Vels); with wide (spread-out) curves: lack of timidity or embarrassment (Vels).

Rounded writing is illustrated in examples 1, 2, 18, 25, 46 and 47 (pp. 261, 268, 272, 286 and 287).

Shark's Tooth

Category: form

Description

This is another form of the Supported form of connections (p. 128). It is a curved form of the supported connection. It appears in the middle zone, usually in the letters m, n or u, in their angular form.

Interpretation:

General It is an indication of an instinctive, cunning ability. The writer is sly in his negotiations, artful and agile in his affairs; deceitful and hypocritical. Dissimulating and lying in a very convincing manner. Max Pulver names it as one of the signs of insincerity (p. 205).

Shark's-tooth writing is illustrated in examples 38 and 50 (pp. 281 and 289).

Simple

Category: form
Synonym: elementary
Antonym: complicated

Description

The letters are restricted to their elementary form and bear no mannerisms, ornamentations, or superfluous strokes. Not to be confused with simplified writing in which the letters are reduced to their essential structure. Simple writing may also be a simple stylized writing.

Interpretation:

General Crépieux-Jamin compares this type to the zero in arithmetic; on its own, it means nothing, it depends much on the rest of the signs.

Favourable If simple and organized: simplicity, modesty, sincerity. Associated with clear, spontaneous, rapid, combined and simplified writing it shows honesty, activity, objective intelligence, ability to synthesize, and moral integrity (if also horizontal and well spaced out). Moral principles, good equilibrium. Self-control.

If the writing is enlarging and rounded it will indicate ingenuity, simplicity of heart, guilelessness and trust.

Unfavourable Puerility. Mediocrity. Obsession with routine. Conformity. Lack of imagination. Simple-mindedness.

Young children or mentally backward people often have an unorganized and simple writing.

Simple writing is illustrated in example 16 (p. 267).

Simplified

Category: form
Synonym: reduced
Antonym: complicated

Description

The letters are reduced to their strictly essential minimal structure necessary for legibility and clarity. Not to be confused with simple writing in which the letters have kept their calligraphic style.

Interpretation:

General It shows a cultured mind, active and adaptable. Libido in progression.

Favourable Introversion. Functions of Thinking. Intuition. Education. Culture. High level of intelligence. Clear and disciplined mind. Originality of thought and conception. Clear judgement. Independence of ideas. Ability to assimilate and separate the essential from the inessential. Precision. Seriousness of character. Morality, simplicity, distinction. Good taste, order, aesthetic sense, eclecticism.

Unfavourable The only negative quality of this writing, according to Klages, is the absence of a sense of form (*Expression du Caractère dans l'Écriture*).

Oversimplified writing is not necessarily unfavourable. It may indicate creativity, productivity and an inventive mind.

Simplified writing is illustrated in examples 1, 3, 5, 8, 43, 46, 66 and 69 (pp. 260, 262, 263, 264, 284, 286, 300 and 303).

Soaring

Category: form
Synonym: lanced
Antonym: heavy, dragging

Description

A variation of lanced and prolonged upwards writing. There is a movement of a stroke (at the beginning, at the end or at times even in the middle of a word), extending upwards more or less vertically, forming a slight curve. It usually appears in apparently calm, monotonous writing, such as that of the Phlegmatic group of people (p. 230).

Interpretation:

General Imagination. Mysticism. Impulsiveness.

Favourable Ardent imagination. Idealism. Inspiration. Vivacious creativity. Rich imagination. Sensitivity. With a simplified and combined writing it shows intelligent activity.

Unfavourable Exalted ambitions. Tendency to impulsiveness. Taste for mysticism. Excessive pride. With supporting signs: madness.

Soaring writing is illustrated in example 22 (p. 270).

Spelling

Category: form
Synonym: correct (spelling)
Antonym: incorrect (spelling)

Description

Spelling, also, is indicative of the personality of the writer and should be taken into consideration.

Interpretation:

Note There are always reasons why an educated adult misspells his or her words. These reasons can be either psychological or physiological.

General When misspelling is not the result of ignorance or illiteracy – which will be easily visible in the handwriting (unorganized writing), it can be caused by lack of attention, lack of ability to concentrate, bad memory, general frivolity of personality, bad coordination. Often it will indicate a pretentious person (depending on the rest of the signs – dissimulation, insincerity, secretiveness etc.). On the other hand, it may indicate an intellectual preoccupation in which case it will be an occasional and accidental lack of control; the Formlevel and the rest of the handwriting will direct us towards or away from this interpretation.

Sometimes, certain illnesses, e.g. mental illness, brain damage, are heralded by spelling mistakes in an educated writing, long before any physical symptoms appear.

Excessive physical tiredness is often the cause of misspellings, as are also various forms of intoxication: too much smoking, alcohol, overeating.

Extreme unhappiness, causing nervous disorders, is another reason for spelling mistakes.

Correct spelling is often only a sign of good visual memory or of a particular knack for good application, especially in writing with signs of disorganization or unorganization. We should not exaggerate the value of a correctly spelled, organized writing. Many paranoiacs with a fair education are excellent spellers.

Paranoiac tendencies consist of exaggerated self esteem, false judgement, mistrustfulness, spirit of revenge and persecution, social inadaptability.

'Spelling' is illustrated in example 23 (p. 270).

Spirals

Category: form

Description

A centripetal movement. A curve which starts from a central point and turns around itself, enlarging like the shell of the snail. It is another form of complicated writing. It appears mainly in capital letters but also in some small letters (like the c) in the initial and the final strokes of the middle zone.

It is an intentional sign.

Interpretation:

General Vanity. Egocentricity. Exaltation. Narcissism. Desire to attract attention and interest.

When the spiral appears in the initial stroke or upper zone: narcissism, coquetry, presumptiousness, egoism, triviality, arrogance, vanity, capricious nature.

When the spiral appears in the final stroke: exaggerated egoism, lack of equilibrium between the self and society; avidity for possessions; inadaptability. To form the spiral movement the final stroke has to turn towards the left – the self – an area from which the writer is meant to have progressed away.

When the spiral appears in the middle zone: egocentricity, narcissism, vanity, touchiness, dissimulation, selfishness.

When the spiral appears in the lower zone: predominance of selfish instincts, need for material possessions, kleptomania (Vels).

Spiral writing is illustrated in examples 22, 48, 62 and 71 (pp. 270, 287, 296 and 304).

Square

Category: form
Synonym: with corners
Antonym: angular, arcades, garlands

Description

The letters, or parts thereof, are connected at their base with a straight horizontal line forming a right angle with the preceding and following strokes, in the form of an open square. All curves become square.

Interpretation:

General Conformity. Affectation, Mannerisms. Distant amiability. Deep-rooted inhibitions. Repression of feelings. Desire to appear attractive (in women). Desire to appear brilliant (in men).

In any event, it is a pretentious writing which, in the mildest case, will show a preoccupation with clarity and legibility and, at its worst, a selfish conformity and rigid attitudes acquired from education and social status.

Square writing is illustrated in examples 9 and 39 (pp. 265 and 281).

Stylized

Category: form
Synonym: neat, official, tidy, italic
Antonym: formless, shapeless, negligent

Description

The effortful reproduction of any of the calligraphic models. The result is order, precision, legibility, with little variation, if any, and homogeneity. Speed is usually moderate or slow. It is used for envelopes or official manuscripts.

Interpretation:

General Stylized writing is not used to dissimulate the real character but only to make a manuscript orderly and more legible. It is often used by very disorganized people whose normal writing may be illegible, carried away, effervescent, etc. So stylized writing will show a need for orderliness, discipline, clarity and simplicity at the sacrifice of speed and spontaneity.

Stylized writing is illustrated in examples 12, 13, 30 and 52 (pp. 266, 275 and 290).

Supported

Category: form
Synonym: deviated connection
Antonym: garlands, arcades

Description

The connecting stroke retraces the previous one before it continues to form the next stroke of a letter, e.g. .

Interpretation:

General This form of connection is often found in many stylized writings, e.g. Sacré-Coeur, in which case it indicates conformity and lack of culture, together with some rigidity of character which has stopped the writer from evolving.

When it is seen in an ordinary writing it shows that the writer is in the habit of hiding the truth. It can also be interpreted as hypocrisy or lying.

Supported writing is illustrated in examples 12, 22, 30 and 51 (pp. 266, 270, 275 and 289).

Swords

See Particular Signs, p. 203.

Triangles

See Particular Signs, p. 203.

Typographic

Category: form
Synonym: print
Antonym: calligraphic, copper-plate

Description

The letters are in imitation of 'print' style, mainly the capitals and some small letters.

The style of writing is usually another form of simple, simplified, clear and sober writing.

Interpretation:

General Good education, culture, erudition. Originality. Aesthetic sense; many great masters of the Renaissance had this writing (Leonardo da Vinci, Michaelangelo, Titian, Rafael). It is a graceful writing used by people who have read much; the image of the print is fixed in their memory and has attracted them with its clarity and simplicity. It shows, therefore, visual memory.

Unfavourable If the writing lacks flow, spontaneity and speed, it is simply an imitative writing and falls into the category of artificial or stylized writing. The Formlevel is lower and the interpretation negative. It shows pretentiousness, preciousness, possibly fraud.

Typographic writing is illustrated in examples 15, 16, 36, 36a and 44 (pp. 267, 278, 279 and 284).

Ungraceful

Category: form
Synonym: unpleasant, unaesthetic
Antonym: graceful, orderly

Description

This type includes vulgar, disproportionate, disorderly, negligent writing, with sharp angles; it is dry, narrow, unstable or widely spread on the page with disproportionate flying strokes and uncontrolled, imprecise movements. The pressure is irregular, from thick and pasty to thin and sharp.

Interpretation:

General Unpleasant, nagging, peevish character. Brusque, irksome, overbearing, insufferable.

This writing often appears in people who suffer from some nervous conditions.

Bitterness, suffering of any kind, anxiety, spite, anger, and all excesses may temporarily produce this kind of writing.

Also, intoxication from alcohol, morphine, drugs, tobacco, etc. may make the writing agitated, disorderly, discordant or carried away, thus indicating a deep alteration of the nervous system and deranged health.

Often, children of people addicted to any of the above elements are innocent victims and their writing is often ungraceful through no fault of their own. In this case, disorderly, twisted, vulgar and discordant writing appears at an early age and it is extremely difficult to improve it.

Ungraceful writing is illustrated in examples 23, 32 and 50 (pp. 270, 276 and 289).

Upper Extensions

Category: form

Description

Tall or short, narrow or full, embellished or simplified, rightward or leftward, light or heavy, connected or disconnected, etc. They will be interpreted according to the Symbolism of Space (pp. 20–21).

Interpretation:

General Upper extensions are generally the expression of our conscious ability to produce spatial images (Pulver). They represent our intellectual and spiritual life.

When they extend high (tall) they show imagination, originality, inventiveness, independence of thinking and, if they are exaggerated, inadaptability, adventurousness, tendency towards chimaera, imbalance. If they are exaggerated and narrow: diminished intellectual abilities (with supporting signs). If they are low (short) they indicate a balanced and reasonable attitude of a well-adapted person. If they are too low the writer is dependent and limited.

If they are narrow, they express a diminished ability to think in abstract terms, according to the rest of the signs. If they are full they indicate an ability to recreate, to narrate, a tendency towards spiritual matters (depending upon whether they are turned towards the right or the left), sense of space and intellectual abilities.

Embellished upper extensions are indicative of a hypertrophic imagination, exaggeration and of a taste for the concrete pleasures of life.

A simplified upper zone shows the introversion of a spiritually orientated person.

Interpretations are many and vary according to pressure, continuity, speed and slant. For example, if atrophied, upper extensions indicate touchiness. If pressure is also weak; religious and moral attitudes. If pressure is strong it shows, simultaneously, spirituality and artistic tendencies. If it is also ample and connected to the next letter, confidence, serenity and lack of meanness.

It goes without saying that, as always in graphology, the value of a sign is relative to all other signs. The presence of one sign alone does not indicate any precise quality or fault.

Upper extensions are illustrated in example 31 (p. 275).

See also 'Prolonged Upwards' p. 62.

Vulgar

Category: form
Synonym: crude, banal
Antonym: distinguished, noble, original

Description

It is inharmonious, disproportionate, discordant, crude and without charm. It is not necessarily a gross writing. It lacks rhythm and originality.

Interpretation:

General It is usually the writing of people without much education or taste. It shows lack of grace and crude, perverted, even baleful attitudes. This is a most worrying writing.

At its best it will indicate conformist attitudes and banal tastes.

Vulgar writing is illustrated in examples 23 and 32 (pp. 270 and 276).

Whips

Category: form

Description

This is another form of Flying Stroke (p. 138). When present, it is a dominant sign. It is formed by a movement thrown first towards the left or right, extending over several letters, then turning smoothly in the opposite direction.

It can appear in t bars, the d or most capital letters.

Interpretation:

General Its interpretations are many and varied. Generally, it shows a vivacious character inclined to verbal outbursts and to snubbing others.

Favourable Imagination, idealism, vivacity. Independent ideas and judgement. Audacious and active character, full of energy and speed in action.

Unfavourable Violence. Impulsiveness. Vehemence. Brusqueness. An authoritarian and inopportune character who wants to dominate others. Exalted, undisciplined, selfish, ambitious, choleric, brutal, 'fantastic', whimsical.

Whipped writing is illustrated in examples 14 and 31 (pp. 267 and 275).

Speed

Abbreviated

Category: speed
Synonym: shortened
Antonym: complicated

Description

The words are cut short, e.g. bcs for because, or replaced by a symbol such as + for 'and' etc.

Interpretation:

General With a harmonious writing and a good Formlevel, see Simplified writing (p. 124).

In a low Formlevel the writing will be crude and discordant.

Abbreviations are collective signs. They don't necessarily save time, neither do they facilitate reading.

Tact and consideration for the reader forbid the use of abbreviations in a letter. They are acceptable only in taking notes or in drafting a letter.

Abbreviated writing is illustrated in example 68 (p. 302).

Accelerated

Category: speed
Synonym: speeding up, gradually increasing pace
Antonym: slowing down, decelerating

Description

The deliberate change of speed from steady to rapid in the same word, line or page (to approximately 150 letters per minute).

Interpretation:

General The acceleration of a writing is indicative of the general activity of the writer. It is usually found with simple, simplified, progressive, combined, resolute, flying strokes, grouped or hopping writing.

Favourable Adaptability. Ability to accelerate the rhythm of work (mental or manual) to cope with an emergency. This is a matter of practice and discipline which would, of course, show the dedication, persistence and desire for perfection of the writer.

Unfavourable If the acceleration produces agitation, messiness, illegibility and disorganization of the writing then it shows nervous tension. A Phlegmatic temperament, when pushed to fast action, loses legibility and control of the writing movement. On the other hand, a Nervous temperament, in the same situation, will immediately adapt to the situation. Hyperemotive or very inhibited people have great difficulty in coping under pressure and, instead of accelerating, slow down, lose control of their motor reactions and the writing dissolves.

Accelerated writing is illustrated in example 11 (p. 266).

Carried Away

Category: speed
Synonym: over-excited
Antonym: calm, peaceful, sedate

Description

This is on the borderline of Organized writing (p. 174). It is an extreme form of Flying Strokes (p. 138). It is caused by extreme rapidity (flying t bars). Movements are ample and vivacious.

Interpretation:

General Anger, impulsive combativity, ambition, excitability, violent emotion, extroversion.

Favourable Emotivity, passion, sensitivity, if the Formlevel is high. Imagination, will-power, activity, ambition, dynamism. Quick reactions.

Unfavourable Lack of inhibition. Impulsiveness. Impatience. 'The writer will impose his will with little consideration for others.' (Pulver) Short-tempered and arrogant, the writer explodes easily into fury. Tendency to exaggeration. Violence. Sometimes also nastiness.

Carried-away writing is illustrated in example 33 (p. 276).

Constrained

Category: speed
Synonym: restrained
Antonym: easy, comfortable, free

Description

The impeded appearance of a writing. Hesitant. The writing progresses with difficulty. The natural flow may be hindered by a number of different reasons: excessive care and attention in the formation of letters; the desire to hide or dissimulate certain traits of character; the inhibiting presence of someone (e.g. a graphologist) watching the writer; external causes like excessive cold or heat, change of attitude, etc.; mechanical causes like the use of an unsuitable pen or paper, an uncomfortable position, copying etc.; lack of adequate writing ability.

A constrained writing is usually squeezed, angular, low, slow or retarded, retouched, inverted, fragmented, inhibited, twisted, suspended, disconnected, disguised and conventional.

Interpretation:

General Reduction of spontaneity. Reserve. It expresses a conflict between a conscious intention and an unconscious force, disturbing the flow of ideas and consequently of their expression. Inhibition.

Favourable Reserve, conservatism.

Unfavourable Reduction of spontaneity. Lack of sincerity. Difficulty in exposition. Tendency to dissimulate certain traits of the personality.

Reduction of social ability. Feeling of inferiority.

Constrained writing is illustrated in example 41 (p. 283).

Controlled

Category: speed
Synonym: held back, restrained, contained
Antonym: spontaneous, thrown, flung

Description

All movements are controlled and restrained, particularly the final strokes. It is compatible with, and similar to, orderly, neat, regular, simple and simplified writing as well as dry and angular writing.

Interpretation:

General Reflection. Self-control. Controlled writing indicates a person who restrains his expressions and actions.

Favourable Prudence. Reflection. Gentleness. Sense of personal, professional and social responsibility. Sagacity. Introversion. A need to make a decision only after having examined, analysed and scrutinized all sides of a problem. Sense of economy. Perspicacity. Vigilance.

Unfavourable Indecisiveness. Lack of activity from fear of being compromised. Inhibition. Dogmatism. Stupid stubbornness. Fearfulness. Exaggerated scruples, resulting in hesitation, anxiety, depression, dissimulation.

Regression of the libido (egoism, narcissism, egocentricity) if there are also signs of excessive inhibition (suspended letters etc.).

Controlled writing is illustrated in examples 12, 44 and 69 (pp. 266, 284 and 303).

Dynamic

Category: speed
Synonym: stimulated
Antonym: inhibited, depressed, constrained

Description

Dynamic is the opposite of constrained writing. It is characterized by *élan* and vigorous and ample movement. The trait is well-nourished; the flow is free, spontaneous and uninhibited. The direction of the lines is usually upwards (climbing). Form is progressive. Speed is rapid, and the freedom of movement produces irregularities in the height and width of letters.

Interpretation:

General Activity. Nervous tension. Energy. Dynamic writing is mainly a positive sign, particularly when it is also harmonious and has rhythm. Negative interpretations are very rare.

Favourable Feeling of well-being. Zeal. Ability to achieve. Love of life. Optimism. Good health. Quick thinking. Enthusiasm. Need of air and space.

Unfavourable Impatience. Nervous tension. Irritability. Imprudent attitudes. Lack of foresight if it is also effervescent. Unjustified optimism. The writer will act impulsively and is unable to be patient, calm or persevering.

Dynamic writing is illustrated in examples 4 and 37 (pp. 262 and 280).

Effervescent

Category: speed
Synonym: agitated, bubbling
Antonym: calm

Description

Very irregular direction and dimension, with rather thin strokes, jerky, agitated.

Interpretation:

General This writing is mainly caused by the general effervescence of the writer's disposition. Many people of a Melancholic Sanguine temperament have this kind of writing.

Favourable Activity, ardour, deep sensitivity. With a high Form-level it indicates a high level of intelligence, decisiveness, inventiveness, even genius.

Unfavourable Impatience. Lack of order. Inconsistency. Instability. Self-indulgence. Moral values may leave a certain amount to be desired.

Effervescent writing is illustrated in examples 14 and 54 (pp. 267 and 290).

Flying Strokes

Category: speed
Synonym: careless, dashing
Antonym: restrained, prudent

Description

An impulsive, rapid movement which produces exaggerations, prolonging mainly the initial strokes of capital letters upwards. Also t bars and i dots are thrown ahead of their respective letters high in the upper zone.

Interpretation:

General Similar to 'carried away'. Extroversion. Spontaneity. Exuberance. Tendency to exaggeration.

Favourable With a firm stroke it shows activity, initiative, impulsiveness, *élan*, affirmation. Tendency to be whimsical. Feeling of superiority. Domination (if the writing is also large). Expansion.

Unfavourable Violence. Zeal that does not last. Superficial judgement. Lack of prudence. Depending on the rest of the signs, brutality. Silliness, superficiality. In excess, mental debility.

Flying strokes are illustrated in examples 33 and 46 (pp. 276 and 286).

Illegible

See Form, p. 108.

Irregular

See Continuity, p. 160.

Poised

Category: speed
Synonym: steady, sedate, calm
Antonym: carried away, exhalted, thrown

Description

Written without haste. It can be described as a 'slowed down' writing. The letters are complete, of moderate dimension. T bars and i dots are more or less precisely placed and, on the whole, the writing shows no great variations in spacing or speed (around 130 letters per minute).

Interpretation:

General The interpretation of this writing depends a great deal on the rest of the signs.

Favourable With a harmonious, firm, combined and simplified writing it shows calm, good self-control, prudence, power of observation, reflective rather than impulsive intelligence and precision of thoughts and expressions. Consistency in action. Ability to memorize. Good judgement. Objectivity. Nobility of character. Adaptability to different situations. Precision.

Unfavourable With a flabby, feeble writing with little or no pressure it shows mediocre intelligence, a taste for routine; submission to habits, lack of will-power, timidity and stubbornness. Also passivity, docility and boredom. The writer may be sweet and sociable but also negative and unlikely ever to change the world.

Crépieux-Jamin says 'steady writing is a poor virtue and the virtue of the poor'. He puts it on the fringes of unorganized writing.

Poised writing is illustrated in examples 1, 2 and 13 (pp. 260, 261 and 266).

Precipitated

Category: speed
Synonym: hurried, impulsive, hasty
Antonym: slow, steady, poised

Description

Although this writing has some rapport with Carried Away writing (see p. 134), it is caused by different elements in the writer's nature. A writing is called precipitated when there is filiformity, when the letters are not well formed and are left unfinished. The disconnected strokes are small and thrown apparently without control. Irregularities are numerous, mainly in the dimension of the letters and the spacing. Legibility is difficult, at times impossible. Speed is excessive (over 200 letters per minute).

Interpretation:

General Can be accidental; as for instance, if the writer jots down something in a great hurry. In this case it will have the same interpretation as accelerated writing.

Favourable Great resources of activity. Ardour. Quick thinking. Versatile intelligence actively manifested. Effervescent imagination. Determination to succeed despite difficulties.

Unfavourable Lack of attention and reflection. Overactivity. Thoughtlessness. Lack of consideration. Irritability. Instability. Impatience. Tendency to undertake risky and dangerous activities. Offensive or hurtful attitudes. Jealousy, hate, deceptive behaviour (if supported by other signs of a similar meaning). Inadaptability. Exaggerated enthusiasm followed by aggressive behaviour if disappointed.

A deliberately precipitated writing (where there are gaps in the flow of speed together with intentional illegibility) may be one of the signs of insincerity or dishonesty (p. 205).

Precipitated writing is illustrated in example 65 (p. 299).

Rapid

Category: speed
Synonym: swift, fast, quick
Antonym: slow

Description

The writing shows an economy of movement; it is spontaneous, simplified, connected, with combinations which save time. The t bars and i dots are either placed to the right of the letter or connected to the following letter, or missing. The slant is moderately to the right, the direction is progressive and upwards. The letters progressively widen and are not all completed, the final stroke is sharp pointed. The size (middle zone) is moderately small (under 3 mm). The words diminish towards their end. The stroke is precise. The left margin widens. The general impression is vivacious (with control), fluent, rather light, with freedom of movement, dynamic and gliding on the paper. (Around 180 letters per minute.)

Interpretation:

General Activity, active intelligence. Initiative.

Favourable A rapid writing is generally of higher Formlevel. It shows culture and general intellectual superiority. Facility to adapt to varied situations. Ability to identify a problem quickly and solve it. Productive activity. With good pressure, taut, deep, clean, precise and in relief, it shows decisiveness, dynamism, persuasiveness and the ability to realize one's aims. Little time for introspection.

Unfavourable If the writing is disproportionate and messy with many corrections and lacking harmony it shows anxiety, instability, impatience, impulsiveness, excitability, imbalance, superficiality. No time for introspection.

See also Flying Strokes (p. 138) and Dynamic writing (p. 136).

Rapid writing is illustrated in examples 8, 10 and 46 (pp. 264, 265 and 286).

Resolute

Category: speed
Synonym: decided, determined, sure
Antonym: hesitant, slack, loose

Description

Firm, dynamic, accelerated, climbing, well proportioned.

Interpretation:

General Self-confidence, decisiveness, lively spirit, briskness.

Favourable When harmonious a resolute writing is indicative of a high-quality character; a leader of people (explorers, statesmen, courageous soldiers, etc.). This is the kind of man or woman who can change the world and make history.

Unfavourable If there are signs of pride and arrogance (inflated or ornate letters, raised higher than others, etc.) then the writer is presumptuous and arrogant and risks making errors of judgement through being too involved with himself and not being objective enough to consider all elements of a situation or problem.

Resolute writing is illustrated in examples 10 and 37 (pp. 265 and 280).

Slack

Category: speed
Synonym: slovenly, loose
Antonym: firm, resolute

Description

A slack writing is without tension. It can be angular or curved but will have no relief or firmness. The movement drags along and the endings are long and slack. Punctuation and spacing are negligent. The whole emanates a lack of harmony and discipline.

Interpretation:

General Lack of vitality. Self-indulgence. Negligence. Depression. Nonchalance. 'We must consider this kind of writing as one of the most detestable writings in graphology.' (Crépieux-Jamin) Lack of morality. Lack of activity. Laziness. If there is weakness of the stroke and the form, this only enhances the lack of discipline and order of the writer and his inability to fight depression, laziness and immorality.

Slack writing is illustrated in examples 24, 35 and 38 (pp. 271, 277 and 281).

Slow

Category: speed
Synonym: indolent, apathetic
Antonym: swift, fast, rapid

Description

The writing is slow when the forms are complicated, calligraphic, designed and ornate; the spacing is very wide or it is squeezed; the writing is loose, heavy, well-nourished or weak; movement is directed towards the left; accents, t bars, i dots are too precise; there are frequent interruptions in the flow and many corrections; the words consistently enlarge; movement changes direction frequently; margins, right and left, are rigid; initial strokes are curved and/or complicated and final strokes are curved towards the left; the speed is less than 100 letters a minute.

The main origins of slow writing are physical or mental weakness, ignorance (lack of education), taste for complications, inhibitions or a heavy/strong pressure (Crépieux-Jamin).

Interpretation:

General Tranquillity, prudence, inactivity, slowness – a Phlegmatic temperament.

Favourable In a good Formlevel, self-control, reserve, reflection, observation, attention. Ability to analyse and classify situations. Moderation. Modesty. Even temper. Passivity.

Unfavourable Lack of spontaneity. Timidity. Lack of initiative. Lack of intelligence. Lack of courage. Tendency to laziness. Lack of will-power. If the writing also is unorganized then it shows lack of education and writing ability. Slow writing is usually done by people with a resigned nature, weak willed, ill or very old. With signs of vanity or narcissism then slow writing indicates stubbornness and nagging; a snarling, peevish, ill-tempered, vicious person.

Slowness, together with certain other signs (p. 205), indicates insincerity, dissimulation and dishonesty.

Slow writing is illustrated in examples 12, 19 and 20 (pp. 266 and 269).

Slowed Down

Category: speed
Synonym: retarded
Antonym: accelerated, precipitated

Description

Great care in forming the letters and in the laying-out of the text. Numerous corrections and additions. Numerous interruptions of the flow. Ornamentations of the letters (mainly the initials), complicated writing, with shaky strokes, hesitant, twisted, alternating between broad and narrow.

Interpretation:

General 'All the reasons for a slowed down writing are occasional because, if a writing was always slowed down, it would be simply a slow writing. The occasional use of the signs of slowness – complicated writing, thick strokes, very large, inhibited, hesitant, disconnected, weak, ornate, etc. reveals the slowing down,' says Crépieux-Jamin.

Desire for perfection, clarity, precision, application.

Favourable If the slowing down is caused by special attention being given to the particular writing, it produces neat writing which is a sign of seriousness, care, order, method, prudence and scruples. If the sign is constant then it might be an indication of great hesitation caused by an over-demanding superego (schizoid tendencies – Vels).

Unfavourable Excessive sensitivity. Lack of sincerity. Silliness. Concealment of the real tendencies of the writer. If ornate then it shows vanity, affectation, coquetry. If it is not due to external causes, e.g. uncomfortable positioning of the body or the support, cold, tiredness, fear etc., and if there are other supporting signs (shakiness, twisting etc.) it may be indicative of an abnormal state (e.g. loss of memory, intoxication, alcoholism, addiction to drugs, depression).

Slowed down writing is illustrated in examples 32, 36a and 52 (pp. 276, 278 and 290).

Spontaneous

Category: speed
Synonym: free, natural
Antonym: complicated, constrained

Description

A simple and natural movement, spontaneous and without any signs of constraint. The speed is not particularly great, it follows the personal rhythm of the writer. The modes of expression of spontaneous writing vary according to the writer's temperament.

Interpretation:

General Spontaneity, simplicity, sincerity of character.

Favourable Honesty, simplicity of manners, sincerity of emotions. Confidence in self and others. Nobility of character. Generosity.

Unfavourable Lack of constraint. Absent-mindedness. Excessive talkativeness if it is paired with an invasive writing occupying all the paper, leaving little or no margin. In this case spontaneity becomes silliness (Crépieux-Jamin).

Spontaneous writing is illustrated in examples 3, 4, 5, 6 and others (pp. 262 and 263).

Continuity

Agitated

Category: continuity
Synonym: restless, choppy, excited
Antonym: calm

Description

This is a variety of Irregular writing (p. 160). It is mainly characterized by discordant and animated irregularities, together with imprecise forms.

Interpretation:

General Hypersensitivity of the individual. The writer is nervous, impatient, agitated.

Favourable Vivacious emotivity. If a precipitated writing then ardent imagination. If the writing is combined, connected, simple and simplified it will show a brilliant mind and great activity; a fearless and decisive character who does not want to waste his time.

Unfavourable Impatience. Irritability. Excitability. Vulgarity. Lack of logic. Easily impressed. Mobility. Difficult character. See also Animated, Disorderly, Irregular, Precipitated, Jerky (abrupt), all aspects of Agitated writing (pp. 91, 42, 160, 140 and 162).

Agitated writing is illustrated in example 33 (p. 276).

Amended

Category: continuity
Synonym: retouched, with corrections
Antonym: spontaneous

Description

Any addition or correction added after the letter had been formed. It is usually aimed at making the writing more legible.

Interpretation:

General If the writing is clear then amendments reveal scruples, anxiety and worry. If the same letter is repeatedly amended it shows obsession and mania.

In general, it is a sign of inhibition and anxiety which influences speed, fluency and Formlevel.

If it is occasional it is not of great significance. But if it appears ten or twenty times on one page it is a sign of severe mental illness.

It is important that the graphologist establishes, first, when the corrections were done: during the progress of the writing, after the end of the page or during the re-reading process; in the latter case the interpretation will depend on the nature of the corrections rather than on the fact that corrections were undertaken.

In the first case there would be discontinuity of, and indecision in, the writing flow and breaks in the stroke, coinciding with the correction. In the second case the writing will be resolutely connected (or in groups) and the stroke (speed, colour, pressure) will not show any interruptions. When corrections have been made on re-reading it shows method, clarity and a sense of improvement.

When corrections are made during writing they are an indication of grave inhibition, scruples, worries, anxieties, narrowness of mind and/or field of consciousness, inability to concentrate on the work in hand, distraction of attention. The writer is more conscientious than active, more meticulous than intelligent.

Amended writing is also a sign of meanness and pettiness (look for supporting signs).

Often it accompanies signs of depression, old age, senility, paralysis or delirium.

With signs of disorder, pride and hyperemotivity amended writing will show severe nervousness, emotional fatigue, agitation, inconsistency, impulsiveness, irritability, inadaptability. It is also a sign of paranoia and schizophrenia (with supporting signs). If a whole word has been passed over twice (or more) without signs of correction or addition, and if this is repeated for more than five–seven words on a page it may be an indication of schizophrenia.

Amended writing is illustrated in examples 7, 9 and 32 (pp. 264, 265 and 276).

Automatic

Category: continuity
Synonym: mechanical, stereotyped
Antonym: irregular, nuancée

Description

Extreme form of regular and monotonous writing. Simple forms with mechanized movement monotonously repeated.

Interpretation:

General Mental debility. The brain does not participate in this writing movement. Lack of intelligence. Melancholia. Neurasthenia. Paranoia. Epilepsy. If it is voluntarily automatic it will show inadaptability, stubbornness, obsession, stupidity.

People who wish to dissimulate their writing (anonymous letters etc.) may use this style. It is easily detectable through the rest of the categories and signs.

Automatic writing is illustrated in example 35 (p. 277).

Broken

Category: continuity
Synonym: ruptured, interrupted
Antonym: connected

Description

The stroke is interrupted suddenly without the writer's knowledge, and continues leaving a discontinuity, i.e. the trace that the pen leaves on the paper is broken, has gaps.

Interpretation:

General In general, a broken stroke is the written expression of a spasm. This spasm may be caused by circulatory, hormonal or nervous imbalance. It is often seen in people who suffer from nervous diseases, cardiac deficiencies, tuberculosis or dyspnoea.

The effect, psychologically, is anguish; distress and anxiety are characteristic of these diseases.

Obese people sometimes have this sign in their writing.

It can also have external causes; a bad quality pen or paper, turbulence in an airplane, etc. Great care should be taken in the interpretation of this sign; a magnifying glass should be used to assess the quality of the writing instrument.

If the graphologist is not very experienced it would be inadvisable to try to interpret this sign.

Broken writing is illustrated in examples 11 and 40 (pp. 266 and 282).

Calm

Category: continuity
Synonym: placid, poised
Antonym: flying strokes, agitated

Description

A modest writing, moderate in all categories (speed, pressure, form, continuity, direction, dimension). Phlegmatic temperament.

Interpretation:

Favourable Calm writing shows equilibrium, measure, harmony, security of action and of thought. Impartiality. Self-control.

Unfavourable If the writing is, at the same time, weak, flabby and crude then it shows indifference, insensitivity, nonchalance, apathy.

Calm writing is illustrated in examples 16, 19 and 35 (pp. 267, 268 and 277).

Combined

Category: continuity
Synonym: linked up
Antonym: unorganized

Description

Original forms produced by the rapid and simplified connection of two or three letters of one word, for the sake of speed and legibility. It is the highest degree of evolution of organized writing.

The fundamentals signs for this writing are connected, simple, simplified, nuancée, supple, clear, rapid, elegant, alternating curves and angles (mixed).

Interpretation:

General Intelligence. Inventiveness. Suppleness of mind. Intellectual agility.

Favourable General intellectual superiority. Ability to vary, aptitude to choose. Good association of ideas. Imagination. Good memory. Inventiveness and suppleness of mind = intelligence. Ability to pay attention. General culture. Independence of thought. Rapid and original thinking. Quick reasoning.

Good ability to assimilate new ideas. Lucidity. Initiative. Creativity. Ability to see essential points of each situation. Thinking. Intuition.

Unfavourable With a weak, flabby stroke: laziness, tiredness.

With a precipitated, effervescent writing: precipitated decisions, not always correct. Not meticulous. Nervousness.

Combined writing is illustrated in examples 3, 4, 5, 7 and 46 (pp. 262, 263, 264 and 286).

Comfortable

Category: continuity
Synonym: free, natural
Antonym: constrained

Description

A simple and spontaneous writing with harmonious movement and pleasant forms. It goes hand in hand with Natural writing (p. 116). A flowing style without much heavy pressure, although it can be velvety (well nourished).

Interpretation:

General Imagination, ability, distinction, charm.

Graceful and supple behaviour of a spontaneous, harmonious and evolved nature.

It indicates a person without constraints, discord or neurosis. The writer is relaxed, confident, easy to get on with and has a well-coordinated character. Agreeable, cultivated and civilized.

Comfortable writing is illustrated in examples 4, 14 and 46 (pp. 262, 267 and 286).

Connected

Category: continuity
Synonym: continuous
Antonym: discontinuous, disconnected

Description

Whole words, or groups of more than five or six letters, are written without pen loosing contact with paper.

Interpretation:

General Ability to follow up a sequence of thought. Deductive, systematic thinking. Ability to rationalize. Taste for routine.

Favourable Good association of ideas. Good memory. Logical reasoning. Foresight. Easy contact. Good coordination. Activity. Adaptability. Sociability. Consistency. Need to keep in touch with reality (by keeping contact with the paper). Deductive thinking. Perseverance in effort and action. Richness of character.

Unfavourable Unmethodical mind, impetuosity with tendency to exaggeration. Stubbornness. Narrow-mindedness. Lack of perspicacity. Conformity. With supporting signs, e.g. monotonous, calligraphic, etc., persona type (Jung). Mediocre intelligence. Absurdities. Lack of initiative. Selfishness. In excess: neurosis.

It may also be a sign of laziness or physical weakness; the writer cannot be bothered, or hasn't got the strength, to lift pen off paper.

Connected writing is illustrated in examples 3, 4 and 69 (pp. 262 and 303).

Constant

Category: continuity
Synonym: uniform
Antonym: uneven

Description

Regular in size, slant and speed. This writing must also be rapid and spontaneous. The strokes will be even, without breakages, of even thickness and direction. It is often rhythmic.

Interpretation:

General Constant writing shows stability, regularity in work, reliability, loyalty of sentiment, courage, honesty, firmness, resistance to fatigue, stamina, orderliness, sense of duty.

This kind of writing has no negative interpretation.

Constant writing is illustrated in examples 4, 10 and 47 (pp. 262, 265 and 287).

Disconnected

Category: continuity
Synonym: juxtaposed
Antonym: connected

Description

The letters, within the words, are separated; they stand alone one by one.

Interpretation:

General Disconnection is an interruption of the flow of writing. It is important to establish Formlevel and dominant signs before attempting any interpretation. The reasons for disconnection may be many and varied, even contradictory; they will depend upon the other signs as well as where the disconnection appears. As a rule, and very roughly, it shows inhibition, diminished abilities, objective criticism.

Favourable With a spontaneous, orderly, slightly slanted writing it shows an orderly mind, receptive, reflective and curious. When it is also occasionally combined: intuitive thinking, inventiveness, knowledge, education, originality. Good association of ideas.

Unfavourable Lack of clarity of judgement. lack of ability to follow the logical process of an idea. Diminished activity. Clumsiness. Inhibition. Lack of practical sense. Weakness of judgement. Inconsequential activity. Egoism. Egocentricity. Jealousy. Stinginess. Dispersion. Timidity.

Disconnected writing is illustrated in examples 1, 13, 16 and 32 (pp. 260, 266, 267 and 276).

Discordant

Category: continuity
Synonym: incongruous, uncoordinated
Antonym: harmonious, orderly, coordinated

Description

All excessive irregularities and partial exaggerations produce a discordant writing.

This sign applies to all seven categories (layout, dimension, speed, pressure, continuity, form and direction). Each discordant writing is so only in one or two categories, rarely in three; and only in pathological cases in more.

Discordant writing totally lacks harmony and proportion.

Interpretation:

General Discordance in form indicates versatility, tendency to dishonesty (depending on the intensity of the sign); in speed: indecision, instability; in pressure: hesitation; in direction: inconsistency, mobility, variability; in continuity: instability, indecision, superficiality; in dimension: lack of judgement, low morality; in layout: frivolity, disorder, lack of discipline.

The most serious discordances are those appearing in dimension and form.

Discordant writing is illustrated in example 23 (p. 270).

Disorganized

Category: continuity
Synonym: disarranged
Antonym: organized, arranged, clear

Description

A writing can only be called disorganized when there is evidence of previous organization, either from old samples of writing or from signs in the same text. (Not to be confused with Unorganized writing; p. 174).

Disorganized writing is a writing which has dissolved (in any direction) through a multitude of reasons. Crépieux-Jamin divides these reasons into two categories: active, when the movement is ardent, excessive and inconsiderate (passion); and passive, the result of laziness, lack of attention, negligence, thoughtlessness, etc. – all negative qualities.

Interpretation:

General It is important to discover the cause of disorganization in a writing. It is not evident from the writing alone. The reasons are multiple but the most frequent are – paralysis, Parkinson's disease, alcoholism, intoxication of all kinds, cramp, old age, accidents to the writing hand or of the brain, ataxia, hereditary nervous illness.

An unusual emotional state, or inadequate conditions at the time of writing, may also create a disorganized writing, accidentally and temporarily.

Disorganized writing is illustrated in example 40 (p. 282).

False Connections

Category: continuity
Synonym: hesitant, inhibited
Antonym: connected

Description

Momentary stops in the flow of writing (mainly between two letters in one word); the writer starts again exactly from where he stopped, reconnecting (soldering) the stroke. This may produce a small dot of ink and a change of pressure.

Interpretation:

General Fatigue. Uncoordinated movement. Lack of writing fluency. Hesitation. People who write in a language which is not their own often produce this sign of hesitation. Also, when copying a text, the writer may stop in the middle of a stroke to verify the spelling.

Otherwise, this sign appears in unorganized writing (children's, illiterate or pathological).

It is also an indication of inauthenticity, particularly if the writing is slow.

Often, with rapid, more or less angular movements and simplified forms, false connections will indicate the writer's need to maintain the continuity of his ideas.

False connections are illustrated in example 19 (p. 269).

Faltering

Category: continuity
Synonym: undecided, irresolute
Antonym: firm, resolute

Description

The writing is imprecise, fragile in its direction and form. Slightly shaky, wavy and without relief. Uncertain. Discordant. Twisted.

Interpretation:

General Any writing showing some form of debility, physical or mental. Also old people and people convalescing from long illness or operations. It is an indication of feebleness.

Faltering writing is illustrated in example 40 (p. 282).

Fragmented

Category: continuity
Synonym: disjointed, oversimplified
Antonym: dotted, stippled, connected

Description

The letters, mainly of the middle zone, are divided into two or three parts. It is an oversimplified writing.

Interpretation:

General Diminished energy and activity. Sometimes written by very old people, or small children before they acquire the ability to coordinate their strokes. Some graphologists see it as an indication of circulatory or respiratory troubles; if the pressure and the whole structure of the writing support this, it may well be so. In any case the writer would be well advised to undergo a check-up.

Favourable In rapid writing with flying strokes it shows inspiration, intuitive understanding, rapid reasoning, 'vision'; the writer sees life through his subconscious as distinct from the Sensation type (p. 219) who will only perceive the realities of life directly through his senses (Vels).

Unfavourable Anxiety. Physical or psychic inhibitions. Doubts. Hesitation. Worries. Fears. Social inadaptability. Lack of suppleness. Capriciousness. Instability. Tendency to prey on other people (Michon). Hyperemotivity (Beauchataud). The writer is not integrated in society; he has difficulty in expressing his emotions.

The disconnection of upper extensions form their middle zone, i.e. d or h, has been found to indicate an experience of disassociations between male and female, e.g. separated parents.

Fragmented writing is illustrated in example 39 (p. 281).

Free

Category: continuity
Synonym: emancipated
Antonym: constrained

Description

Similar to, but more free than, comfortable writing. Free writing has more freedom of movement. It may contain some exaggerations which are not necessarily discordant. It is a mobile writing.

Interpretation:

General Frivolity and lightness of character. Pretentiousness.

Favourable With a rapid movement, combined letters and good relief, it will indicate popularity, extroversion, sympathy, urbanity, and worldliness. Independence. Curiosity. Ardour. Sensitivity.

Unfavourable If the exaggerations are too much, then the writing loses its charm. If it is also slow then it shows silliness, pretentiousness and unjustified self-confidence.

Free writing is illustrated in examples 5, 37, 54 and 68 (pp. 263, 280, 290 and 302).

Grouped

Category: continuity
Synonym: syllabic, in groups, partly connected
Antonym: connected, disconnected

Description

In groups of no more than two or three letters connected together.

Interpretation:

General The function is Thinking (auxiliary Intuition).

This writing represents the unending game between activity and inhibition. Its general meaning is suppleness, agility and an aptitude to vary, the most precious qualities for anyone to possess.

Favourable Intellectual adaptability. Good equilibrium between intuition and deduction. Productive intelligence. Vivacity. Spontaneity. Critical observation. Good coordination between ideas and actions. Initiative. Ingenious, inventive mind. Independence of judgement (Beauchataud). Ecclecticism; the writer chooses and assimilates only the best out of any situation (Vels). Clarity of mind. Ability to classify things in order of importance and similarity. Encyclopaedic mind. Originality. Intelligence.

Unfavourable Disconnected thoughts. Nervousness. Lack of harmony. Instability. Difficulty in establishing a link between personal tendencies and those of the people around him. Ambivalence. Inhibition. Doubts. Lack of expansion. Hesitation.

The above interpretations do not apply to the grouping of letters in an Unorganized writing (p. 174).

Grouped writing is illustrated in examples 5, 6 and 46 (pp. 263 and 286).

Hesitant

Category: continuity
Synonym: undecided, irresolute
Antonym: resolute

Description

Lacking in firmness, shaky, slow, of uncertain and irregular direction. It is another form of retouched and complicated writing, full of irregularities. The general effect gives an impression of lack of written fluency.

Interpretation:

General Severe inhibition. Inability to take decisions. Systematic hesitation. Infirmity of character. Nervous tension. Disappointment. Anxiety to the point of illness. With supporting signs, strong ambivalence (contradictory tendencies). Imprudence. Tendency towards chimaera. Excessive emotivity which destroys stability, security and calm. Feeble character.

Hesitant writing is illustrated in examples 15 and 41 (pp. 267 and 283).

Homogeneous

Category: continuity
Synonym: systematic
Antonym: heterogeneous, varying

Description

The writing does not vary from page to page or from one document to another – it is very consistent and constant in its forms and written movements, despite all difficulties.

Interpretation:

General The interpretation of this writing depends on the rest of the signs. Consistency. Equilibrium.

Favourable With a spontaneous and original writing it shows that the writer is secure in himself. Responsible and consistent in his behaviour.

Unfavourable If the writing is very regular or monotonous the writer is non-emotive; he lacks adaptability, suppleness, receptivity and compassion. He tends to be subjective and perhaps even (with other supporting signs) egoistic and materialistic.

Note: If the writing is also meticulous and sober it may be that the writer's profession requires precision and accuracy, e.g. engineer, mechanic, architect, accountant.

Homogeneous writing is illustrated in examples 10, 12 and 47 (pp. 265, 266 and 287).

Hopping

Category: continuity
Synonym: nimble, alert, sprightly, irregular
Antonym: calligraphically connected

Description

Small groups of letters, varying, symmetrical and combined.

Hopping writing is mostly rhythmic and gives the impression of progressing with little jumps from group to group of letters. It may also have some flying strokes.

Interpretation:

General Activity. Vivacity of mind. Impetuosity. Promptness of action. Intuition. Imagination. The writer is typical of a Mercury type (p. 255); prompt, independent, quick in thought and action, easy and agile in motion.

Hopping writing is illustrated in examples 17 and 33 (pp. 268 and 276).

Inhibited

Category: continuity
Synonym: suspended, slowed down
Antonym: dynamic, accelerated

Description

Includes a number of other types such as constrained, suspended, hesitant, etc. The writing rhythm is constantly interrupted one way or another.

Interpretation:

General Inhibition. It reveals all that which interrupts the flow of energy, psychic or physical. General nervousness. Irritability. Conflicts. Morbid self-observation. Susceptibility. Doubts. Hesitation. Lack of confidence. Feeling of inferiority. Distrust. Obsessive ideas (with rigid, mechanical, regular, overconnected writing). Emotional suffering.

From the above it must not be concluded that inhibited writing is solely negative. Inhibitions serve to contain and regulate excessive tendencies. People without inhibitions are usually insufferable.

Favourable Prudence. Steadiness. Tolerance. Sensitivity. Sincerity. Modesty. Self-sustained individual.

Unfavourable Depression. Anxiety. Nervousness. Fear. Lack of confidence in self and in others. Feeling of inferiority. Insecurity. Confusion. Disarray. Excessive timidity. Awkwardness. Inadaptability. Instability.

Inhibited writing is illustrated in examples 15 and 41 (pp. 267 and 283).

Irregular

Category: continuity and layout, dimension, pressure, form, speed, direction
Synonym: varied
Antonym: regular

Description

Moderate irregularities in all categories without the writing becoming discordant.

Irregularities may appear only in some categories, or in all; for this reason it must always be specified which irregularity is meant; for instance, 'irregular pressure', 'irregular direction' or 'irregular dimension'.

Interpretation (for all categories):

General All irregularities reveal emotion. The smaller and the more often they appear, the deeper and stronger the emotions they represent; the bigger the irregularities the more superficial are the emotions they represent, e.g. between jerky writing and bubbling (effervescent) writing there is nuancée writing which, with its constant but discreet irregularities, without agitation, contradictions or exaggerations, shows a perfect harmony of the mind and the heart.

Favourable Sensitivity. Imagination. Intuition. With supporting signs (firm, rapid, combined, etc.), it shows initiative, activity, dynamism. Creativity. Vivid intelligence.

Unfavourable Predominance of emotions over reason. Weak will, Easily influence. Instability. Inadaptability. Indecision. Unhappy inner life. Impressionability. Uncertainty.

Irregularity of Layout

Instability. Easily distracted. Lack of concentration. Negligence. Mobility. Easily influenced.

Lack of self-discipline. Bad distribution of time and energy.

Irregularity of layout is illustrated in examples 17 and 58 (pp. 268 and 293).

Irregularity of Dimension

(Enlarging and Diminishing writings (pp. 56, 54) are also examples of irregular dimension.) Sensitivity. Capacity for affection. Susceptibility (with angular writing). Inhibition. Variability of self-confidence.

Irregularity of dimension is illustrated in examples 7, 14 and 17 (pp. 264, 267 and 268).

Irregularity of Pressure

Variations of energy. Nervousness. Aggression. Irritability. Excitability. Argumentativeness. Sensuality. Psychosomatic troubles. Irregularity of Pressure is illustrated in example 6 (p. 263).

Irregularity of Form

Vibrant and changing sensitivity. This sign may indicate falseness of character. Duplicity (with slow writing) (see p. 143).

Irregularity in the Upper Zone Sensitivity. Mental activity. Creativity. Constructive imagination. Inspiration. Inventiveness.

Irregularity in the Middle Zone Sensitivity. Contradictory qualities. Instability. Egocentricity (with supporting signs). Emotional inadaptability. Nervousness.

Irregularity in the Lower Zone Materialistic impressionability. Inadaptability. Problematic sexuality. Domestic or financial worries. Dissatisfaction. Anxiety. Nervousness.

Irregularity of form is illustrated in examples 14 and 17 (pp. 267 and 268); in the upper zone in example 14; in the middle zone in examples 14 and 17; and in the lower zone in example 14.

Irregularity of Speed

Strong sensitivity. Anxiety. Nervousness. Suppleness of mind. Ability to see different opportunities and act upon them. Creativity. Schizoid tendencies. Inconsistency. Feeling of insecurity etc., depending on the rest of the signs.

Irregularity of speed is illustrated in example 6 (p. 263).

Irregularity of Continuity

Sensitivity. Inactivity. Inhibitions. Influencability. Lack of discipline. Dispersion of thoughts.

Irregularity of continuity is illustrated in examples 6, 17 and 39 (pp. 263, 268 and 281).

Irregularity of Direction (line)

When the lines do not follow a more or less uniform direction – they rise, they descend, dive or stay horizontal on the same page – the writer is of a Melancholic temperament (p. 251). He is moody; he changes from enthusiasm to depression, from friendliness to aggression, from hope to despair, from tolerance to irritability, within a matter of minutes.

It is an indication of instability, susceptibility and neurosis.

Irregularity of Direction (stroke)

If the irregularities are subtle they indicate intellectualism, imagination, suppleness and curiosity of mind and a large field of consciousness. If the irregularities are pronounced they show ambivalence, nervousness, indecisiveness, difficulty in concentrating and possible aggression (if the writing is also sharp-pointed).

Irregularity of direction is illustrated in examples 6 and 17 (pp. 263 and 268).

Jerky

Category: continuity
Synonym: bustling, abrupt, choppy, 'ataxic'
Antonym: calm

Description

Another variety of Irregular writing (see above). Brusque changes in direction, dimension, pressure and form, producing angles where angles should not be (as if written on a jerky surface). Also called 'ataxic'.

Interpretation:

General Nervous, Melancholic temperament. Fatigue. It is the typical writing of hypermotive people who are, by definition, touchy, mistrusting, easily frightened and constantly trying to control their emotions. This continuous effort produces excessive nervousness, moodiness, irritability, aggression, excitability, irregularity of activity, fatigue, instability, shakiness of the hands, etc.

Jerky writing may indicate a pathological state of health, for instance: intoxication, glandular imbalance, obsessional neurosis, nervous fatigue and ambivalence, (i.e. inner conflict of contradictory forces such as complexes and their compensations, conscious and subconscious, etc.).

Great care should be taken not to confuse small jerky signs of sensitivity in a rapid or precipitated writing with the jerky type which should be of poised or, at the most, of accelerated speed.

Jerky writing is illustrated in examples 24 and 60 (pp. 271 and 294).

Lapses of Continuity

Category: continuity

Description

Interruptions of the flow of writing. Little gaps in the middle of words. Sometimes these gaps are even wider than the distance between two words.

Interpretation:

General These are unconscious movements indicating various forms of inhibition, like shyness, embarrassment, timidity, inferiority complex, inadaptability, hesitation, nervousness, clumsiness, or any feeling in opposition to self-confidence.

Favourable Strong, introverted emotivity. Prudence. The writer stops to think before taking a decision.

Unfavourable Excessive worry. Anxiety. Lack of confidence in self and others. Hesitation. Inferiority complex. Inadaptability or difficulty in communicating thoughts and emotions, either through lack of adequate education, great nervousness or unclear thinking. Difficulty or inability to solve problems with speed and confidence.

This sign is often seen also in the writing of manic-depressive people.

Lapses of continuity are illustrated in example 6 (p. 263).

Mingling Letters

Category: continuity
Synonym: letters close together, overlapping
Antonym: spaced-out letters.

Description

The letters within a word are very close together (the normal distance between two letters is the width of the letter o of the same writing), touching or even overlapping.

Interpretation:

General With a typographic writing in which the distance between the letters is very small but they are not touching, this sign may simply indicate that the writer is accustomed to books, has read a lot and has a picture of print writing at the forefront of his mind.

If the letters do overlap, it is a regressive sign since the movement has to go backwards in order to overlap the previous letter.

In conjunction with relevant signs its interpretation will vary from calculated amiability, to commercial or marketing sense, to dissimulation.

In any event, it is usually a sign of egocentricity.

Mingling letters are illustrated in examples 18 and 53 (pp. 268 and 290).

Monotonous

Category: continuity
Synonym: uniform, without life, automatic
Antonym: varied, nuancée, irregular

Description

Lack of diversity. The writing is constant, regular, with no variety of strokes, no rhythm and with weak pressure. Uniform and without life.

Interpretation:

General Lack of personality. Lack of emotivity and activity. Insignificance. Liking for routine. Conformity. Boredom. Diminished interests in life. Apathy. Indolence. Melancholia. Possible stupidity, imbecility. Mentally automatic. Neurasthenia.

Monotonous writing is illustrated in examples 19, 48 and 50 (pp. 269, 287 and 289).

Nuancée

Category: continuity
Synonym: varied, irregular, vibrant, subtle
Antonym: monotonous, automatic

Description

Small irregularities of dimension, spacing, slant (of words and letters) etc., which do not affect the harmony and enhance the rhythm.

Nuancée writing must be orderly, spontaneous (natural), simplified, simple, sober, connected or in groups, proportionate, vertical or slightly slanted to the right, never slow. Legible, clear, in relief (distinct), aerated, combined, harmonious and rhythmic.

Interpretation:

Favourable The best indication of a harmonious coexistence between high intellect, strong intuition and profound sensitivity, which produce unlimited receptivity, clarity of mind, objectivity, altruism and tolerance.

This sensitivity comes from the depths of the human soul, sensitizes the mind and stimulates the manifestation of intelligence and of the superego.

It is this sensitivity which produces great works of art and inspires great ideals.

Vibrant intensity of feelings animates the writing and makes this the easiest of types to analyse. The experienced graphologist will read in it the writer's mind like an open book; he has nothing to hide – no need, no worry, no time to hide. He is concerned about the world, not about himself.

'Nuancée writing is *noble* writing.' (Crépieux-Jamin)

Nuancée writing is illustrated in examples 2, 6 and 69 (pp. 261, 263 and 303).

Organized

Category: continuity
Synonym: arranged, well designed
Antonym: unorganized

Description

An organized writing should show no effort. The letters are clear and well formed; margins and spacings follow the rules of legibility without signs of struggle.

Interpretation:

General An indication that adequate writing fluency has been acquired. Nearly all writing is basically organized and is a necessary condition for further graphological analysis.

Favourable Cultivated intelligence. The ability to put order into his or her thoughts and express them clearly on paper. Adaptability. Conscientiousness.

Unfavourable With a monotonous, even, slow writing it shows the persona of the writer, the kind of person who will be assessed as 'adapted', who will fit his role in life with calm acceptance. The kind of person who will hold on to his job to the end but, if his thin layer of varnish is scratched off, we see a miserable little person, insecure, uncertain of himself and others, lost in a confusion of mixed values.

Organized writing is illustrated in examples 1, 2 and many others (pp. 260 and 261).

Overconnected

Category: continuity
Synonym: hyperconnected
Antonym: connected, disconnected

Description

Excessive connections. Not only letters but also words are connected by a long horizontal stroke.

Interpretation:

Favourable If the overconnection does not affect legibility, it will show great mental activity, ability to think quickly and reach a decision efficiently. With supporting signs, i.e. dynamic, progressive, sober writing, in relief (distinct pressure), etc., productive activity. High principles. Morality. Facility to improvise. Strong intuition if the writing is also irregular and light.

Unfavourable Narrowness of mind. Logic pushed to extreme – sophistry. Stubbornness. Obstinate character, attached to stale principles, traditions and prejudices. Sectarian mind (Beauchataud). Obsessiveness. Tendency to illusion. Impulsiveness. Lack of measure. Imbalance. Disorder. Fanaticism. With supporting signs: fatigue; the writer hasn't got the strength to lift pen from paper.

Overconnected writing is illustrated in examples 11, 14, 64 and 65 (pp. 266, 267, 298 and 299).

Resting Dots

Category: continuity
Synonym: dotted, spasmodic
Antonym: flat

Description

A sudden stop of the pen during the progress of a stroke producing a dot. It is another variant of the Spasmodic group of signs (p. 78).

It can appear at the beginning of a letter, in the middle or at the end.

Interpretation:

General When it appears at the beginning of a letter it signifies hesitation before action.

When it appears in the middle it shows a slow, lazy, inactive character, gauche and clumsy who cannot progress smoothly in action.

When it appears at the end it shows a weak person without *élan*, incompetent and rather inflexible.

In all cases it manifests pronounced materialism.

Resting dots are illustrated in example 25 (p. 272).

Rhythmic

Category: continuity
Synonym: cadenced
Antonym: regular

Description

'Small irregularities constantly repeated, similar but never identical.' (Klages) It is the frequent but irregular repetition of the irregularities of movement.

Klages puts rhythm as one of the basic elements of the Formlevel, 'The rhythm of a writing cannot be measured, it can only be felt.'

To avoid any possible confusion, I should mention that the FL does not necessarily indicate vitality, physical dynamism or the capacity to be affectionate. The FL shows only the quality of the soul (psyche) of a person.

Interpretation:

General Independence of thought and action. Decisiveness. Movement. Precision in action (the writer does not waste time). Objective judgement, critical sense. Determination. Receptivity. *Élan*. Optimism. Confidence in self and life. Diversity of sensitivities. Equilibrium of the four functions (Thinking, Sentiment, Intuition, Sensation). Good balance between the two attitudes (introversion/extroversion), and harmony between the conscious and the unconscious. Also harmony between the social and the intimate self. Stability of character.

The writer dislikes emotional scenes. He has not got a very developed sense of responsibility (he does not need it). He is usually a perfectionist, but he is not often fussy about food.

In pathological cases it shows sadistic perversity.

Note: Rhythm is not necessarily consistent in all 'rhythmic' writings.

Rhythmic writing is illustrated in examples 1, 2, 3, 4, 5, 6, 10 and others (pp. 260, 261, 262, 263 and 265).

Shaky

Category: continuity
Synonym: jerky strokes
Antonym: regular strokes

Description

The strokes (particularly the vertical ones) are shaky.

Interpretation:

General A shaky writing, in most cases, indicates a pathological state. In neurology there are various causes of tremor. These include involuntary, occasional shaking, i.e. Parkinson's disease, which is not constant and can disappear when conscious effort is made; intentional shaking, i.e. multiple sclerosis, produced in movement and stopping at rest; constant shaking (such as intoxication, senility, etc.) which is intensified in movement. Most neurological diseases produce shaky handwriting. When it is not pathological it is indicative of extreme sensitivity, apprehension, strong emotion, nervousness, anger, clumsiness, puberty, etc.

Too much coffee or tea, alcohol, nicotine, morphine, opium, cocaine, etc. will also produce shaky writing.

There may be external causes as well, such as cold, physical tiredness, or fear.

The solution to the problem of shaky writing is of intense complexity. There is much research still to be done in this field. The graphologist will be well advised to be very careful when faced with a shaky writing and refrain from giving any medical diagnosis.

Shaky writing is illustrated in examples 12 and 17 (pp. 266 and 268).

Stable

Category: continuity
Synonym: regular, even, consistent
Antonym: unstable, proteiform

Description

The writing shows no great changes although it is not monotonous or stereotyped. It is consistent, systematic and regular in its forms, and does not easily change. To call a writing stable, therefore, we need more than one document written at different periods of time.

Interpretation:

General Stability of character. Confidence in one's own values, background, overall judgements and ideas.

This kind of writing applies to many types; its detailed interpretation depends on other signs.

Stable writing is illustrated in examples 12, 13 and 47 (pp. 266 and 287).

Sticks

Category: continuity
Synonym: staccato, choppy
Antonym: connected

Description

The writing is disconnected and the letters are separated in two, three, or four fragments and reduced to little sticks. A variation of oversimplified writing.

Interpretation:

General This sign has been seen in the writings of people who suffer from either circulatory or respiratory deficiencies or from nervous diseases. Also, some mentally retarded people or children produce the same fragmented letters. It shows inability to coordinate the stroke.

Generally, apart from physical reasons, this writing indicates hesitation and fatigue. It appears also in cases of general decrepitude. Old and very tired people use this writing for economy of movement, particularly if the down stroke is also shaky. Its principal result is extreme slowness.

If the writing is large and pressure firm, the interpretation is less negative; it may show frivolity, imagination or capriciousness, albeit with some tiredness too.

See Simplified writing (p. 124).

Structured

Category: continuity
Synonym: organized
Antonym: unstructured

Description

The 'architectural' formation of letters: well constructed, balanced and fluent. Similar to Organized writing (p. 166).

Interpretation:

General It indicates the individual maturity of the writer, his creative force, activity, receptivity and ability to realize goals.

A badly structured writing may indicate lack of harmony in the writer's subconscious, causing various symptoms from shyness or lack of courage to dissimulation, lying or general insincerity.

The overall appearance of the writing and the rest of the signs will guide the graphologist towards the right interpretation.

Structured writing is illustrated in example 25, and others (p. 272).

Sublimated

Category: continuity
Synonym: modified, subjugated
Antonym: natural

Description

A fluent and 'assured' writing showing few signs of lack of naturalness. The overall appearance is 'silent'. The dominant signs are more or less the same from one sample to another. The main characteristics are: small, simplified, connected (very often over-connected), rapid to accelerated, curved, with short and simple upper and lower extensions. The stroke is rather firm and the pressure mostly velvety (well nourished). The slant is usually vertical or slightly slanted to the right. Form is generally wide with an occasional narrow m or n. Layout is aerated or spread out (indicates emotional isolation).

Sublimated or modified writing is seen mostly in men of upper-middle-class education in England.

Interpretation:

General The effort to absorb the imposed persona (in this case a 'stereotyped' social attitude) was made at an early educational age (between eight–ten and seventeen–eighteen) during the graphologically and emotionally formative years. The writer had to conform in order to survive emotionally, sometimes even physically. His innermost dignity and individuality have been insensitively exposed and often publicly ridiculed.

Conformity was the only alternative strength. Thus the imposed convention percolated deep into the writer's subconscious. The true self has been buried underneath the scars of the wounded human dignity, never to appear again. The acquired personality has taken over. The adult man is a socially acceptable creature, able to keep his upper lip stiff when needed and to hide his unspoken misery in the world of his dreams.

Favourable Well-developed practical sense. Ability to think things out and to find practical solutions to problems. Ability to conform to a social and cultural model.

Discipline. Ability to 'soldier on' against all the odds. Self-control (including facial control). Apparent tolerance. Apparent sociability. Apparent easy communication.

Unfavourable The writer is never truly relaxed. His feeling of security is based on the validity of the values imposed on him which he has learned to comply with, adopt and imitate. His unconscious is extremely strong in most cases. The buried nature hits back, trying to break through. This produces various neuroses, fantasies and, more often than not, sexual perversions, homosexuality, 'kinkiness', impotence or indifference, in some cases (with supporting signs, i.e. clubs, spasmodic pressure, breakages of the written stroke, etc.), viciousness or even brutality, all hidden behind a 'civilized' facial expression and an easy-going, 'relaxed' and 'no nonsense' social attitude.

Mistrustfulness. Hypocrisy. Extreme scepticism. Arrogance. Apparent 'superiority' complex. Bizarre notion – or lack – of common sense.

Overdeveloped sense of privacy, often to the degree of unfriendliness or even enmity.

Sublimated writing is illustrated in examples 11, 43 and 64 (pp. 266, 284 and 298).

Suspended

Category: continuity
Synonym: inhibited, unfinished, retained
Antonym: easy, disengaged

Description

One letter stops short of the baseline; it may be at the beginning, the middle or at the end of a word.

Interpretation:

General Suspended letters are always a sign of inhibition.

Favourable Gentleness. Prudence. Carefulness. Constant surveillance of self. Scrupulousness. Careful and objective judgement. The writer watches his actions and will not take a decision or make a judgement unless he has studied all the facts. This may lead to dogmatism (Vels), particularly if the writing has firm down strokes, or, at least, to firmness of behaviour. With a light, irregular writing: Intuition. Introversion.

Unfavourable Inhibition. Crippling scruples. Nervous apprehensiveness. Anxiety. Insecurity. Fatigue. If the writing is of a low Formlevel: dissimulation, insincerity; the writer might lie out of fear, feebleness, insecurity, feeling of inferiority, etc., depending on supporting signs.

Suspended writing is illustrated in example 17 (p. 268).

Unfinished

Category: continuity
Synonym: truncated, incomplete
Antonym: complete

Description

The letters are not quite finished or the words lack letters. Dots, t bars, etc. are missing.

Interpretation:

General When the writing is voluntarily abridged and simplified it shows economy of time and effort for the sake of speed. On the other hand, when the writing has suspended letters, slackening strokes and is slow, it indicates impatience, laziness, inhibition, debility or negligence.

With other supporting signs it will show trickery, inconsistency.

In a good Formlevel this sign will show speed of thought, activity (nervous Melancholic temperament). The writer does not waste time when pursuing his targets.

Unfinished writing is illustrated in examples 14 and 17 (pp. 267 and 268).

Unnecessary Lines

Category: continuity

Description

Some letters have a little horizontal line at the top or at the bottom. Usually these are the letters ħ f ℓ, p̄, d̄ or q̲.

Interpretation:

General Sanguine temperament. The writer is excitable, enthusiastic and energetic. He knows it and tries to control his enthusiasm and excitability. These little bars serve him as brakes serve a car. They are a sign of inhibition.

Crépieux-Jamin considers this sign, together with the double bars (ŧ) and the double dots (j̈, ï) as one form of double-jointed writing.

Unnecessary lines are indicated in examples 21, 26 and 32 (pp. 269, 273 and 276).

Unorganized

Category: continuity
Synonym: clumsy, uneducated, infantile, elementary
Antonym: organized, disorganized

Description

The result of lack of written fluency. It is evident from the elementary formation of letters, lack of certainty in the stroke, slow speed, clumsy forms and spelling mistakes.

Interpretation:

General Lack of education and culture.

It is the writing of young children or people who have not received even a primary education. If written by an adult, with at least a basic form of education, it will indicate mental debility, puerility, gaucherie, lack of tact and finesse.

In either case unorganized writing does not easily reveal the individuality of the writer.

Unorganized writing is illustrated in examples 15 and 23 (pp. 267 and 270).

Unvarying

Category: continuity
Synonym: even height, uniform
Antonym: jerky, irregular

Description

All letters are of the same height in their respective zones. Pressure is usually pasty and even throughout the writing. Speed is poised, slow and uniform, without variation.

Interpretation:

General It is a sign of stability and regularity, the writing being generally harmonious, orderly, simple and regular.

Favourable Level-headedness. Good equilibrium. Regularity in action. Straightforwardness.

Unfavourable When it is automatic, artificial, complicated, constrained and monotonous, which it can be easily, by definition, then the interpretation of the writing is also automatic, artificial, etc.

Unvarying writing is illustrated in examples 19, 30 and 48 (pp. 269, 275 and 287).

Variable

Category: continuity
Synonym: inconsistent, unstable, changing
Antonym: invariable, consistent

Description

The writing appears different from one document or page to the next, or even from line to line.

Interpretation:

General Easily impressed. Instability. Excessive emotivity. Nervousness. Tendency to lie. A sign of dishonesty: many delinquents try to vary their writing for obvious reasons. Infidelity. Versatility. Extreme selfishness. People who have 'many writings' are people who easily change jobs, positions, partners – in business or in love – a clear sign of egoism, disloyalty, nervousness and superficiality.

Lack of ability to concentrate, lack of attention. Lack of discipline. Inconsistency. General primarity of character (p. 227). Weak will. Inability to follow up an idea.

Sometimes a writing may change over the years. This is a slow process; the changes happen gradually and they affect, especially, the categories form, dimension and direction. The reasons for this transformation may be favourable, e.g. the development of character, evolution of the personality through education, experience, psychotherapy or psychoanalysis; or unfavourable, e.g. disorganization of the writing through illness (mental or physical), moral, economic or intellectual deterioration (which can transform the personality quite dramatically), or the breakdown of a marriage, redundancy, emigration or imprisonment.

Variable writing is illustrated in examples 33–33a and 37 (pp. 276 and 280).

Direction

Direction is divided into two sections: line and stroke.

Concave

Category: direction (line)
Synonym: grooved
Antonym: convex

Description

The lines or words bend in the middle. This is a variety of Descending writing (see below).

Interpretation:

General It shows depression, but the writer makes an effort to pull himself together. It may be a temporary depression, in which case the sign soon disappears, or a more profound and permanent one in which case the sign persists everywhere. The writer, in any case, is worried. This sign may appear and disappear, often in the writing of very sensitive people.

The writer has well-developed defences. His will-power is strong and will not succumb to emotion and depression. His morale is strong if not always high. An initial weakness which will not last. Physical illness affecting morale and the emotions of the writer. This sign may also appear when the writer is under stress or during periods of grief or profound disappointment.

Concave writing is illustrated in examples 22 and 38 (pp. 270 and 281).

Convex

Category: direction (line)
Synonym: curved upwards
Antonym: concave

Description

The lines curve upwards in the middle. This is another variety of Descending writing (see below).

Interpretation:

General Physical and/or moral depression. Activity which is not sustained. Any initial energy or perseverance soon collapses. Will-power is not strong enough, the effort cannot be maintained for long and the writer falls back into depression.

Lack of strength to accomplish tasks. Lack of energy.

Convex writing is illustrated in examples 18 and 53 (pp. 268 and 290).

Descending

Category: direction (line)
Synonym: falling lines
Antonym: rising lines

Description

The lines slide downwards as the writing progresses from left to right. Sometimes even the t bars, the signature, the paraph, etc. follow this same direction.

Interpretation:

General If the writing is taut (shows tension), the lines are parallel and there are no other supporting signs, the graphologist must conclude that this sign is accidental due to bad positioning of the paper and/or the elbow.

With other supporting signs it expresses a weakness. Energy is lacking and capacity for work is low.

The writer feels beaten, guilty, impotent and discouraged for various reasons.

It may be caused by physical pain. It can be an indication of fatigue caused by illness, as well as lassitude, boredom, sadness, etc.

Unfavourable If the writing is also small, light, pale, flabby, hesitant with many corrections, retouched, regressive, twisted, jerky or negligent, it will show debility, neurasthenia, passive neurosis, etc.

The writer is likely to let himself be influenced quite easily. He is weak willed. Tendency to moral corruption, infidelity, hypocrisy, egoism.

This writing has different interpretations for different temperaments and characters. Depression, sadness, debility, etc. are not expressed in the same manner by all people. Crépieux-Jamin says:

'Each one of us reacts in different ways, many depressed people are astonished when they notice that their writing does not fall.'

Descending lines are illustrated in examples 22 and 46 (pp. 270 and 286).

Diving

Category: direction (line)
Synonym: falling, plunging
Antonym: climbing

Description

The lines plunge downwards, particularly the final words of the line, as the writing progresses from left to right. See also Descending lines (above).

Interpretation:

General Depression. Fatigue. Anxiety. Lack of ability to react. Discouragement. Loss of hope. Tendency to suicide, but only with supporting signs. In some writing it is also an expression of pain, bodily or emotional suffering. Possible illness – physical or mental.

Diving writing is illustrated in example 40 (p. 282).

Galloping Downwards

Category: direction (line)
Synonym: falling tiles
Antonym: horizontal

Description

The words or syllables slide downwards but not necessarily the line, i.e. the last letters of each word or syllable are hanging downwards.

Interpretation:

General A constant fight against depression or fatigue. The writer is sad and tired but full of goodwill and starts again and again, trying to maintain his efforts, but without success.

Galloping downwards writing is illustrated in examples 38 and 41 (pp. 281 and 283).

Galloping Upwards

Category: direction (line)
Synonym: rising tiles
Antonym: horizontal

Description

The words or syllables climb upwards but not necessarily the line, i.e. the last letters of each word or syllable are higher than the first letters.

Interpretation:

General Unsustained zeal. The writer is unable to maintain a constant effort. He is euphoric and eager but lacks stamina.

Galloping upwards writing is illustrated in example 17 (p. 268).

Horizontal

Category: direction (line)
Synonym: straight
Antonym: climbing, descending

Description

The lines run parallel to the top and bottom edges of the paper.

Interpretation:

General Calm, even-tempered. Self-control. Orderliness. Tranquillity.

Favourable With a combined, aerated writing, progressive, rapid, harmonious and in relief it will indicate serenity, composure and harmony of tendencies. Punctuality. Discipline. Strictly channelled activity.

Unfavourable Indifference. Non-emotive character if the writing is homogeneous, uniform (unvarying) and calm. Coldness. Apathy.

Horizontal writing is illustrated in examples 12 and 49 (pp. 266 and 288).

Irregular

See Continuity, p. 160.

Rigid

See page 189

Rising

Category: direction (line)
Synonym: ascending lines
Antonym: descending lines

Description

The lines climb upwards as the writing progresses from left to right.

Interpretation:

General If this is not accidental, i.e. caused by bad placing of the paper in relation to the body (which the experienced graphologist will be able to see from the combination of speed with direction), and if the rising is not more than 8–10°, it shows dynamism, optimism, love of life, good humour, joy, liveliness, activity, ardour, initiative, extraversion, good health. These characteristics must be supported by other signs.

If the lines rise more than 10° (climbing lines) the above qualities will be exaggerated and will show arrogance, exaltation, megalomania, loss of contact with reality, presumptiousness, aggression and, with supporting signs, sadism.

More rarely, the cause of climbing lines may be a strong, deep-rooted depression which the writer tries to fight against. This possibility has to be supported by signs revealing great sensitivity, excitability, nervousness, tiredness and combativity.

Rising lines are illustrated in examples 8 and 45 (pp. 264 and 285).

Stable Baseline

Category: direction (line)
Synonym: straight baseline
Antonym: wavy lines

Description

The letters and words progress on a straight baseline regardless of the direction of the lines – whether rising, horizontal or falling.

Interpretation:

General Consistency in action. Sense of responsibility. Tenacity of will. Moral courage and stamina.

In a low Formlevel (regular, rigid or unorganized writing) it will indicate stubbornness, lack of flexibility and adaptability.

A stable baseline is illustrated in examples 10, 44 and 49 (pp. 265, 284 and 288).

Undulating Words

Category: direction (line)
Synonym: sinuous words
Antonym: rectilinear letters

Description

The letters in one word do not all touch the baseline. This sign is a variety of Irregular writing (p. 162).

Interpretation:

General Instability caused by strong emotivity. Anxiety.

Favourable Great sensitivity. Ability to sense things intuitively. Sensitive attitudes with people. Suppleness, diplomacy, quick adaptability to new situations. Delicacy of feelings.

Unfavourable Possible ambivalence and lack of inner harmony (particularly if paired with an oscillating slant from right to left). Aggression, worry. Disposition to obsessional neurosis. Dissimulation. Lack of sincerity (with supporting signs), excessive emotionalism. Versatile tendencies (homo or bisexual), with supporting signs, i.e. rounded lower extensions, deviated pressure, etc.

If the writing is unorganized none of the above may be applicable. It may only indicate embarrassment and/or lack of written fluency.

Undulating words are illustrated in examples 17, 33a and 63 (pp. 268, 276 and 297).

Wavy Lines

Category: direction (line)
Synonym: serpentine, sinuous, undulating
Antonym: rectilinear

Description

The lines undulate. Not to be confused with the direction of the lines. Wavy lines may be descending, plunging, horizontal or rising.

Interpretation:

General Hesitation. Emotivity. Anxiety. Instability. Impressionability.

Favourable Mental activity. Suppleness. Diplomacy (with a simplified, combined, aerated writing). *Savoir faire*. Versatility. Intuition (with a light, irregular writing).

Unfavourable Hesitation. Meanness. Dissimulation. Tendency to lie. Lack of sincerity. Lack of self-confidence, impressionability, nervousness. Instability, cunning, lack of firmness and backbone. Weak-willed (if there are supporting signs). Hypocrisy, deceit (if the writing is organized). Infidelity.

With supporting signs it can indicate ambivalence (contradictory tendencies), anxiety, aggression, bitchiness, exaltation, homosexuality – in extreme cases, even sadism or obsessional neurosis.

Wavy lines are illustrated in examples 23, 36–36a, 40, 56 and 63 (pp. 270, 278, 279, 282, 292 and 297).

Centrifugal

Category: direction (stroke)
Synonym: rightward direction of final stroke
Antonym: centripetal

Description

The general tendency of this writing is towards the right. The final strokes of letters or words are extended towards the right, either straight or slightly curved upwards.

It is another form of progressive writing.

Interpretation:

General If the extensions are exaggerated it shows absent-mindedness, precipitate thought, lack of prudence.

Favourable In a good Formlevel it is an indication of altruism, kindness, generosity, spontaneity of feelings, devotion, conciliation.

Unfavourable With an angular, rigid writing with clubbed and/or flying strokes it shows impulsiveness, impatience, aggressiveness, violence, moodiness. A difficult character.

Centrifugal writing is illustrated in examples 8 and 38 (pp. 264 and 281).

Centripetal

Category: direction (stroke)
Synonym: leftward direction of final stroke
Antonym: centrifugal

Description

The final strokes of words or letters are deviated towards the left, upwards or downwards.

Interpretation:

General Egoism. Calculated reserve. Anti-social attitudes. Egocentricity. Fury.

When the final stroke is also spasmodic with excessively sharp points (needle-like endings of the strokes), it shows extreme violence which could reach criminal tendencies.

Centripetal writing may be one of the signs of dishonesty (p. 205).

If this sign is present in an unorganized, slow and stylized writing it may simply be a gesture of relief; a pause from the effort needed to write. In this case the interpretation will invoke neither egoism nor dishonesty.

Centripetal writing is illustrated in examples 42 and 50 (pp. 283 and 289).

Irregular

See Continuity, p. 160.

Leftward

Category: direction (stroke)
Synonym: left slant
Antonym: forward slant, right slant

Description

The writing leans to the left beyond the vertical.

Interpretation:

General It is generally accepted that this type of writing indicates an attitude of defence. It shows introversion when it is moderate, but also extreme extroversion-hysteria-paranoia when excessively slanted to the left, with full loops in upper and/or lower zones, big movements and uncontrolled speed.

Favourable The writer tries to hide his emotions. He refuses to suffer and reacts againt his sensitivity, renouncing it. Many nuns have a backward slant to their writing.

Unfavourable Inferiority complex. Unhappiness. Lack of self-confidence. Often repression of homosexual tendencies (with descending lines). Dissimulation. Affectation. Constraint. Rebellion against authority. Mistrust. Fear. Timidity. Negation. Aggression. Lack of discipline. Repressed emotionalism. Irritability.

Selfishness (Klages). Arrogance. Suspicious nature. Criticism; usually false. Inadaptability. Unpleasant personality. Tendency to lie or hide the truth in order to defend oneself. Negative attitudes.

The writer mistrusts other people's affection for him or her.

Opposition to authority, society and established conventions (Beauchataud). This is one of the most difficult signs to interpret correctly. Great care should be taken and consideration given to the other dominant and supporting signs.

Leftward slanting writing is illustrated in examples 20, 27 and 28 (pp. 269, 274 and 275).

Progressive

Category: direction (stroke)
Synonym: advancing
Antonym: regressive

Description

The overall movement of the writing is directed towards the right with speed and economy.

Not to be confused with centrifugal writing which contains exaggerated strokes. Progressive writing is simple, simplified, sober, connected, accelerated, combined and rounded.

Interpretation:

General Sociability. Natural interest in and affection for people. Adaptability. Easy contact with others (physical or mental). Expressiveness. Open behaviour. Extrovert thinking. Intuition.

Favourable Good and rapid coordination of ideas. Graciousness. Honesty. Friendliness. Allocentrism (see Glossary and p. 247). Self-detachment. Generosity. Activity. Imagination. Confidence in people. Intelligence; spirit of enterprise. Initiative. General superiority and culture. Expansion. Ability to understand social, political and economic problems.

Unfavourable If the writing is spread out, it shows lack of prudence, direction and discipline. Vanity, need for new sensations, easily impressed.

With supporting signs: ostentatious character. Ability to explode. Tendency to exaggeration (with inharmonious writing).

Progressive writing is illustrated in examples 5, 8 and 66 (pp. 263, 264 and 300).

Regressive

Category: direction (stroke)
Synonym: tending leftwards, centripetal
Antonym: progressive

Description

Certain strokes which should be directed towards the right are directed towards the left. The emphasis is mainly on the final strokes, initial strokes, capital letters, t bars and signature.

Regressive movement can be angular or curved. Hooks, loops, spirals, arcades, lassos, etc. can be regressive. Also, double-joined writing is a form of regressive writing.

Interpretation:

General This sign is opposed to intelligence, honesty and activity. By its sheer direction (against the normal flow of the writing), it is in opposition and shows hardness and coldness. Its positive or negative interpretation will depend upon the zone in which it usually appears.

Egocentricity, egotism, narcissism. The writer worries about his own problems and is rather indifferent or shows only a superficial and frivolous interest in other people's concerns. Attachment to possessions.

Favourable Reserve. Individualism. Shyness. Selectivity. Need for independence. Indifference about other people's opinions. Solitude. Introversion.

Unfavourable Inadaptability. Lack of spontaneity. Lying. Tendency to dissimulation. Rumination. Narcissism. Stubbornness. Lack of consideration for others. Lack of honesty and moral values. Children, mentally retarded or neurotic people and delinquents often have regressive writing (Vels). According to the rule that every exaggeration indicates the opposite it will show extroversion or even hysteria when the regressive strokes are over-pronounced.

Regressive writing is illustrated in examples 26 and 28 (pp. 273 and 275).

Reverse

Category: direction (stroke)
Synonym: inverted, clockwise
Antonym: progressive

Description

A clockwise movement to form the ovals and/or loops. Arcades in general are a reverse (clockwise) movement unless they are formed from right to left (centripetal writing); t bars, if they form an arch, are also a reverse movement.

Interpretation:

General During puberty people are inclined to try to establish their independence by resisting discipline. At that time 'd' can turn into 'δ', indicating a revolutionary tendency. This particular sign becomes rarer in maturity.

Real independence is self-discipline which has nothing to do with a reversed d or 'need for emancipation'.

Favourable In a good Formlevel (rapid, combined, simplified): intelligence, independence of mind.

Unfavourable Inner contradictions. Argumentativeness. Lack of discipline. Inadaptability. Egoism. Provocativeness. Resistance. Obstinate and stubborn character.

Reverse writing is illustrated in examples 3 and 4 (p. 262)

Rightward Slant

Category: direction (stroke)
Synonym: leaning to the right
Antonym: vertical, left slant

Description

The letters slant to the right, forming an angle of approximately 54° with the baseline.

Interpretation:

General The writer needs the continuous presence of other people near and around him. Positive impressionability (adaptability) when the writing is curved and in garlands, and negative (combativity) when it is angular.

This writing is typical of the function of Sentiment (in extroversion).

If the pressure is light it shows impressionability, weakness, tenderness, sympathy, subjectiveness. Easily influenced.

Favourable Sociability. Easy communication with people. Warmth of heart. Compassion (particularly if the writing is in garlands). Passion. Femininity. Sweetness of manner. Amiability. Sensitivity (if the writing is curved and irregular).

Unfavourable If this writing is also monotonous; blind passion or tenacity. Narrow mindedness. Obstinacy. If the pressure is spasmodic: strong sensuality. In general, this writing indicates that the heart rules the head.

Rightward slanting writing is illustrated in examples 2, 3, 4, 5 and others (pp. 261, 262 and 263).

Rigid

Category: direction (line and stroke)
Synonym: firm, angular, inflexible
Antonym: sinuous, wavy, weak

Description

Inflexibility of direction. Extreme, unbending regularity, giving the impression of automatism. Not to be confused with Automatic writing (p. 148).

Interpretation:

General Rigidity of ideas. Stubbornness. Hardness.

Favourable Probable qualities of this type are precision, straightforwardness, moral strength, stability, principles, seriousness, punctuality, etc. If there are minor irregularities they show hidden sensitivity.

Unfavourable Selfishness. Inadaptability. Lack of social sense. Austerity. Severity. Arrogance. Inflexibility. Sytematic opposition. Inferiority complex. Fanaticism. Intransigence. Aggression. In extreme cases: sadism, obsessional neurosis.

Rigid writing is illustrated in examples 10, 30 and 38 (pp. 265, 275 and 281).

Twisted

Category: direction (stroke)
Synonym: distorted, crooked, bent
Antonym: straight

Description

The down strokes, which should be straight, are distorted: ℓ, ℓ
Should not be confused with Wavy strokes (p. 204).

Interpretation:

General This sign appears generally during periods of transition: from childhood to puberty to adulthood and during menopause. It manifests nervous, glandular or circulatory disturbances which occur during these particular periods in life.

It is indicative of a temporary diminishing of vitality due to various causes (look for supporting signs). The libido is mostly in regression or blocked. Overworked people – particularly housewives – often produce this sign. Postoperative and postnatal conditions also produce twisted down strokes. It is a sign of an emotional upheaval (usually temporary), of instability, great sensitivity and nervousness – an unsettled period in life. Tiredness is the result of all such situations. Puberty and the 'change of life', in both men and women, is the most common cause although we must not exclude pathological reasons.

Twisted writing is illustrated in examples 50 and 53 (pp. 289 and 290).

Vertical

Category: direction (stroke)
Synonym: straight, perpendicular, upright
Antonym: slanted right or left

Description

The up and down strokes form, with the baseline, a right angle. The writing is perpendicular to the baseline of the writing.

Interpretation:

General Firmness of attitudes. Stability. Self-control. Coldness.

Favourable Reserved attitude. Stability. Reflection. Firmness.

Independence. If the writing is firm and with good pressure in the down strokes: strong will-power, decisiveness. The writer is reasonable and has good control over his emotions. His judgement is clear and firm. He is consistent and reliable in character and thought. Good ability to control his desires, tendencies and sentiments. This does not mean that he does not have strong feelings and emotions. It only means that he has control over them rather than they over him.

Unfavourable Lack of enthusiasm for life. Lack of spontaneity. Pride. Selfishness (with supporting signs). Insensitivity. Distrustful character. Lack of warmth. Indifference to other people's problems. Hardness, coldness of attitude (with angular writing and straight baselines). Aloofness, inflexibility, arrogance (with angular, super-elevated writing and rigid direction).

With supporting signs it may indicate pathological states of health.

Vertical writing is illustrated in examples 15 and 16 (p. 267).

Very Slanted to the Right

Category: direction (stroke)
Synonym: lying, recumbent
Antonym: vertical, left slant

Description

The right slant is between 30–45°.

Interpretation:

General Lack of self-control. Exaggerated impulsiveness. Exaltation. Lack of self-discipline. Weakness of character. Lack of control. Abandonment to passions. Dramatization of feelings. Subjectiveness. Overexcitement of sexual and sensual impulses; often exhibitionism. Desire to attract attention, to be loved.

With exaggerated, prolonged lower extensions: deep homosexual tendencies, particularly if the writing has feminine traits and is regressive (descending, the f in the shape of an 8), with spasmodic or deviated pressure, etc.

The writer needs physical manifestations of affection. Egoism. Jealousy. Envy. Irritability. Aggression (particularly if the writing is also thrown, sharp-pointed, rapid and angular).

Writing which is very slanted to the right is illustrated in example 35 (p. 277).

Particular Signs

Accents etc.

Category: particular signs

When the accents or i dots are placed high, it is a sign of idealism, intellectual interests, ambitions or illusions (depending on supporting signs).

When they are placed on the right of their respective letters they show headlong activity, haste, lightness of spirit, flight.

If they are placed precisely they show care, order, reflection or consideration.

If they are heavy and placed low, they indicate materialism, calculation, laziness (with a slow, pasty writing).

If they are placed on the left of their respective letters, the interpretation will depend on the form and speed of writing. If they are progressive and the writing is Rapid or Precipitated (pp. 141 and 140), they show speed of thought, carelessness, lack of attention to detail. If the writing is slow and the dots and accents are heavy and correctly formed it is a sign of laziness and carelessness due to weakness of character.

Exclamation and other marks used in abundance are a sign of extreme extroversion, primarity (see p. 227), exuberance, exaggeration, hysteria or obsession.

In some Latin countries – as, for instance, in Spain – it is fairly common to form the i dots and full stops in the shape of a little circle (examples 14 and 38). Depending on the general style of writing, this may be indicative of the warmth and emotionalism which is a national characteristic. In any event, it shows a sanguine temperament: extroversion, ebullience, passion, impulsiveness, joviality, easy contact, coquetry, gaiety and strong vitality.

Capital Letters in the Middle of Words

Category: particular signs

Description

There are capital letters in place of small letters.

In some countries children are taught this style of writing at school, e.g. in Ireland, the capital R is copy-book style.

Interpretation:

General Indicates lack of judgement and a tendency to exaggeration. It is usually a sign of simple disorderliness and messiness. The writer is not fussy about the right order of things. He needs double the normal effort to be punctual or tidy. Even truth sometimes suffers in the hands of such writers.

When the lines also rise, the writer is in a state of effervescence. His imagination runs away. He may not even realize he is lying or exaggerating. He feels good, rich, beautiful, powerful. The writing may also increase in speed, the pressure becomes strong, sometimes precise or in relief.

This can also be a sign of alienation in which case this state does not last long. The writing will soon start to lose its vigour, the lines will fall, the direction will become uncertain and speed and pressure will decline.

Capital letters in the middle of words are illustrated in example 18 (p. 268).

Final Strokes

Category: particular signs
Synonym: end strokes
Antonym: starting or initial strokes

Description

All strokes appearing at the end of a letter, a word or a line.

Interpretation:

General If the final stroke is short: d e a : a phlegmatic sign, good control, tolerance or indifference, serenity or insensitivity – see the rest of the signs. If the final stroke is sharp-pointed: a e d g t : if short it may indicate a sharp, penetrating mind or an inclination to criticize; if long it shows aggression and impulsiveness, particularly if repeated and frequent.

If the final stroke is clubbed: a , e : may be favourable if short and controlled. It shows well-disciplined activity; if long it can be either a sign of brutal and violent behaviour (with supporting signs), or a sign of generosity and allocentrism. It will depend on the rest of the signs and the Formlevel; if the clubbed end descends it may show severe depression, not necessarily manifest: a d. Example 21 (p. 269).

A final stroke turning leftwards when it shouldn't: n = n, i = i : egoism, secretiveness, mistrustfulness (only when consistently repeated).

An open final stroke in the form of rising garlands (like a fishing hook): e a : suppleness of behaviour, self-interest, captivating abilities often seen in American-style writing. Example 22 (p. 270).

Vertically prolonged final strokes: t d : can be tiredness, strong instincts, activity (particularly if it is also clubbed) or materialistic interests. Example 60 (p. 294).

Little hooks: a p : usually an unfavourable sign of selfishness or dishonesty (see Hooks, below).

Hooks

Category: particular signs

Description

Tiny little superfluous strokes which appear usually at the beginning of an initial stroke of a letter, at the end of the final stroke of a letter (or word, line, or text), forming a pointed angle with the rest of the (initial or final) stroke.

Interpretation:

General The interpretation is extremely variable and depends solely on which zone they appear, which way they point and how long (or visible) they are.

Generally, hooks indicate tenacity and resistance. If they are in the upper zone as initial starting strokes they show that the writer is well encrusted in his theories (usually intellectual) and remains inflexible.

If they are in the middle zone the stubbornness is more in the general attitude of the personality. They are the trademark of people who will not give up; passively or actively, they stick to their own feelings or activity.

If the hooks appear in the lower zone this sign is more often unfavourable. It shows a passion for material acquisitions and an attachment to possessions. Love of money and, in general, ownership. The writer will be aggressive and malignant, vindictive, selfish and probably dishonest (with a complicated, disorderly, angular, sharp-pointed or clubbed writing with spasmodic pressure).

Hooked writing is illustrated in example 42 (p. 283).

Lassos

Category: particular signs
Synonym: large loops
Antonym: rigid

Description

The lasso is formed by a horizontal flying stroke curving and returning, so forming a large loop and a bow, or two large loops in one stroke. Often the lasso starts from a preliminary leftwards turn. It can appear in the body of the writing as well as in the signature and the paraph.

It is related to Flying Strokes (p. 138).

Interpretation:

General Egoism.

Favourable Imagination. Inventiveness. Agility. Dynamism. Tenacity. Commercial talents. Captivating mannerisms.

In women: coquetry, decorative talents.

Unfavourable Selfishness. Authoritarianism. Stubbornness. Calculated captivating mannerisms. Vanity. Possessiveness. Cunning. Intrigue. Imposters often use this sign.

Lassos are illustrated in examples 14 and 54 (pp. 267 and 290).

Lyrical d

Category: particular signs

Description

The upper extension of the letter d curves gently and gracefully towards the left.

Interpretation:

General In an otherwise progressive writing this form, albeit regressive, indicates the idealistic or romantic tendencies of the writer.

It is also called the 'poetic d'; it shows a poetic inclination and lyrical imagination; meditation and introspection.

Lyrical d writing is illustrated in examples 7 and 8 (p. 264).

Shark's Tooth

See Form, p. 122.

Signature

Category: particular signs

The signature can never be interpreted as an isolated sign, it can only be studied in connection with the text to help complete and confirm an interpretation of the writing as a whole.

Whatever the qualities of a writing, we cannot be certain of these without the signature. In truth, we know little about the writer without his or her signature.

In order to analyse a writing, therefore, the signature is needed. Its role is decisive – whatever we have deciphered from the handwriting may be confirmed or rejected by the signature. In cases of disparity the signature is pre-eminent; it is the key to the writer's real personality and inner life.

The first thing a signature reveals is the writer's vitality: his or her ability to realize his potential; the direction he gives to his life; how he puts his abilities to use.

In the writing we see the writer's potential; in the signature, whether and how he uses this potential. The choice depends more on history and psychic strength than on personality and temperament.

The second element revealed in the signature is the writer's own evaluation of himself; his personality and how he rates himself among his fellow beings.

The third element expressed is the degree of reliability and morality: sincerity and honesty, or otherwise.

The fourth element deals with the writer's family history: the summation of his childhood, personal history, situation in the family home and the way he felt about it; the attachment, or not, to a memory of past happiness or misery – all reflected in his future, directing it this way or that.

In analysing a signature we should first have a proper signature, not just initials. Also, it helps if we know the exact name – and its spelling – of the writer.

The Symbolism of Space (pp. 20–21) is very useful in an interpretation of signatures, in the same way as a compass helps a navigator map out a journey. If the extensions tend to the north, the writer's tendencies reflect the activities of the brain, through intellectuality, spirituality, to psychic utopianism. If the extensions point due south, the writer is more oriented towards practical activities, instincts and materialistic interests. If there is a tendency towards the east, the writer looks towards the future with open arms. If the strokes turn west, it indicates a denial of the present, fear for the future, withdrawal and dissimulation; the writer turns towards his sources, towards the past, trying to avoid whatever is to come.

The signature is also a symbol of the writer's activity in life. Often his profession is pictured quite clearly in its design. In this case, it helps if we know more about the writer than sex and age. For example, the following signature could be interpreted as that of an intellectual – however, this does not apply here. He is, in fact, a man who has made his fortune in shipping and his signature is clearly the outline of a three-masted ship.

The text will tell us about the writer's attitudes towards his environment, towards the world, and his social behaviour. The signature will express the writer's attitude towards himself; his inner feelings about his own value.

Hundreds or even thousands of pages have been written about the study of signatures. There is hardly room here to elaborate in detail on this subject, important and even imperative as it may be for the building-up of a portrait. (For further reading on this subject, see R. Crépy, *La Signature*, which is one of the best of its kind; published in 1983 in Paris by Delachaux–Niestlé.) We shall concentrate, therefore, on the basic, general rules of interpreting the signature in connection with the text.

1 a. If the *forms*, e.g. angular writing in a filiform sign, are *different* from those of the rest of the text (discordance between signature and text), there is disassociation between social and intimate behaviour. Duality of personality. Lack of harmony between the writer's social attitudes and private reality. At the extreme, it indicates dishonesty, amorality, hypocrisy, etc.

b. If all categories are similar (continuity, speed, pressure, etc.) but, as a whole, *inharmonious*, it is a sign of deeply rooted neurosis. The writer is unaware of his own situation, whatever this may be. He identifies completely with the social role he has adopted, thus blocking any chance of allowing himself room to evolve and progress.

If the whole is *harmonious* the writer is in harmony with himself. His behaviour is always in accord with the circumstances of his life, in private or in public. He is loyal, natural and honest (with supporting signs).

2 a. If the signature is the same in form and style but is *larger* than the text, there is a discrepancy between what the writer is and how he likes to appear. This may (with supporting signs) indicate an inferiority complex compensated by arrogance or pride. If there are no supporting signs for the above, however, then it shows only that the writer values himself higher than, at the least, the person he is writing to. Also (with supporting signs) self-admiration, narcissism, vanity, neurosis, paranoia (with disproportionate upper extensions).

b. If the signature is *smaller* than the text then it shows an inferiority complex (always with supporting signs), or humbleness, timidity, inhibition, or unsatisfactory attitudes at home, e.g. meanness.

3 a. If the signature shows signs of *greater speed* than the rest of the text, the writer is really more confident in himself than he shows. He has good potential for improvement in many fields of his activity.

b. If it is *slower* than the text the writer is trying to master his impulses. He is reserved, his attitude may be defensive (with supporting signs). He is careful, he slows down to give himself time to control his impulses.

4 a. If the *pressure* of the signature is *heavier* the writer is avoiding compromises and has fear of confrontation. He feels stronger alone; his self-confidence is greater.

b. If it is *lighter*, the writer needs to retreat into the comfort of his privacy. Social contacts threaten his self-confidence. He dislikes expressions of feeling. He has to force himself to communicate with others.

5 a. If the letters of the signature are *more connected* than those in the text it shows fluency of thought (in a high Formlevel with medium to small letters). The writer can 'think' better when he is alone. He tends to get distracted by the presence of others.

In a low Formlevel it indicates anxiety and social inhibitions.

b. If the letters are *less connected* in the signature, the writer may be tired, he needs to 'go home', to rest alone, to recover strength and recharge his batteries.

6 a. If the signature *slants* more to the *right* than the text the writer is more at ease in intimate circles. He can communicate more easily and express his feelings better.

b. If the signature is *vertical* but the text slanted, the writer is reserved by nature; he dislikes intimacy and feels more comfortable in the presence of others. He may be displeased with his present private situation.

7 a. If the signature is *placed* to the *right* of the page, it is where it should be, as it is taught in European schools.

It shows extroversion (always in accordance with the text and the rest of the signs), easy communication with others, activity, initiative, optimism.

In the United States, the fashion is to sign to the left of the page. The electric typewriter prefers it! The organization of the page is such as to force the person to sign on the left.

b. If the signature is placed in the *middle* of the text, it shows inhibition. The writer is hesitant, possibly shy and withdrawn (with supporting signs).

c. The more the signature moves to the *left*, unless it is part of the American 'block style' (see above) which will be evident from the rest of the text (see Margins, p. 46), the more the writer is withdrawn, discouraged and depressed. His self-confidence is punctured, he tends towards melancholia, isolation, possibly suicidal tendencies (Pulver).

8 When the signature is *rising* it shows optimism, ambition, activity, *élan*, possibly an *arriviste*.

9 If it is *descending* it indicates pessimism, discouragement, stubbornness, obsession or tiredness.

10 A signature followed by a *full stop* shows prudence, inhibition, mistrustful attitude towards the world.

11 A signature *underlined* with a firm horizontal stroke indicates confidence, will-power, tenacity. If the line is undulating it shows coquetry.

12 A *centrifugal* (upwards) end stroke shows *élan* and physical courage.

13 A *large paraphe encircling* the name indicates that the writer feels a need to protect himself from danger. Feebleness. General inhibition. Anxiety. Often, agoraphobic people encircle their signatures. It is also a sign of dissimulation or dishonesty.

14 The paraphe in *lasso* is usually a sign of suppleness. The writer has mental agility, diplomacy, cleverness.

15 When the final stroke of a signature extends firmly downwards (*centripetal*) and stops abruptly, nervousness and irritability are indicated. Also, firmness and will-power of the writer. He is an achiever in concrete, material things. If this lower extension is barred by another stroke, forming a cross, it shows combativity.

16 If a final paraphe *returns towards the left* in the shape of lightning, *underlining* the name, it shows hardness, ruthlessness, vindictive instincts. If it returns over the top of the signature it shows egoism and apprehension of society.

17 If the final stroke *returns to the left over* the signature, crossing it out, it is a sign of self-destruction. In this case the signature will rarely be on the right – it will be either in the middle or on the left under the text.

18 If the signature is *illegible* the writer is distrustful, mean and petty.

19 If the signature is *simple, clear* and *without any paraphe*, it indicates an honest, open character, confident of his value who has nothing to hide. Also (depending on the Formlevel and the rest of the signs), simplicity of mind or naivety.

20 If the signature *runs between two parallel lines*, it shows that the writer likes to follow a set path of action. He feels more comfortable 'on rails'.

All the above interpretations are basic and general. Everything depends on the Formlevel and the signs in the rest of the text.

Spirals

See Form, p. 126.

Starting Strokes

Category: particular signs
Synonym: initial strokes
Antonym: final or end strokes

Description

Any stroke appearing before the first letter of a word or a line of words.

Interpretation:

Generally, starting strokes represent dependence.

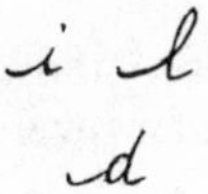

open garland: a 'commercial' sign; slightly superficial, not necessarily disagreeable. Often called the stroke of amiability.

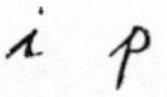

short connected straight rising stroke: decisive and stiff – this little stroke indicates just that. Traditionalism gives a certain feeling of security and so do old habits.

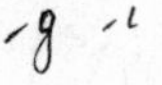

short disconnected light rising stroke: an 'I object!' sign, often precautionary. It usually goes with signs of hesitation in the rest of the writing. A rather 'dry' heart.

long initial stroke starting from the lower zone: an active sign, albeit 'unloved' – this represents the era of childhood when the writer was 'seen but not heard'. An intense need for affection.

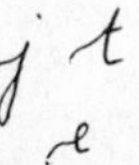

arched starting stroke: inhibitions. It represents reserved behaviour (rather than a permanent characteristic). Often against the family and the past. Disloyalty, possible hypocrisy.

spiral: a sensible and practical sign. The writer takes precautions before making a decision to act.

initial dot: pedantry. A ponderous writer, rather slow and hesitant.

superelevated starting stroke: pride (or arrogance), confidence (or recklessness), noble feelings (or haughtiness), intellectuality (or pedantry).

no starting stroke: independence, quick thinking, decisiveness, precision. The writer does not waste time or energy.

It goes without saying that all the above are valid only when endorsed by supporting signs.

Strong Regressive Strokes

Category: particular signs

Description

An intensely regressive movement of the stroke. The pen moves upwards towards the left and curves down in the form of a reverse arcade.

Interpretation:

General Whether in the lower zone, , in the middle zone, = , or in the upper zone, = , this sign shows egocentricity as well as egoism, and a wish to monopolize at close quarters. The writer has little sensitivity for other people's feelings or needs.

If the end of the regressive stroke is also sharp-pointed it shows hurtfulness, meanness or nastiness.

In a stylized writing the above interpretations may be milder.

Strong, regressive strokes are illustrated in example 41 (p. 283).

Swords

Category: particular signs

Description

Some lower extensions, paraphes or signatures take the shape of a sword. They may be straight or slightly curved.

Interpretation:

General The interpretation of this sign is similar to that of Flying Strokes, Prolonged Downwards and Animated writing (pp. 138, 61 and 91). Extroversion. Combativeness. A lively, irrepressible nature which enjoys and thrives in battles and wars.

Swords are illustrated in example 14 (p. 267).

Triangles

Category: particular signs

Description

They appear usually in lower extensions, letters f, g, y, etc., and in t bars. May also appear in the letters s and z and less often in the ovals of the middle zone.

Interpretation:

General The triangular movement is usually accompanied by a firm pressure and indicates a desire to command and impose one's desires, ideas, opinions or decisions upon others. Tendency to dominate at home or in intimate circles.

If the final stroke points upwards with a sharp-pointed ending it shows aggression, argumentativeness, stubbornness, obstinacy, authoritarianism, combativeness.

If it is closed high, near the middle zone, with strong pressure towards the final rightward stroke, it may show hardness or antisocial behaviour.

If the final stroke of the triangle descends low and towards the body of the letter ( ) it shows stubbornness and a refusal to progress.

Not a very communicative sign, the writer may be anchored in his opinions, reserved, fearful of his position, secretive, etc. with supporting signs.

If the triangles are in proportion, the writing is in relief and harmonious, it will indicate self-confidence and an ability to pursue one's aims with tenacity and courage.

Triangles are illustrated in example 31 (p. 275).

Wavy Strokes

Category: particular signs

Description

Any undulating stroke which should be straight as, for instance, t bars, initial and end strokes, or any down strokes in the body of the letter (not usually horizontal strokes). Should not be confused with Twisted writing (p. 190).

Interpretation:

General Indicates lightheartedness and imagination.

Favourable Cordiality. Jovial disposition. Good sense of humour. *Fantasie*. Lightheartedness. Sympathy. Flexibility. Adaptability. Agility. Verbal or intellectual lucidity. Need to expand, to 'grow'. Finesse. Spirituality. The rest of the writing will guide us towards the correct interpretation.

Unfavourable Escapism. Lack of morality or sincerity. Astuteness. Weakness of character (with slack tension and weak writing). Tendency to avoid responsibility. Hypocrisy. Lack of frankness or straightforwardness.

If the pressure of the wavy strokes is uncertain, weak and mainly in the vertical strokes it may be that the sign is not that of wavy strokes, but rather that of Twisted writing (p. 190).

Wavy strokes are illustrated in example 8 and 15 (pp. 264 and 267).

Signs of Insincerity

We all lie at some time in our life and we all hide something from someone, if need be.

There is no one sign to indicate insincerity, hypocrisy or criminality as such. There is, however, a combination of signs which, when present, should be examined with particular attention and care.

The following signs (listed in alphabetical order) may be completely innocent and normal, but could become indicative of insincerity, hypocrisy or even criminality if present in certain combinations and under certain conditions.

These are: ambiguous forms, amended, arcades, artificial, bizarre, clubbed, covering strokes, diminishing (excessive), double curves, enlarging, fragmented, irregularity of forms, lapses of continuity, left slant, mingling letters in middle zone, negligent, one letter replaces another, ovals open on the left or underneath, in reverse, shark's tooth, slow, spirals, supported, trenchant, unnecessary dots, wavy lines.

Take note also: if there are marked differences between text and signature, excessive similarity between text and signature, excessive irregularity of pressure, exaggerated width or height of letters, exaggerated ornamentations.

It is not advisable for students or inexperienced graphologists to interpret any of the above signs as insincerity, hypocrisy or criminality, as these can only be assessed when present in certain combinations and in a specific context.

Graphology is a constructive science. It does not judge or put a value on people. Positive thinking, objectivity and understanding are fundamental qualities for all serious graphologists.

Pathological Signs

Some graphological signs may indicate a malfunction in certain areas of the body or mind.

These are: amended, automatic, broken, congested, constrained, cramped, descending, discordant, disorganized, diving, faltering, fragmented, jerky, pale, shaky, spasmodic, twisted, unnecessary dots, weak.

Although these signs, when present, indicate a certain malfunction, it is not wise to try to make a full medical diagnosis from them alone.

Whereas it has been proven that early detection of a malfunction (say, in the respiratory system) is possible from the written signs, it is impossible to tell what causes it (pneumonia, TB, cancer or simply smoking too much). It is therefore wiser to advise a general medical check-up rather than presume on a risky diagnosis. It is not improbable that one day graphology will be able to help medical doctors more accurately and perhaps this day is not far off. It is only a matter of research and organized documentation.

6

INTERPRETATION OF SIGNS

The purpose of graphology is to understand the human mentality, character and general psychological make-up through handwriting.

In this process we trace the cause from the effect, through logical connections only.

Before starting work on a writing, establish the age and sex of the writer and whether he is left or right-handed. It is also important to discover, whether the writer is fluent in the language in which he is writing. Other useful information concerns nationality, level of education, profession, etc.

The document must be adequate, i.e. one full page of prose (not poetry or copy from another text) on unlined paper, handwritten with a fountain pen or ballpoint (not felt-tip pen or pencil), fully signed and dated. Ideally, we should have more than one document, preferably with an interval of about six months between each.

After setting the document in front of you, first open your mind to it and all its favourable and unfavourable aspects. Chase away any personal preoccupations or feelings in order to stay receptive to the writing.

Look at the totality of the writing to get a first *general impression*, e.g. its intensity of energy or lack of it.

Establish a few basic factors: whether it is harmonious or otherwise, organized, unorganized or disorganized, spontaneous or artificial, natural or copy-book, typographic or any other style, and the Formlevel.

It helps to retrace the movement of the stroke with a pointed instrument or a pencil without lead.

Now start the definition. Observe all the particularities of the writing and write them down. Pick out the *dominants*; these are the most striking signs, the ones which give the writing its special character. They can be almost any of the signs. Each writing has six to twelve dominants and from twenty-five to fifty or sixty signs.

Write down all signs, even the smallest and most insignificant. A magnifying glass is helpful at this stage. It is surprising how many details the naked eye misses.

Read carefully the description of each sign (including those of Hegar, p. 28) before you decide to attribute it or reject it.

To make sure nothing has been overlooked, use the list of signs for each category and check each one against the sample of writing; mark down the ones that apply.

At this stage a determining frame emerges and we proceed with the *synthesis of signs*. This is the stage at which one group of signs gives an indication of the writer's intellectual potential, a second group shows emotional state and depth and a third highlights the writer's activity, energy, motivation, etc.

The next stage is the *psychological typology*.

From the work already done it becomes clear which is the dominant psychological function, temperament and character of the writer. At this stage choose the psychological typology you wish to use; the more information the better.

Now we can build up the writer's psychological *portrait* from the synthesis of signs and psychological classification. This portrait is the only part of graphology that relies on subjective elements.

Personality can be viewed from many angles. Which angle the graphologist chooses should depend solely on the use to which the portrait it is to be put. Portraits of the same writing done by different graphologists will differ, however, because each graphologist will tend to emphasize one or other trait of the writer's personality, depending on his or her own concept of life, particular tastes or character and temperament.

More often than not this is one of the reasons why two different graphologists will produce two seemingly different portraits of the same writing; the incompetence of one or other of the two graphologists, or both, might otherwise explain it.

One way of ensuring some impartiality and accuracy is to construct a list of some twenty-sixty or even 100 questions and answer the relevant ones for each case (after doing the initial work).

Here is an example of such a list:

Extrovert or introvert?
Imagination or otherwise?
Vitality: medium, weak or strong?
Will-power: weak or strong?
Diplomacy or otherwise?
Initiative or otherwise?
Independence?
Sociability?
Practical sense?
Orderliness?

Loyalty?
Sensibility?
Adaptability?
Activity?
Tenacity?
Sensuality?
Intellectuality?
Emotivity?
Motivation?

and so on. . . .

Part II

PSYCHOLOGY

7

INTRODUCTION OF SIGNS

The expression 'self-awareness' became first of all, a cult phrase and now a cliché; sometimes even a piece of 'esoteric nonsense'. Those who care to discover self-awareness may, instead of developing their ability to truly understand self and life, erect a barrier around their existence by, for example, becoming blindly attached to a cult. They stop searching. They stop trying. They think 'that's it'.

But self-awareness is never finished. We have been told that the ordinary human being uses only 3 per cent of his brain capacity. Jung told us that our conscious is like a nutshell floating on the ocean of the unconscious. So self-awareness is a colossal task unlikely ever to be fully achieved. But if we start the right way we stand a better chance of living in harmony with ourselves and others.

Learning to observe is obviously the best way to begin. We must start by trying to understand the psyche, character, temperament and all the abilities and limitations of ourselves and others. Then observe the body.

Psyche is life itself; the non-physical part of it, the abstract side. Wisdom, heroism, will, wish, genius and spirit are parts of psyche. It is not as it is sometimes thought, 'spirit', 'soul' or God. Psyche does not involve faith nor need saving. Good and evil do not apply and death does not affect it. When a person dies, he surrenders his psyche with his last breath. The ancient Egyptians were the first to say that, after a person dies, his psyche flies about and rests before it enters another person. The Greeks call butterflies 'psyches'.

Character is what we are born with and it is neither good nor bad. It is just a fact. Character '*is*', just like hair, eyes or height, and there is nothing we can do about it, but we can do a great deal with it. If we know what we – and others – have available, then our possibilities – and I am convinced, our abilities too – will double or treble; otherwise they will go to waste through ignorance, conflict and intolerance.

Whereas character is '*what is*'; constant and invariable, temperament is '*what becomes*', is variable; this variability, however, moves within well-determined limits for each human being.

By the end of the nineteenth century psychology had reached a point at which psychologists, through their relentless analysis of the mind, had lost sight of the human being as a whole. They had forgotten that the object of their study was the man or woman. It was the period of 'analytical psychology'. Clinical observations and experimental results were reduced to dead statistics and the essential differences between one human being and another still remained a mystery.

But the door is always left open for the serious researcher into the human mind. More recently, intuitive psychologists have begun to consider the human being as a single unity.

Psychology is not only about finding the wrong (abnormal), it is also about seeing the right, establishing the facts as they are in a given person. The equivalent of, say, 5′8″ tall, blond hair, blue eyes, hooked nose, etc., i.e. being able to describe the non-material as clearly as the visible parts of a man. Not the pathological, or the good, or the bad, just the facts.

Psychology is a field of study. It has limits. If we go beyond the limits we find ourselves in neighbouring areas: philosophy, medicine, religion, physics, destiny, etc. There is nothing wrong with visiting neighbouring fields, of course. But what interests us here is the specific one of psychology. We have not exhausted it and never will. It seems, however, that we have discovered its limits. First, Freud started walking and observing the field, then Jung went further until he found the boundaries with other fields – and went on walking. He was an illuminated man, Jung, he had the 'sacred flame' in him. Although he has been criticized as a metaphysical mystic, he simply discovered connections that, unless we follow through the same process of thinking, we cannot understand. It is a very worthwhile experience to read Jung without prejudice and with an open mind. He was a gnostic. He managed to go very deep into the human soul, well beyond the conscious, and reach the concept of Christ.

Of course, having discovered the boundaries does not mean that we know everything there is in our field. Far from it. We are still discovering. Consider intelligence: what exactly is it? how do we measure it? how can we develop it? how does it affect the psychological structure of the individual? how many kinds of intelligence are there? are there many kinds? is talent a form of intelligence? The same with habits, with behaviour, with emotivity, with activity. We are only at the beginning.

There are many ideas and systems, developed in the last seventy years, on how to assess people from their handwriting. Most of these have been tried and tested for decades and the ones that have been proven correct and scientific have been adopted as common practice.

As a matter of interest, in a recent publication, *La Graphologie*, put together by Pierre Faideau and twenty-two other writers (Paris, December 1983), it is stated that there does not yet exist a complete work which will allow graphology to benefit to any real extent from the Freudian approach to the personality.

The newest theories of Maslow, Eysenck, Fromm and others are still also on trial.

From the psychologists available, the most favoured by graphologists are Jung, Le Senne, Pophal, Hippocrates, St Morand, and Kretschmer. In this section we concentrate on Jung, Le Seene, Hippocrates, St Morand and Maslow.

I have found the study of graphology a voyage of profound discovery. For twenty-five years I have experienced all the difficulties and fascinations of unveiling the immense complexities of human nature. It is indeed the only means of truly understanding people quickly; and wishing to do so is the only strong motivation which can see us through a lifetime of continuous search and learning.

This section on psychology and its application to graphology is addressed to all the people who wish to understand the hows and whys of their fellow human beings as well as of themselves.

8

SYTEMS OF PSYCHOLOGY APPLIED TO GRAPHOLOGY

Jung – Types and Attitudes

Extrovert–Introvert

Jung based his two typologies on the concept of the unconscious which is unknown to us but very active.

He divided living beings into two fundamental groups: extroverts, whose general attitude and energy is directed mainly outwards, and introverts, whose general attitude is directed mainly inwards. These two attitudes are as old as civilization itself, he said.

Extroverts and introverts are found everywhere: in history, in art, amongst primitive people as well as amongst the most erudite; in animals too: horses, dogs, cats and dolphins.

This classification of two opposed types coincides with the psychomorphological types of Dr Corman, Sheldon and Kretschmer (ectomorph, endomorph, mesomorph – and their extremes). William James, the American psychologist, noticed that 'tender spirit' corresponds to the extrovert and 'resistant spirit' to the introvert. Many others also noticed these two antagonistic tendencies.

The extrovert's libido (psychic energy) is directed outwards. His reaction towards things is spontaneous and immediate. He has great interest in people and objects. He is sociable, he thinks, judges and acts in accordance with his world and its fashions. He is a charmer, a good mixer with people. He dislikes solitude. He likes external life passionately. He spends himself and gives himself without reserve. He is extensive but not necessarily intensive. He considers anything that has to do with the inner life as unnecessary and morbid. Generally, he gives the impression of a good balance because he adapts quickly and easily to circumstances. But this easy adaptability often hides an empty inner life or a flight from life. In extreme forms extroversion leads to hysteria.

The introvert, who is constantly embarrassed by the extrovert, has opposite qualities to the extrovert. For him, the interest lies not in the object as it is but as he himself sees it. That's why he is often considered egoistic or egocentric. But this judgement would be superficial since neither the extrovert nor the introvert monopolize egocentricity and egoism. The introvert becomes more rewarding as one gets to know him. He may often be clumsy, timid, closed and nervous; he keeps his opinions to himself, he lacks adapatability and suppleness, but he possesses a greater depth of sentiment and thinking. In a crisis the extrovert will seek the company of people and other distractions. The introvert will take refuge within himself.

Without the extroverts, the introverts would never meet each other.

The extrovert fears a loss of contact. The introvert fears conflict.

Exaggerated introversion leads to obsessional neurosis and, in psychiatric cases, to schizophrenia.

These two attitudes are not the result of any social class or education. All beings have both possibilities and in different situations, in the course of life, the same individual will be introverted or extroverted.

No one attitude is better than the other, but there are fashions. Recently, we in the West, for instance, have appreciated extroversion more. Up to the last century this was not so. For Hindus, on the other hand, introspection and meditation are considered more essential. The Yogi, through meditation, follows an inner voyage towards his objective: the union with Brahman, the superior Being, the One.

Introversion, as well as extroversion, can lead towards either an inflated ego (egocentricity) or detachment from the ego (allocentrism).

The art of life consists of a rhythmic movement between introversion and extroversion.

The *writing of an extrovert* shows a clear tendency towards expansion; ample and centrifugal movements, spread out, dilated, slanted, precipitated and dynamic; a tendency towards the right, prolongations upwards and downwards, variability of forms (examples 4, 10, 14, 27 and others).

The *introvert's writing* is altogether more constrained and covers less space. Slant, pressure and dimension are slightly irregular. The writing is more sober on the whole, simplified, thin, often squeezed, with short finals, wide spaces between words or letters, suspended letters, arcades or small garlands. T bars are placed on the left, the d tends to turn to the left, margins are rather narrow and/or narrowing. Connections may be filiform. The whole is discrete, vertical or slightly to the left. The introvert avoids all visible exteriorization (examples 1, 7, 16 and others).

Libido

The human psyche is a combination of functions which helps us adapt to our environment. It is a whole system of psychic energy or *libido*. Unlike Freud, who considered libido as specific sexual energy, energy, Jung understood libido to be the totality of energy in which sexuality is only a part. Libido is the intensity of psychic activity. The quality of this libido changes through the energetic process but the quantity stays the same. For instance, if we lose the object of our psychic energy we shall, subconsciously, try to find a substitute: a new activity, a new direction, otherwise the libido will create neurosis or even physical illness.

Take a man who has reached retirement age. He has been used to work all his life; his psychic energy, accustomed to a certain path of activity, suddenly falls into a void. He finds himself with nothing to do. The prospect of all those interminable years may transform him either into a tyrant at home or push him into a depression, the extent of which he has never known before. The only thing which can save him is another interest, a new direction of his psychic activity, a transference of his energy.

The movement of the psychic energy is either progressive or regressive.

Progression requires a constant effort to adapt and we can never successfully adapt to the needs of the outer world if we are not equally adapted to the conditions of our inner life, i.e. if we are not in harmony with ourselves.

Regression is a refusal to make this effort. We all go through periods of regression in the course of our life. For most of us it is a temporary but necessary retreat to recharge our batteries before meeting life again. It is a biological fact that, if we stay in one condition permanently, we shall inevitably produce the opposite result. The unconscious reacts to all exaggerations of the conscious.

The libido may be directed towards an infinite variety of situations in life. When it is oriented inwards it develops the imagination or mystic powers of the unconscious.

People with strong libido who have been forced to direct it inwards (through captivity, lack of means or physical mobility, etc.) have often produced the greatest works of their life, e.g. the prisoner of Alcatraz, works that perhaps they would never have produced under different circumstances.

Progressive libido gives a feeling of power, hope and well-being. It directs the man towards the future and future accomplishments. It is a dynamic and positive attitude which gives confidence and attracts success, good health, harmony, and alertness of energy.

Regressive libido is a state of depression, tiredness, discouragement, when everything appears difficult and uninteresting. The person turns his back on the present and future and faces the past, his 'good old days'. This attitude leads, of course, to failure, disappointment and lack of confidence.

The most difficult state of the libido is to be *blocked.* This is the extreme state of a regressive attitude. It is the situation of the man who, having fallen into a bad patch, cannot find a way out. He feels dried up, bored and has not got the vitality to see the light, to get out of the tunnel. He loses interest in living, gives in and returns to childhood memories. Then this situation becomes a neurosis and almost all neuroses are regressive. A blocked libido may be caused by any shock or frustration which reverses the flow of dynamism from its natural expression.

Dreams express the libido. Handwriting expresses all the fluctuations of the libido. The intensity of the stroke will indicate vitality. Suppleness will show the degree of adaptability to the world. Direction manifests tendencies and aspirations.

It is not easy to assess the libido from the handwriting because the conscious is mixed with the unconscious during the act of writing.

Libido – Signs

Strong Libido The writing is firmly pressed on the paper, large, in relief, regular, dynamic, rhythmic; there is unity and stability of the stroke and precision of forms. Examples 27, 37 and 64 (pp. 274, 280 and 298).

Weak Libido The writing is light, pale, irregular, unstable, weak or filiform, montonous, small or very small, with descending lines, undulating or galloping, with a diminished lower zone. Lower extensions are either closed low or without loops, and directed leftwards. The writing can also be low, shaky, diminishing, slightly slanted; the stroke is blurred, strokes disconnected or fragmented and letters suspended. Examples 19, 29, 35 and 40 (pp. 269, 275, 277 and 282).

Progressive Libido The writing is rhythmic, dynamic, harmonious, regular and in relief, rapid or precipitated, grouped, progressive, expanded or with flying strokes; the lines are rising. I dots and accents are placed high and forward, the signature is to the right. The left margin progressively enlarges. Examples 3, 4 and 45 (pp. 262 and 285).

Regressive Libido The writing is monotonous, regressive, narrow, extremely small, with feeble or atrophied lower extensions. Slanted to the left, inhibited, slow, slack, with descending lines or galloping downwards; half-finished letters, twisted strokes, missing t bars or placed very low. The signature is placed to the left and without vigour. Examples 20, 28, 39 and 41 (pp. 269, 275, 281 and 283).

Blocked Libido The writing is heavy, pasty and dark, without dynamism, slow, very squeezed, muddy, automatic, with movements towards the left, twisted strokes and inhibited generally. Examples 18, 26, 30 and 63 (pp. 268, 273, 275 and 297).

The Four Functions

The four functions help us adapt to the world and to ourselves. They are the principal psychic functions of *thinking, sentiment* (or feeling), *sensation* and *intuition*, all quite distinct from each other. One function will tend to be dominant in any one individual, for example, a person may perceive a situation through his feelings. What we mean is that this person uses sentiment (rather than thinking, or any other function) to perceive the world. The dominant function does not, by itself, indicate the intensity with which an individual perceives a situation.

The four functions partly operate in the unconscious but the more conscious they become the more subtle, productive and useful they also become.

The functions act in the following manner:

Sensation – perceives and states whatever is around us.
Thinking – gives the significance of the things we perceive, what they are, what they mean.
Sentiment – gives the value of the things we perceive; it establishes our connection with objects, it produces the conditions for acceptance or rejection.
Intuition – detects the possibilities inherent in the things we perceive. It is spontaneous and comes from the subconscious.

Everybody has these functions in different degrees. The dominant function is called the *principal* or main function. The secondary one is the *auxiliary* and the third and fourth are less developed, pushed more or less into the unconscious.

Occasionally, one function is very well developed and all the other three are very weak. It may also be that no one function is more developed than the others and they are either all very weak or all equally well developed. The latter state is very rare.

A person with the dominant function of thinking is objective and logical and discards sentiment and its subjective judgements.

A person who has sentiment (or feeling) as a dominant function is in immediate contact with the object and judges it as 'I like it or I don't like it.'

A person who has sensation as a dominant function feels vividly all that touches his senses (he may be weak in intuition).

A person who has intuition as a dominant function understands things in their totality immediately, but may be inefficient when it comes to the practicalities of life.

Thinking is logical and can be passive or active. Passive thinking does not depend on will whereas active does. Jung called the capacity to direct thinking: intellect (what William James called 'associative intuition'), and undirected thinking (the passive): intellectual intuition.

Sentiment is the function of the heart. It is subjective. When it is very intense it can become affection. Sentiment, like thinking, evaluates. It, too, can be passive or active. It is passive when it is attracted by any situation and it is active when it is directed, values situations and makes a choice.

Both thinking and sentiment are rational functions.

Intuition sends messages from the subconscious. It is a subconscious conception and has the characteristic of certainty and infallibility.

Sensation is a physical stimulus coming not only from without (sensation extrovert), but also from within (sensation introvert). It is perception through the senses. It is a basic function which has no connection with judgement or reason.

These last two functions, intuition and sensation, are irrational.

A rational dominant function can have, as an auxiliary, an irrational one only. For example, thinking can have, as an auxiliary, intuition or sensation (sentiment will be weakest). In the same way, an irrational dominant function will have a rational function as auxiliary.

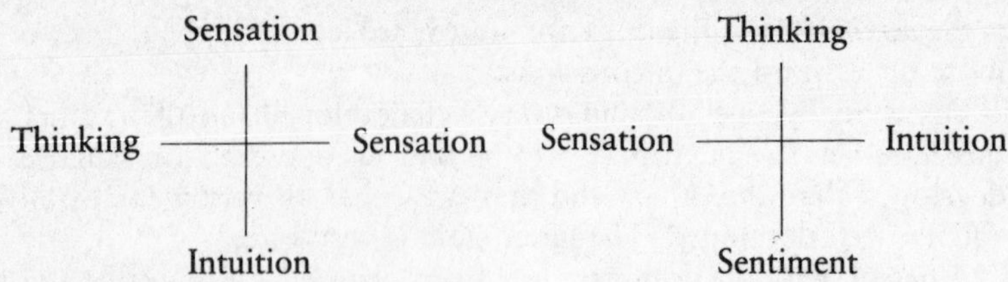

If sensation is at the top of the cross (main function), intuition will be at the bottom and the auxiliary will be placed on the left (either sentiment or thinking), and so on.

These pairs of functions produce eight possible combinations.

The Four Functions – Signs

Abbreviations: intr = introversion, ex = extroversion,

Thinking The writing is sober and simplified. Small and rather fine. Well spaced or aerated, combined, connected, small and rounded. Orderly, progressive, with sharp end strokes and weak or short lower extensions. Printed (typographic) capitals. The signature is usually simple and unpretentious. Examples 8 (intr), 11 (ex), 46 (intr).

Sentiment The writing is mostly large, spread out, expanded, with garlands or angular garlands, slanted to the right without much alteration of direction. The final strokes are in open curves, the pressure is slightly pasty, velvety. Most of these signs must appear together, with very few variations. Examples 12 (intr), 22 (ex), 25 (ex), 47 (ex).

Sensation The writing is large or medium, pasty, often muddy, right slanted, compact, with a dominant lower zone. Examples 4 (ex), 27 (ex), 54 (ex).

The sensation introvert has somewhat different signs: the writing is slightly artificial, at times even stylized. Smaller and complicated with pasty pressure. Examples 10, 18, 26, 51.

Intuition The writing is light and fine, with airy rhythm, juxtaposed or grouped, combined, ample and simplified. It has originality in the upper zone; the lower extensions are usually formed in the shape of cups. Generally the writing is quite irregular. Examples 5 (ex), 7 (intr), 14 (ex), 58 (ex).

Each one of these functions can be extrovert or introvert.

This typology, like all others, does not make value judgements. All types have their good and bad points and we should not take a moralistic stand on them.

Animus – Anima

Anima is the female element in man, animus is the male element in woman.

Anima and animus are dynamic forces in both sexes; they motivate and animate the soul towards more expression, constructiveness and communication with the unconscious. (This last process is called integration.)

Anima, for Jung, is the archetype of life. It represents all the feminine tendencies of the man, such as sentimentality, prophetic intuitions, vague moods, feeling for nature, artistic inclinations, the capacity to love personally, the relationship with the unconscious, etc. It will make a man sentimental or emotional, artistic, intuitive, subjective, moody and introspective.

Animus represents all the masculine psychological tendencies of the woman, such as objectivity, practical reasoning, concern about moral laws, intellectuality, etc. It will give a woman an imposing personality, aggression, authoritarianism, intellectuality, strength of character and more creativity.

The written signs of anima are large and curved, with garlands, spread out (wide), right or left slanted and rounded forms.

The main function will be sentiment. Examples 2, 22, 23, 24, 28 and 38 (pp. 261, 270, 271, 275 and 281).

The written signs of animus are small and simplified, sharp-pointed, sober, combined. Examples 8, 16 and 33 (pp. 264, 267 and 276).

The strongest function will be thinking.

Persona

Persona is a mask; it is 'the representation of our being. It represents what each of us think we are towards others and not what we really are.'*

'Persona is a complex developed for reasons of adaptability or convenience. It does not blend with our individuality. It concerns only our communication with the exterior world.'

It is a 'false self.' All human beings have a persona which is what we wish to present to others. Some people, however, blend their persona with their reality. That stops them from evolving, progressing and growing. They project themselves into a 'role'; they

* C. G. Jung, *The Psychological Types.*

desire to be accepted and recognized as what they would like to be and not as what they truly are – they think their true self is not good enough. In the long term the individual loses the concept of his or her reality and identifies with his or her persona; their greatest concern then is to avoid being unmasked.

The written signs of persona are many and varied: all exaggerations, all stylizations which mechanize the writing through regularity of movement, and any stereotyped writing deprived of movement and life examples 18, 30 35, 38, 51 and 52 (pp. 268, 275, 277, 281, 289 and 290).

Young people in puberty or older people who never grow up are particularly subject to persona. Emotional immaturity causes it. In the majority of young people the writing will eventually disengage itself from the inhibitions, inexperience and ignorance of youth, and will become individualized through acquiring its own personal rhythm and movement.

Le Senne – Study of Character

Characterology is the science of character study and has two main schools: the 'narrow', which is the one we shall touch on and which deals with the congenital, permanent skeleton of the mental structure, and the 'wide' (mainly used by the German schools of psychology) which embraces the effects this mental structure has upon the individual. Alfred Adler analyses not only the nature of character but also what a person does with it.* Of course he, like many others, ends up getting lost in the study of human destiny.

Earlier this century in France, René Le Senne studied personal differences of character for many years. At the same time in Holland, Professors G. Heymans and E. Wiersma of the University of Groningen were on a similar track and, simultaneously, these two schools developed a system of characterological types which is not only intellectually understandable but can also withstand scrutiny and analysis.

René Le Senne in his book, *Traité de Caractérologie*, gives a clear definition of character: 'The totality of congenital dispositions which form the mental skeleton of a person.'

This definition has three elements:

1. Character is not the whole being. It is only what we possess as a result of our heredity; a fundamental structure formed

* Le Senne, *Traité de Caractérologie*, PUF, 1960.

by genes passed on to us by our distant and recent ancestors. There is nothing in a character that is not congenital.
2. This character is solid and permanent. It is the structural identity of the individual.
3. This structural identity is mental but is only the skeleton of psychological life.

Character, says Le Senne, completes the body and conditions the mind. The body develops in collaboration with character.

To avoid any confusion between character and 'personality', it is as well to define the latter: personality includes both character and all elements acquired in the course of life. It is the concrete totality of self of which character is only the fundamental and invariable part.

To sum up, there are two basic truths about character: every person has his or her character; all characters are invariable.

Factors Constituting Character

There are three factors that constitute character. These are emotivity; activity; and responsiveness.

First and foremost, we must establish that people are distinguished only by the degree of intensity of those factors, never by their presence or absence.

Emotivity (E) is the tendency to be moved by events. It is common to everybody, but some have it more than others. The more emotive a person is, the more easily he or she is affected by events and vice versa. All events touch us. The difference lies only in the intensity, in how deeply they touch us. Whatever happens around us provokes an agitation of mind. An event acts upon us as a motivating agent and provides energy.

The intensity of emotivity is seen in action as well as in knowledge. In action when emotivity is charged, the intensity – if it does not change direction – is more or less violent. We can say the same thing about a raised voice, becoming red in the face and agitated by emotion or speaking with a calm voice and poised attitude. The only difference is in intensity.

As regards knowledge, emotivity is seen as an attachment by the individual to the cause which affects him or her.

The intensity of sentiment penetrates and motivates the whole being. Active or non-active, the individual will react in one way or another and manifest the seriousness of the situation – to him.

Since emotivity is a force, an energy ready to be mobilized, the outward manifestation of it depends on the direction it takes. This, in turn, depends on whether the individual is active or non-active. Let us take an emotive-active person. Feelings will be expressed in thought, word and action, but will be resolved through some form of action. Anything else will be experienced as an obstacle, a brake that slows down the action. The emotive non-active person, however, reverses the energy from outwards to inwards. Such a person has no path through which to channel the energy and so the force will remain unmobilized.

Two observations must be made here:

1. The essence of emotivity is the aptitude to be moved by events of minimal importance. The word 'importance', however, is subjective and can differ from one person to another, depending on tendencies and interests. For instance, an emotive ambitious man will be moved by success, money, position, etc.; an emotive mother may be moved by events that happen to her children. therefore, we should not be surprised if an individual appears cold towards something that doesn't interest him. The diagnosis of emotivity presupposes a knowledge of the interests of the subject observed. Even regarding universal concerns, like fear of death or disease, there are variations in the degree of preoccupation. But there must be no confusion. The emotive person will always be moved in accordance with his interests and tendencies more than the non-emotive.
2. When assessing emotivity we must not forget that some people mask the effects of their emotivity. These individuals, without diminishing or suppressing the effects, manage to dissimulate them in a way which escapes observation. Not all emotives are expansive. The observer will detect the emotivity, when it is not manifested, by various little symptoms like a tic or a tone of voice or, indirectly, from statements, judgements or memories of the person in question. In this category of individual, we find the responsive element (the third factor constituting the character) to be 'secondary', i.e. introverted, as against 'primary', i.e. extroverted (see below).

We have considered the intensity of emotivity. Let us now see the various ways this energy may be dispensed.

The release of energy can be achieved in many ways during the course of our life; either little by little or in a brusque, explosive manner. The curve of intensity can ascend or descend, i.e. it can start slowly and go on increasing until it wears off, or it can reach immediately (or almost immediately) its maximum and slowly decrease.

The main characteristics of emotivity are:

1. The relative importance between the objective gravity of an event and the subjective agitation with which a person reacts.
2. Concern: anxiety, restlessness, uneasiness.
3. Mental mobility.
4. Change of mood: visible and invisible.
5. Alternations of mood from exaltation to depression, from enthusiasm to hate, etc.
6. Impulsiveness, the impact of the moment upon the individual, is also a result of emotivity. This impulsiveness is closely linked to responsiveness. To people who live in the present, impulsiveness is immediate and reactive. To others, who suppress their feelings, the result can be explosive. It manifests the influence of old, accumulated experiences which finally find a way and a time to be discharged, such as contained anger which finally explodes.
7. Excitability. It takes very little to excite an emotive person.
8. Intolerance. The intensity of feelings favours intolerance.
9. The intensity of manifestations of the emotive person is the result of intensity of emotivity. The decrease of intensity of emotivity determines the decrease of manifestations. Thus a decrease diminishes anxiety, activity, expressiveness and a disposition towards sympathy. It favours objectivity and veracity.

To conclude the subject of emotivity we must say that, although emotive people can understand those who are not, they more or less resent their 'insensitivity'. They find them hard or unintelligent and often tend to dismiss them. For the non-emotive, the emotive remains forever a mystery.

The written signs of emotivity are small and constant irregularities of all kinds, jerkiness, tension of the stroke, frequent interruptions, in small writing there will be little flying strokes, the pressure will be irregular but strong or heavy, the ovals may be open; large writing may have some disproportions, it will be animated, more or less angular, enlarging, sinuous, rapid or dynamic.

Non-emotivity is manifested by regularity of the stroke, order, closed writing, vertical or slightly slanted in either direction, evenness, rather small size, even pressure but not very heavy, contained or monotonous writing, poised or slow and straight lines.

Activity Whereas emotivity keeps its energetic essence, we cannot say the same about activity (A). Here we must distinguish very clearly between activity called 'manifested' and 'characterological' activity. For instance, a person may appear active but for two different reasons: first, because of emotivity; second, directly from activity. In both cases he would be considered 'active'. But in the case where activity is the result of an outside stimulus, or if the person is strongly emotive, he or she would be 'falsely active'. The characterological term of 'activity' can only be applied to a person whose disposition to activity comes from within himself. The non-active acts against his liking, against his will. It does not give him pleasure to act. He acts only when and because he is forced. Whereas, the active acts because he must. It is a congenital impulse that pushes him to act. We can even say that the active person lives to act. When an obstacle appears in his way he considers it an invitation to action. Some actives will even choose a task because of its obstacles. Alpinists tackle the mountain tops 'because they are there'. The inactive will write about them instead.

An emotive-active person is a man of action and ambition. A similar but non-active individual is directed more towards his own private life, the intimate consciousness of his feelings.

The active person is active in everything in life. Always occupied, time is constantly running short for him, even at leisure periods. He rarely postpones jobs or decisions. He is persevering, independent, lively, agile, punctual, objective, practical, truthful. He is also more active sexually than the non-active.

To conclude: if emotivity expresses the subject's dependence on the object, activity expresses the influence of the subject upon the object.

The written signs of activity are: firm and dynamic writing, rising, animated, in relief, angular or semi-angular, homogeneous with strong t bars, vertical or right slanted, firm, i dots slightly towards the right, little hooks anywhere, prolonged up and down, pressure is well nourished, speed is rapid.

Non-Activity is manifested by rounded or round writing, slow, complicated forms, monotonous, unspontaneous or artificial, weak and flabby strokes, false connections, double curves, irregular spacings, i dots missing or placed very high.

Responsiveness In 1902 in Leipzig Otto Gross published his discovery of the distinction between the slow and rapid reaction of the nervous tissue of the brain. This distinction was adopted by the Dutch school (Heymans and Wiersma) to describe 'primary' and 'secondary' ways of response.

People of *primary response* (P) live mainly in the present moment. Their joys and sorrows are short-lived. Their reactions are fast and explosive but soon run out of steam. On the other hand, people of *secondary response* (S) are influenced for a long time by their feelings. Their reactions are slow and prolonged. They live in the future. For them the present is the basis for the future which, in turn, depends on the past.

In all people every stimulation triggers a reaction. No one is indifferent to the present and no one is uninfluenced by the past. But when the effects of a present stimulation recall the impressions of past stimulation then primarity prevails and the person is of primary character. If, however, the impressions of past stimulation persist without interruption into the present, the person is of secondary character.

To conclude, let us say that, for primary people, impressions produce the maximum effect immediately and for a short period of time; here, 'experience' means the live presence of a fact or situation. For the secondary people, impressions slowly carve their effect on the nervous system; 'experience' signifies the accumulation of impressions received. 'We write easily on sand but it wipes off easily; we carve with difficulty on marble but the engraving stays forever', said Le Senne.

The *writing of the primary* individual is lively, agitated, often spasmodic, dynamic, discordant, impulsive, often disproportionate, illegible, with flying strokes, soaring, rhythmic, large or small, diminishing, often filiform.

The *writing of the secondary* individual is sober, orderly, rather vertical or leftwards slanting, angular, closed, contained, constant, moderate, often dry and regressive or small and regular.

The Eight Characters

The combination of the three fundamental factors – Emotivity, Activity, Responsiveness – gives eight characters:

the Emotive, Active, Secondary (EAS)	Passionate
the Emotive, Active, Primary (EAP)	Choleric
the Emotive, non-Active, Secondary (EnAS)	Sentimental
the Emotive, non-Active, Primary (EnAP)	Nervous
the non-Emotive, Active, Secondary (nEAS)	Phlegmatic
the non-Emotive, Active, Primary (nEAP)	Sanguine
the non-Emotive, non-Active, Secondary (nEnAS)	Apathetic
the non-Emotive, non-Active, Primary (nEnAP)	Amorphous

These are the basic, pure characters. But, because of the variability in the degree of the components (E, A, S or P), each of the eight characters may have one or two of the others as auxiliary e.g., the Passionate can also be paraCholeric or paraSentimental or paraPhlegmatic, etc. No character, however, may have, as an auxiliary, its opposite, i.e., the Passionate cannot be paraAmorphous, the Choleric paraApathetic and so on, at least not without producing a highly explosive mix productive of genius or madness.

The pure EAS (Passionate) is aggressive, decisive, practical, efficient, active, perseverent, observant, objective, precise, devoted, patriotic, ascetic, honourable, natural, indifferent towards food and sex, kind towards people inferior to him, prudent, loyal, serious, attached to tradition, a collector.

He has a good memory, compassion, no vanity, vigorous reaction to obstacles, great working ability, a taste for grandeur, sense of social values, rapid conception of situations. He likes order and cleanliness, and there is harmony between words and actions.

Because of his strong attachment to tradition, his political ideas are not always progressive.

Among the great Passionates are Napoleon, Nietzsche, Carlyle, Michaelangelo, Pasteur, Dante, Gladstone, Newton, Tolstoy, Beethoven, Louis XIV, Goethe and Plato.

The pure EAP (Choleric) is impulsive, authoritative, excitable, optimistic, versatile, inventive, combative, violent, subjective, touchy (but will not sulk), mobile, busy, decisive, extroverted, demonstrative, natural, talkative, materialistic, sociable, cordial, obliging, popular, dynamic, quick witted, keen on politics, good humoured, confident with people, easily adaptable, a motivator of people, a keen and uninhibited public speaker with lively sentiments, practical.

He has a taste for change, fast emotional response to the environment, ambition for honours, taste for action, tendency to exaggeration, vitality, appetite, strong sexuality, taste for new things, no fear of obstacles.

He lacks discipline in action, patience when waiting for results; He also likes to satisfy his physical needs – eating, drinking, etc.

Among the great Cholerics are Dickens, Danton, W. Scott, Fielding, B. Cellini, Georges Sand, Casanova, Victor Hugo, Diderot, Leon Gambetta and François I.

The pure EnAS (Sentimental) is unobservant, subjective, retrospective, scrupulous, melancholic, obsessive, sulky, spiteful, grudging, timid, stubborn, prudent, attached to habits, very sensitive to changes and new things, displeased with himself, inclined to boredom, nagging, easily discouraged, honourable, an idealist, romantic, vulnerable, mistrustful, introspective, interested in meditation.

He has variability of sensitivites, long-lasting emotional hurt, lasting impressionability, taste for solitude, variable moods, slow reactions, taste for collecting, poor adaptability, moral feelings, dignity, tendency to half measures, a rapport with nature. He likes old memories (mental rumination). He avoids tragedies. His words and actions accord.

He lacks *élan*, confidence in self and the future, aptitude for practical solutions, interest in machines.

He feels the need for protection, seeks security, can be violent. He reacts against social conformities. He is dogmatic. Dislikes command or to be commanded.

He loves animals and transfers his affections to them, avoiding closeness with people since he is easily hurt; he may therefore be mistaken for a hard person.

Some famous Sentimentals are Thackeray, J. J. Rousseau, Robespierre, Calvin, Kierkegaard, Amiel, Louis XIII and Alfred de Vigny.

The pure EnAP (Nervous) is impulsive, mobile, busy, negligent, unstable, artistic, prevaricating, playful, susceptible, excitable, frivolous, artificial, seductive, indecisive, not persevering, easily discouraged, self-contented, affected, vain, mistrustful, unreliable, unpunctual, sarcastic and capricious (when nL,* p. 246), sad and sorrowful (when L*), rapidly consoled. He is a vagrant in friendship, love and profession.

He has rapid and superficial judgements, big projects which never take off, taste for fashion, taste for entertainment, variability of moods, mobile sympathies, reactive impulsiveness, emotional violence, vivacity of sentiments, poetic feelings, desires for honours, liking for change. He talks much – mainly about himself. He embellishes his talk. He laughs and talks loudly. Laughs at his own jokes. He needs new impressions. Expects immediate results. There is contradiction between his thoughts and his life.

His feelings, exceptionally mobile, move him promptly from tears to laughter, from depression to enthusiasm and vice versa. His emotional energy is wasted on impulsive decisions. There is debility of moral sentiment and disorderly sexuality. He is a big spender. He has a taste for the macabre, absurd and horrible.

Some famous Nervous characters are Baudelaire, Alfred de Musset, Edgar Allan Poe, Oscar Wilde, Byron, Heine, F. Chopin,

* Note: nL = Narrow Field of consciousness
L = Large Field of consciousness (see p. 246)

Mozart, Dostoyevsky, Jean Cocteau, Chateaubriand, Alphonse Daudet, Lamartine and d'Annunzio.

The pure nEAS (Phlegmatic) is calm, even tempered, well controlled, phlegmatic, silent, contained, wary, reflective, circumspect, tolerant, intelligent, constantly occupied, patient, persevering, tenacious, methodical, concise, punctual, patriotic, virtuous, sober, impassive, honourable, a man of habits and principles, interested more in things than people, ceremonious.

He has cold kindness, sexual continence, apparent indifference, dignity, a wide mind, independence of opinions, long-lasting sympathies, objectivity, objective observation, sense of humour, slow decisions. He worries about the future. He has little sympathy but great understanding for his fellow human beings. There is accordance between words and actions.

He may lack imagination but he has a very open mind and great intellectual abilities. He is kind and attached to principles. He is courageous and stoic and if it were not for his tremendous sense of humour he could be considered the greatest bore of all.

Some great Phlegmatics are Hume, Darwin, Bergson, Cavendish, Addison, Gibbon, Montaigne, Owen, Washington, Turgot, and Kant (a truly rare pure Phlegmatic).

The pure nEAP (Sanguine) is calm, polite, witty, constantly working, lover of wealth, practical, courageous, egoistic, observant, objective, positive, tolerant, indifferent, benevolent, sceptical, a cynic, adaptable.

He has rapid understanding, a talent for improvised public speaking, independent judgement, easy rapport with people, easy adaptation, a taste for the abstract, a taste for science, rough sexuality, negative and critical attitude to religion.

He lacks depth, sense of continuity. Solves problems fast. He prefers useful things. His words and actions accord.

He likes wealth (and knows how to make it) and all the pleasures that go with it. He is a great diplomat, somewhat ironical but with a quick mind. When he is a man, he loves women (not particularly for their brains) and is quite liberal with them; as are his views in general and especially in politics. He is a realist and likes sport.

Among the great Sanguines are Louis XVIII, Machiavelli, Mazarin, Bacon, Voltaire, Shaftesbury, Talleyrand, Metternich, Haekel, Montesquieu, Colette and Henri IV.

The pure nEnAS (Apathetic) is sombre, placid, closed, stubborn, unconsolable, introspective, unsociable, secretive, a man of principle, even tempered, honourable, sexually indifferent, not particularly religious.

He has a tendency to melancholia and economical living. He dislikes changes and novelties. No strong predisposition for mental disturbance.

He is grudge-bearing when not spiteful and also likes solitude. He sticks to his principles, is conservative and, when he is not thrifty, is avaricious. He dislikes children and as a teacher may prove cruel. He endures danger and hardship without emotion (since he has little). He thrives under discipline and is a happy soldier. Lacking in imagination, initiative and curiosity of the mind, he floats over life, frustrating people and boring himself. He usually ends his existence drinking heavily as if to fill up the void within.

No Apathetic has left his name in history except Louis XVI but only through heredity of power.

The pure nEnAP (**Amorphous**) is inactive, placid, calm, impulsive, laconic, lazy, insensitive, courageous, selfish, indecisive, tolerant through indifference, difficult to convince, sexually undisciplined, non-demonstrative. He has no religious fervour. He is the servant of his physical and egoistic interests.

He lacks practical sense and his predominant interests are selfish and materialistic. He is brave but not especially patriotic. Although lacking many qualities of character, he is usually gifted with various talents, more than any of the other seven characters: he can 'act' any of them.

He likes being with people, spending money and entertaining. This makes him a charmer which, together with his lack of personality, often misleads people into saying about him: 'He is a mystery to me; I can't quite grasp him.' Of course, there is little to grasp. He is the mirror of any one he chooses – when he can be bothered. Many entertainers, actors, comedians belong to this character.

As far as I know, no Amorphous has reached immortality, except for Louis XV; but he, too, was born to it.

The similarities between the eight characters are due to the similarities of the components (E, A, S or P). For instance, the Passionate and the Choleric share the same two factors (E and A) and are bound to have similar character traits.

No one of the eight characters is better or worse than the others. Each can be good or evil, nice, selfish and so on, depending on education, upbringing, circumstances of life, etc. Prisons are full of all eight characters. It is behaviour that counts, and behaviour can be learned at any age in life.

Tables of Character Traits

The following eight tables will help you diagnose your own character and that of the people around you.

Tick, in each of them, all the elements you honestly believe you possess. The character in which you have ticked the largest number of signs is your predominant character; the one with the second largest number of ticks will be your 'para'-character, and so on.

The EAS (Passionate)

ambitious ☐
authoritative ☐
hidden hardness ☐
impatience ☐
vigorous reaction to obstacles ☐
aggression ☐
intense and efficient activity ☐
objectivity ☐
decisiveness ☐
practical sense ☐
does not lose sight of aims ahead ☐
working ability ☐
always busy ☐
likes to finish what he undertakes ☐
ability to concentrate ☐
attributes importance to the results of work ☐
needs to work in an accelerating way ☐
devoted ☐
persevering ☐
observant ☐
good memory ☐
concise ☐
precise ☐
social interests ☐
rapid conception of situations ☐
impressions have long-term effect ☐
likes history ☐
is attracted to old memories ☐
sense of social values ☐
tendency to collect ☐
attached to traditions ☐
ambition may lead to the satisfaction of material needs ☐

indifferent to food and sex ☐
taste for grandeur ☐
needs to stamp his personality on things ☐
moral qualities ☐
prudent ☐
compassionate and obliging ☐
kind towards his inferiors ☐
loyal ☐
honourable ☐
patriotic ☐
natural ☐
lacks vanity and ostentation ☐
likes cleanliness and order ☐
harmony between words and actions ☐
religious feelings; mainly when he is L (p. 246) and very Emotive ☐
political ideas not always progressive because of attachment to tradition ☐

The EAP (Choleric)

mobility of sentiments ☐
impulsive ☐
authoritative ☐
excitable ☐
improvised and efficient action ☐
quite persevering ☐
impressions have short-term effect ☐
taste for change ☐
versatile ☐
capacity for affection ☐
vivacious feelings ☐
violent ☐
subjective ☐
susceptible ☐
optimistic ☐
touchy (but will not sulk) ☐
active ☐
inventive ☐
combative ☐
mobile ☐
busy ☐
decisive ☐
practical ☐

taste for action ☐
undisciplined in action ☐
likes immediate results ☐
no fear of obstacles ☐
dynamic ☐
initiatory ☐
impatient ☐
impetuous ☐
active in politics ☐
sociable ☐
extrovert ☐
demonstrative ☐
natural ☐
talkative ☐
cordial ☐
obliging ☐
popular ☐
quick witted ☐
good humoured ☐
confident with people ☐
easily adaptable ☐
motivator of people ☐
ambitious for honours ☐
importance of vital needs ☐
materialistic ☐
vital ☐
possesses appetite ☐
strong sexuality ☐
taste for new things ☐
taste for change ☐
likes to satisfy his physical needs; eating, drinking, etc. ☐
likes communication with people ☐
keen and unhibited public speaker ☐
lively sentiments ☐
fast emotional response to the environment ☐
tendency to exaggeration ☐

The EnAS (Sentimental)

vulnerable ☐
sensitive to changes and new things ☐
taste for solitude ☐

mistrustful ☐
lasting impressionability ☐
long-lasting emotional hurt ☐
melancholic ☐
sensitive to weather changes ☐
feels the need of protection ☐
seeks security ☐
poor adaptability ☐
timid ☐
attached to the past ☐
subjective ☐
retrospective (likes old memories) ☐
unobservant ☐
scrupulous ☐
obsessive ☐
sulky ☐
spiteful ☐
grudging ☐
attached to habits ☐
romantic ☐
introspective ☐
interested in meditation ☐
stubborn ☐
moral feelings ☐
dignified ☐
idealistic ☐
displeased with himself ☐
prudent ☐
honourable ☐
variability of sensitivities ☐
variable moods ☐
slow reactions ☐
inclined to boredom ☐
nagging ☐
easily discouraged ☐
tendency to half measures ☐
rapport with nature ☐
lacks confidence in self and the future ☐
lacks *élan* ☐
avoids tragedies ☐
aptitude for practical solutions ☐
reaction against social conformities ☐

can be violent ☐
dislikes commanding or being commanded ☐
taste for collecting ☐
dogmatic ☐
loves animals and transfers his affection to them ☐
avoids closeness with people (since he is easily hurt) ☐
can be mistaken as a hard person ☐
accordance of words and actions ☐

The EnAP (Nervous)

lack of sense of continuity ☐
negligent ☐
mobile ☐
impulsive ☐
prevaricating ☐
busy ☐
playful ☐
unstable ☐
seeks immediate results ☐
rapid and superficial judgements ☐
easily discouraged ☐
big projects which never take off ☐
need for emotion ☐
seeks new impressions ☐
taste for fashion ☐
taste for the arts ☐
taste for entertainments ☐
mobility of sentiments ☐
variability of moods ☐
mobile sympathies ☐
vivacity of sentiments ☐
impulsively reactive ☐
frivolous ☐
intense capacity for affection ☐
touchy ☐
susceptible ☐
excitable ☐
laughs and talks loudly ☐
emotional violence ☐
moves promptly from tears to laughter and vice versa ☐
moves promptly from depression to enthusiasm and vice versa ☐

poetic feelings ☐
vagrant in friendship, love and profession ☐
taste for changes ☐
self-contented ☐
artificial ☐
seductive ☐
affected ☐
vain ☐
unreliable ☐
unpunctual ☐
capricious (when L) (p. 246) ☐
sarcastic (when L) ☐
emotional energy wasted on impulsive decisions ☐
indecisive ☐
not persevering ☐
needs to impress ☐
pays compliments easily ☐
embellishes his talk ☐
talks much mainly about himself ☐
laughs at his own jokes ☐
desires honours ☐
debility of moral sentiments ☐
mistrustful ☐
sad and sorrowful (when L) ☐
rapidly consoled ☐
disorderly sexuality ☐
likes spending ☐
taste for the macabre, absurd and horrible ☐

The nEAS (Phlegmatic)

reduces manifestations of activity ☐
calm ☐
even tempered ☐
well controlled ☐
phlegmatic ☐
silent ☐
contained ☐
wary ☐
patient ☐
pays little attention to appearances ☐
sober ☐

tenacious ☐
concise ☐
methodical ☐
virtuous ☐
impassive ☐
tolerant ☐
great working ability ☐
constantly occupied ☐
tenacious ☐
persevering ☐
intelligent ☐
reflective ☐
circumspect ☐
methodical ☐
broad mind ☐
objective observation ☐
objective ☐
independent opinions ☐
slow in decision making ☐
virtuous ☐
patriotic ☐
honourable ☐
ceremonious ☐
interested more in things than people ☐
dignified ☐
long-lasting sympathies ☐
open minded ☐
intellectual abilities ☐
kind ☐
attached to principles ☐
courageous ☐
stoic ☐
sexually continent ☐
cold kindness ☐
apparently indifferent ☐
lacks imagination ☐
little sympathy but great understanding of people ☐
sense of humour ☐
accordance between words and actions ☐

nEAP (Sanguine)

coldly extroverted ☐
calm appearance ☐
polite ☐
ironical ☐
talent for improvised public speaking ☐
practical sense ☐
rapid understanding ☐
always working ☐
good organizer of his money ☐
solves problems fast ☐
prefers useful things ☐
witty ☐
observant ☐
independent judgement ☐
positive ☐
easy rapport with people ☐
easy and quick to adapt ☐
unsystematic ☐
sceptical ☐
lacks depth ☐
cynical ☐
indifferent ☐
egoistic ☐
tolerant ☐
negative and critical attitude to religion ☐
liberal ☐
diplomatic talent ☐
benevolent ☐
courageous ☐
likes wealth and its pleasures ☐
quick mind ☐
liberal political views ☐
realistic ☐
likes sports ☐
likes the opposite sex ☐
taste for the abstract ☐
taste for science (mainly as a useful instrument) ☐
rough sexuality ☐
lack of sense of continuity ☐
lack of accordance between words and actions ☐

The nEnAS (Apathetic)

placid ☐
sombre ☐
closed ☐
stubborn ☐
inconsolable ☐
unsociable ☐
secretive ☐
introspective ☐
even tempered ☐
honourable ☐
tendency to melancholia ☐
attachment to principles ☐
sexually indifferent ☐
tendency to economize ☐
dislikes changes ☐
dislikes novelties ☐
not particularly religious ☐
lacks imagination ☐
attachment to discipline ☐
lacks initiative ☐
lacks curiosity of the mind ☐
dislikes children ☐
can be cruel ☐
endures danger and hardship without emotion ☐
likes solitude ☐
avaricious ☐
conservative attitudes ☐
bears grudges ☐
spiteful ☐
no strong predisposition to mental disturbance ☐
can be a heavy drinker ☐
easily bored ☐

The nEnAP (Amorphous)

inactive ☐
placid ☐
calm ☐
impulsive ☐
laconic ☐
lazy ☐
insensitive ☐

selfish ☐
indecisive ☐
reckless ☐
tolerant through indifference ☐
rash ☐
not particularly patriotic ☐
non-demonstrative ☐
sexually undisciplined ☐
materialistic ☐
egocentric ☐
servant of his physical and egoistic interests ☐
no religious fervour ☐
lacks practical sense ☐
may be gifted with various talents ☐
can 'act' any of the other seven characters ☐
likes being with people ☐
likes spending money ☐
likes entertaining ☐
lacks personality ☐
appears difficult to understand ☐
difficult to convince ☐
negligent ☐
unpunctual ☐
lacks continuity of thought ☐
tendency to postpone decisions and activities ☐
predominance of physical interests ☐
casual communicator with people ☐
astute ☐

The written signs of each of the characters are as follows:

The Characters – Signs

Emile Caille applied Le Senne's theory to graphology as follows:

EAS (Passionate)

F. A mostly tense and sober writing, simplified and rather angular.
Pr. Firm and mostly regular.
Sp. Rapid.
Dir. Progressive. Often to the right, sometimes rigid. Lines horizontal or rising, rarely sinuous.

Cont. Grouped or connected. Often overconnected. Always with tension, never slack.
Dim. Medium to small, rarely large. Sober.

Examples 2, 3, 45, 46 and 65.

EAP (choleric)

F. Curved, animated, less tense, with big movements. Robust. Natural. Spontaneous. Often with crosses.
Pr. Firm. Well nourished, or thick (warm). Often with clubs and flying strokes. Spasmodic.
Sp. Rapid, at times it can be ordinary.
Dir. Sinuous with irregular slant.
Cont. } Dim. } A bubbly writing, connected or disconnected, but always giving the impression of explosive energy.

Examples 4, 9, 25, 54 and 57.

EnAS (Sentimental)

F. Rather narrow, often tall. Dominance of middle zone, but also often soaring or superelevated.
Pr. Can vary but will remain regular with small irregularities.
Sp. Rather slow (can be poised). Lacks fluency. Large irregular gaps between words. Often inhibited.
Dir. Regularity of slant.
Cont. False connections, connected or disconnected.
Dim. Large middle zone – dominant.

Examples 15, 32, 36 and 42.

EnAP (Nervous)

F. Ornamentations. Unnecessary prolongations. Irregular. Large capital letters (vanity, inferiority complex). Also irregular spacing and layout. Sometimes artificial.
Pr. Irregular, rather light, blurred, often spasmodic, never very firm or regular.
Sp. Precipitated, accelerated, irregular.
Dir. Irregular slant.
Cont. Irregular.
Dim. Irregular. Inconsistent writing. Often graceful, mannered, original.

Examples 9, 14, 17, 26, 31 and 58.

nEAS (Phlegmatic)

F. No exaggerations of any sort. Often alert, vivacious, always controlled and disciplined. Contained, proportionate. Semi-angular, semi-rounded.

Pr. Never too strong or too heavy but always firm with medium tension. Often light or well nourished.

Sp. Supple, accelerated. Between slow and precipitated.

Dir. Never rigid. Often nuancée in the slant, it varies very little (homogeneous). Contained.

Cont. Rather connected. Rarely overconnected. Often grouped and combined.

Dim. Mainly moderate. Well proportioned in all three zones.

Examples 13, 43, 44 and 49.

nEAP (Sanguine)

F. Ample. Rounded. Fluent, with movement. Often embellished capitals; curved, spirals.

Pr. Well sustained, vigorous but may vary from one sanguine to another, from heavy or pasty to light but always constant. At times in relief.

Sp. Sometimes precipitated, more often poised. Rarely rapid.

Dir. Fluent. Often vertical, sometimes slightly right slanted, rarely left.

Cont. Usually grouped or disconnected.

Dim. Very variable from one sanguine to another.

Examples 10, 27, 55 and 62.

nEnAS (Apathetic)

F. Regular, at times even rigid with no surprises. Often monotonous. Stagnant.

Pr. Heavy. Sharp-pointed. Can be firm and neat or blurred and clogged.

Sp. Mostly slow. Rarely poised.

Dir. Mostly right slanted. Rarely vertical or left. Baselines well sustained.

Cont. Mostly connected or grouped.

Dim. Often prolonged downwards.

Examples 19, 20, 35 and 38.

nEnAP (Amorphous)

F. Distended ovals, long and narrow or spread on the line. Often deformed; lacking control. Large capitals spread. Impulsive.

Pr. Flabby. Blurred. Light or pasty, never firm, containing no signs of aggression.

Sp. Slow. Inconsistent. Without great life.
Dir. Lacks firmness. Lines often undulant. Lacks orderliness. Uncertain.
Cont. Lacks backbone, firmness, structure. Habitual simplicity. Conventional.
Dim. Undisciplined.

Examples 23, 56, 59, 60 and 61.

Supplementary Factors

To the three fundamental factors which constitute the character (emotivity, activity and responsiveness) Le Senne added a few 'supplementary factors'. The most important of these are:

1. Broadness of the field of consciousness;
2. Analytical intelligence;
3. Egocentricity/Allocentrism;
4. Will.

Broadness of Consciousness The most significant of these is the broadness of the field of consciousness. In the course of a life the field of consciousness may vary from large to narrow and vice versa, depending on external factors. If the mind sticks to a specific object without any distraction whatsoever, and observes this object isolated from other perceptions, then the field of consciousness is narrow (nL). If ideas and sensations form a continuously flowing unity then the field of consciousness is large (L).

All emergencies narrow the field of consciousness. But the degree to which this effect is produced depends on character; certain minds are larger than others.

G. Heymans in his book, *Psychologie des Femmes*, states that 'in women, on average, the intensity of consciousness is higher and the field of consciousness narrower than in men', (depending on emotivity). This is a debatable statement, but very possible.

The impressions received by a 'narrow' character are more intense because he or she isolates them from surrounding impressions.

The 'large' character tends to receive impressions in perspective with the surroundings, in a more diffuse light and with less intensity.

People with a *large field of consciousness* have aerated and harmonious writing, nuancée, well nourished, with open curves, occasionally stylized and in relief. The Formlevel is high. Examples 5, 6, 17 and 66.

The *writing of nL people* is monotonous, usually cramped and/or small, regular, almost automatic, squeezed or compact, often tangled, regressive, often infantile (unorganized) and weak. Examples 12, 18, 19, 20, 22, 28, 30, and 36.

Analytical Intelligence G. Heymans gives the definition of an intelligent person as 'he who arrives sooner and better than others to the right conclusion'. Le Senne defines intelligence as twofold: 'pure appreciation of value' and 'reflection, abstraction and the consequent analysis of their products'. Here we will take intelligence to be the ability to understand quickly and correctly incoming information in as large and as varied an area as possible, and to make quick deductions from the logical combination of accumulated information and experience, plus imagination and memory. There is, of course, 'Generalizing' intelligence and 'Particularizing' intelligence but these are orientations of intelligence rather than intelligence itself.

The *written signs of intelligence* are varied, uncertain and depend very much on the personality of the writer. They differ from character to character, from temperament to temperament. As a general rule, the writing is supple, rapid and combined, limpid and aerated. Layout is well organized and clear (though not necessarily). Movement is rhythmic, slightly irregular and grouped. Examples 3, 4, 5, 8, 46, 57, 64.

Egocentricity/Allocentrism The human conscious has two primordial tendencies: the 'I' and the 'other'. When the 'I' is put in the centre of attention, the tendency is egocentric (Eg.). For the egocentric conscious 'other' is but an object. On the contrary, when the conscious is identified with 'other' and can see the 'I' from the other's point of view, then the tendency is allocentric (nEg.).

To distinguish Eg/nEg. from egoism/altruism, it must be made clear that each one of the first can be either of the second.

The distinction between Eg. and nEg. is very important in characterology.

The *Eg. writing* is mainly large or medium size, with regressive movements, centripetal short finals or very prolonged towards the right or the left, big loops, spirals, looped garlands, large signature (not necessarily disproportionate), and spindle-shaped strokes, slanted to the left or vertical. Examples 14, 27, 42, 50, 56, 59, 60, 61 and 63.

The *nEg. writing* is progressive, spontaneous, centrifugal, rapid, with garlands or semi-angular garlands, slanted to the right or vertical, with relief or light pressure, medium to small dimensions, and often nuancée. Examples 3, 5, 6, 8, 11, 45, 46, 64, 65 and 66.

Will is not a specifically psychological term. It is the aptitude to actualize (or realize) one's intentions. Each voluntary action, preceded and defined by an idea, presupposes reflexion (intelligence) and responsibility. Actions which do not fulfil this rule do not depend on will.

The procedure of will consists of four stages:

1. the *concept* of a project;
2. the *deliberation* (consideration of best possible action);
3. the *decision* (choice of best action);
4. the *execution* of the concept to the end.

The final product is the proof of authenticity of will.

The most common malfunctions of the will, happen at the stages of '*deliberation*' – where the individual weighs the pros and cons of action and stops there, – of '*decision*' – some individuals will ask around subconsciously trying to get others to decide for them and usually take the less painful, or the easiest path, to avoid responsibility, – or of *execution* – the impulsive or erratic individual will not pursue his goal through lack of consistency.

Although the will is an intentional action, it is closely connected to the needs.

Will is the expression of self, as well as of the whole personality, the unconscious motivations, social education, etc.

The graphic signs of will are: firmness of the stroke, spontaneity and regularity of movement, firm t bars (long or short but always well sustained), angles, clubs, and usually dominance of the vertical axis over horizontal (irrespective of slant), in relief, often precise, robust and homogenous. The signature is determined, often underlined. Examples 4, 7, 10, 21, 27, 37, 49, 64 and 69.

Note: *Obstinate will* does not have the same signs. The writing may be less angular and the t bars may form the figure of 8, the pressure will still be firm, often though thick or blurred.

Carton – Hippocratic Temperaments

Hippocrates, the fifth-century *BC* Greek physician, first developed an understanding of bodily fluids with their associated temperaments. This idea has rung through the centuries. 'These possibilities exist since birth. It is their development which characterizes the growth of each person; it is their realization which will ensure this person's future. All human beings do not have the same possibilities and the mosaic of powers which constitutes their temperament must be known if we want to direct, orient or treat them.'* And Dr Paul Carton in his book, *Diagnostic et conduite des tempéraments*† supports this last statement by saying, 'The study of temperaments is one of the most important means to overall understanding of the human being.'

Temperament is a mental tendency in the individual – congenital or acquired, 'a dynamic state represented by the totality of physical, psychological and biological possibilities of the individual', says Dr Vannier. It dominates one or more of the four fundamental instincts of life: the 'motor' instinct (also called 'unifying') which coordinates decisions taken according to aptitudes, tastes and the physiological and intellectual possibilities of the individual; the 'cerebral' (also called 'psychic') which directs thinking, reasoning, searching and understanding, the 'vital' (or thoracic) which incites respiration and development; and the 'nutritive' (or abdominal or 'material') instinct which sees to the nutritive and reproductive needs.

There are four anatomical systems that serve these dominant and fundamental instincts: the 'osteomuscular' system which holds the whole body together and is therefore called the 'unifying' system; the 'nervous' which, incorporating the brain, the cerebellum, the medulla and the plexus of nerves, coordinates, regulates, conserves, warns, protects, etc.; the 'respiratory' incorporates the heart, veins, arteries and lungs, which feed the whole body with oxygen and keep us alive; and the 'digestive' and 'reproductive' systems incorporate the digestive organs (stomach, intestines), the transforming organs (kidneys, bladder) and the reproductive organs (genitals, external and internal) which constitute the abdominal factory that sees to our material needs of growth and reproduction.

The ancient Greeks, the Egyptians, the Hebrews and the Indians believed that there are four body fluids (also called 'humours') and that each temperament is caused by the predominance of one over the others. These four body fluids are:

the bile – or green bile – corresponding to the Choleric temperament;

the atrabile – or black bile – corresponding to the Melancholic temperament;

the blood, corresponding to the Sanguine temperament; and

the phlegm – or mucus – corresponding to the Phlegmatic temperament.

They went on to say that the fluids correspond with the four primordial elements of fire, earth, air and water, and with the four fundamental qualities of matter: dry, cold, hot and humid, which, in

* L. Vannier, *Typologie et ses Applications Thérapeutiques*, G. Doin, Paris, 1955.

† Librairie Le François, Paris, 1961.

turn, correspond with the four states of matter: ether, solid, gas and liquid.

Dr Carton gives an interesting table of correspondences of the four temperaments:*

	Phlegmatic (lymphatic)	*Sanguine* (sanguine)	*Choleric* (bilious)	*Melancholic* (nervous)
Elements	Water	Air	Fire	Earth
States of matter	Liquid	Gas	Ether	Solid
Organic chemistry	Hydrogen	Oxygen	Nitrogen	Carbon
Vital qualities	Humid	Hot	Dry	Cold
Force	Physical	Vital	Unifying	Spiritual
Sphere	Instinctive	Animistic	Volitive	Intellectual
Parts of the body	Abdomen	Thorax	Limbs	Head
Systems	Digestive	Cardiopulmonary	Osteomuscular	Nervous
Humour	Phlegm	Blood	Bile	Atrabile
Functions	Digestion	Respiration	Execution	Reflection
Manifestations	Instinct	Sentiment	Will	Intelligence
Expressions	Material	Life	Synthesis	Thinking
Ages	Childhood	Adolescence	Old	Adult
Seasons	Winter	Spring	Autumn	Summer
Vices	Sensuality	Hatred	Undisciplined	Foolishness
Qualities	Asceticism	Love	Saintliness	Genius
Nation	Agriculture	Communications	Government	Finance
Industry	Manufacture	Commerce	Direction	Research
Arithmetic	Division	Multiplication	Addition	Subtraction
Colours	Blue	Red	White	Yellow

It is a fact that, among 100 company directors, for example, the vast majority is of a Choleric temperament; the Melancholic temperament is better in research than any other; and, of the people who suffer from, say, cardiovascular discomfort, the majority belongs to the Sanguine temperament.

Everybody has at least three (if not all four temperaments) in their biological constitution, but in differing proportions. A temperament in equilibrium has the four elements – water, air, fire and earth – in balance.

The Phlegmatic Temperament is calm and stable, passive and slow, relatively unconscious. He needs time to absorb situations and impressions. Few things ever trouble him. He likes routine in his life and in his business. He is consistent and wise, loyal in his feelings and traditional in his habits. He avoids exalted and agitated people; they trouble him. He has no enthusiasm in his activities and is slow in the execution of his job. He is precise and punctual, capable and

* *Diagnostic et Conduite des Temperaments*, Librairie Le François, Paris, 1961.

competent despite his apparent carelessness. He doesn't misuse his energy, his movements are sober, precise and slow. He is very observant and has a good memory, particularly for concrete and physical things. But his imagination is weak. He prefers to use instruments of precision. His instinct of preservation is very developed. He is prudent and fears the unknown, danger, fights, violence and avoids them, without shame. But if he finds himself involved in such a situation, he defends himself with ferocious and astonishing tenacity.

He can be an engineer, mechanic, scientist, soldier, employee; because of his abilities of repetition, execution, comparison and measure, he could do any job requiring these qualities.

His *writing* is slow, round, thick, quiet. The rhythm is even, at times heavy, manifesting laziness in the use of muscles. Movement is unctuous and heavy, lacking in enthusiasm. The stroke is blurred, filiform, connected, undulant. The forms are often low, wider on their base – never firm. Examples 19, 35, 48 and 53.

The Sanguine Temperament is sociable, passionate, impulsive and jovial. He is full of *joie de vivre*, likes nature and adapts easily to every environment. Dazzling and overflowing, he is destined to exteriorization. He likes movement, physical activities, contact, adventures and amorous conquests. He has a practical mind and a great heart. He likes travelling and he is usually optimistic, sensual, greedy and full of vitality. He switches readily from cordial behaviour to combative, aggressive reactions.

He may be a commercial traveller, industrialist, financier; good in public relations, marketing, executive positions, advertising, artistic work.

His *writing* is enthusiastic, euphoric, optimistic, exuberant, with ample, dynamic gestures, large, connected, rapid or poised, full, well nourished, superelevated, with spirals, round, dilated, animated, often with unnecessary strokes. Examples 4, 10, 22, 25, 27, 47, 54, 64 and 67.

The Choleric Temperament is disciplined and organized, energetic, firm, serious, sober, reflective, decisive. His intelligence is profound, prompt and brilliant but his memory often fails him. He is dignified, laconic, ethical and just, objective and positive. He respects others and expects them to keep to their word, as he does. He has great ability to concentrate, think and reason. He is the intellectual par excellence. He prefers the 'concrete' to the 'abstract' and, as his feelings are not very well developed, he sees, or prefers to see, only the evident. He is a fierce fighter who doesn't abdicate easily. Emotionally he is vulnerable.

He is mainly found in the academic world. He is also a director in business. His creative and executive talents, together with his tenacity, will-power and energy, could make of him an apostle, a leader or a fanatic.

His *writing* is rhythmic and intense but not always rapid. Sober, firm, precise, moderate, rather angular and constant. He doesn't waste time in big gestures and directs movement towards his object with diagonal strokes, long prolongations downwards (like a runner's spikes), sharp endings and many cross-shaped forms. Examples 21, 34, 46 and 65.

The Melancholic Temperament is perpetually dissatisfied, pessimistic, introverted, reflective, orderly, anxious, meticulous, serious and reserved. He worries, he feels badly placed, inadapted, uprooted in the real world. He rebels against his surroundings, feels hostile in society, he is distrustful. Extremely sensitive and emotive, he can be vindictive, susceptible and grudging, irritable, versatile and egocentric. He has an inquisitive mind and needs to know everything that goes on around him. He has a very creative imagination and speculates on abstract thought. He is the great intuitive thinker. His intelligence is profound and prompt, his mind is complicated.

He is usually unstable in his profession until he comes to terms with his instability. Could be a researcher, philosopher, psychologist, teacher, lawyer, poet or painter (when he is artistic).

His *writing* is rising, rapid, fragile, very irregular and simple, narrow, dry, small or condensed, rigid and mechanical when he is a 'cerebral Melancholic' (examples 2, 8, 12 and 30); or complicated, illegible, confused, bizarre, animated but still irregular and agitated when he is a 'sensitive Melancholic' (examples 5, 9, 33, 48, and 58).

These are the four temperaments. But almost no one has only one, pure temperament. We all have one dominant, a second auxiliary, a third and a fourth, which may vary or alter, sometimes after a traumatic experience or a dramatic change in life. Therefore, the written signs are always modified by the second and third temperament's influence.

Koechlin St Morand – Mythological (Planetary) Types

This system corresponds with the four temperaments and consists of eight types of behaviour characteristic of the planets or the gods after which they are named.

The mythological types are symbolic of the human evolution. They are usually presented in the form of a cycle, progressing anticlockwise (see below).

Diagram 3 *The Mythological (Planetary) Types*

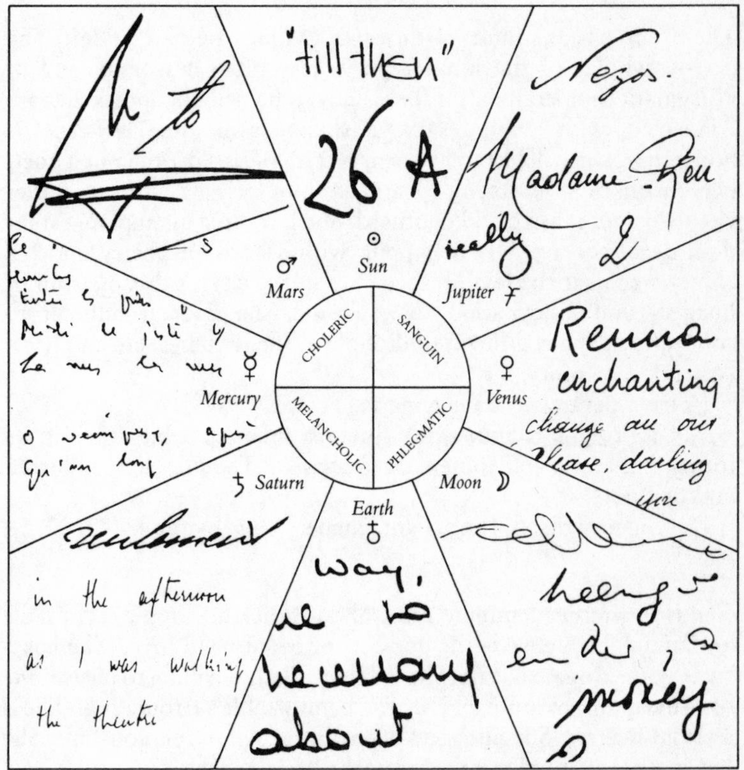

All human beings, if they live long enough, go through a sequence of transformations. We start from Earth which, containing both water and solid matter, is the origin and source of life.

The Earth is simple and practical, thoughtful and concrete. Materialistic, concise, objective, with solid judgement based only on facts. She (often a woman) has original ideas (when superior type). Methodical and orderly, she is the great realist.

Her temperament is a combination of Phlegmatic and Melancholic.

Her *writing* is simple, regular, medium or small, orderly, connected, concentrated and in straight lines. Often inelegant. The strokes descend towards the ground. The t bars are placed low or very low. Loops are basic and simplified. Capital letters are formed without pretentions. Pressure is heavy, pasty. Movement is square on the base line. The i dots are placed low, near the letter.

Dominant signs: heavy, square, clumsy, sensible. Examples 10, 18 and 27.

The Moon has an affinity with water. (Moon affects the tides.) The person who is of the lunar type is very often a woman and of Phlegmatic temperament. If she is active, she will like sports that are connected with water (sailing, skiing, swimming). If she is non-active, she will like to live near water. She is a dreamer or a poet; her unconscious is strong (instincts, impulses, etc.). She is rather vague, naive, evasive and confused. She likes to contemplate rather than decide or act. She is happier with a book of poetry under a cherry tree near the lake, rather than in the city. A dreamer full of imagery and imagination. A romantic, she finds it difficult to concentrate, she is difficult to discipline, she is vulnerable and has a very good memory.

Her temperament is Phlegmatic.

Her *writing* is round, slow, sinuous, inflated, a bit vague in its forms, imprecise and somewhat indecisive. The pressure is blurred and/or runny.

Dominant signs: filiform, light, vague, loops. Examples 17, 23, 54 and 56.

Venus is another feminine type. She is graceful, supple, adaptable and amiable. (Venus is the goddess of beauty and love.) She has a sweet, affectionate nature. She is subjective and willing to please. She likes harmonious atmospheres and comfortable surroundings. She is a jovial hostess. She also gets deeply attached in relationships. She has a sense of rhythm and is attached to the arts.

Her temperament is Phlegmatic and Sanguine.

The *writing* is elegant, always conforming with the current style, of medium size, rounded, mostly connected, with dominant middle zone, rather short lower zone. All forms are in garlands and cups. Starting and ending strokes are curved. The pressure is often velvety or thick; rarely thin.

Dominant signs: curves, also the middle zone and garlands. Examples 25, 47 and 48.

Jupiter is the father of the gods and the ruler of the Universe. He is paternal. A good organizer, realistic, cordial, influential. Spontaneous, but also reflective. He sees big. He is charitable and communicative, authoritative and vain, but also choleric and impatient.

His temperament is Sanguine.

His *writing* is well organized, often conventional and conformist, clear, inflated, large and with arabesques. The lower zone has big loops. Some lassos, mainly in the initial strokes, and often prolonged upwards. It is not necessarily always aesthetic.

Dominant signs: cylindrical movements, large arabesques. Examples 31, 54 and 55.

The Sun is the god of light. His judgement is clear and lucid and based on consolidated points of view. He is orderly and sees the large view. He intensely dislikes mediocrity. He is ambitious and naturally authoritative. He is the chief. A perfectionist, he is also selective and demanding. For some he is an idealist, for others a mystic, but always an aesthetic.

His temperament is Choleric and Sanguine.

His *writing* is a noble writing. Rhythmic, in relief, vertical, tall, well laid out. There are many arcades. The capitals are typographic and the writing is aesthetically proportioned. It is grouped or juxtaposed, prolonged upwards or superelevated. The t bars are firm. Lines are straight, stroke is tense, arcades and curves are firm but supple. Pressure is often spindle-shaped and distinct.

Dominant signs: typographical overall. Tall letters, elegant capitals. Examples 2, 13, 15, 16 and 34.

Mars is the god of war. He is energetic and active, determined, courageous, forceful, combative. He has plenty of initiative and takes on responsibility. He is instinctive, strong willed and impulsive. He only thinks after the event. He is quick on the attack and likes arguments.

His temperament is Choleric.

The *writing* is dynamic, heavy, with flying strokes, turbulent. It is big, carefree, with a slant to the right, animated, prolonged, angular and pointed. It has many crosses and lightning-shaped strokes. Some letters are superelevated, t bars are thrown towards the right and placed high in a gesture of independence. There are clubs and sword-like strokes. Pressure is firm and decisive.

Dominant signs: lightning movements, clubs, crosses. Rising. Examples 21, 22 and 37.

Mercury is the god of commerce and communication. He is astute, receptive and clever. Quick to profit from anything new. He is a good improviser but also an excellent psychologist. He understands quickly the situations between people and would be excellent in psychotherapy, in law, in commerce, as well as in teaching. He is cerebral and intellectual, not always stable.

His temperament is Choleric and Melancholic.

His *writing* is small, rapid, irregular, fine, jumpy, simplified. Often the i dots and accents are connected to the next letter. The lines are sinuous, undulating. The t bars are fine and in the form of aerials. Upper extensions are low and rather sinuous. Capital letters are small, and so is the lower zone (to save time). The stroke is sharp pointed and generally gives the impression of many small irregularities.

Dominant signs: needles, pointed ends, fragile direction of the stroke, rapid writing, small, irregular, with little triangles and lots of interruptions. Examples 1, 5, 8, 33, 44, 45 and 46.

Saturn is the mature, sensitive and receptive grandfather of the gods. He is the profound thinker, scientist, idealist, loner. He never seeks the company of others; he is independent and keeps to himself. His thinking is logical and objective. His imagination is rather poor, but he has great powers of concentration. He is cohesive and can analyse deeply.

His temperament is clearly Melancholic.

His *writing* is sober, concentrated, narrow, angular, dry and lacks warmth. Simple and simplified, with no ornamentation, exaggeration or excess and with descending lines, it is severe and serious.

Dominant signs: angularity, narrowness, continuity, small irregularities. Firmness. Examples 12, 34, 43 and 69.

No one, or almost no one, belongs to one type alone. All of us have three-five types; what matters is which one is dominant.

The planetary types are, by their nature, connected with the temperaments.

There has been a tendency to try to correlate the various systems of typology; with mythological types, the effort has been towards finding corresponding functions and attitudes (C. G. Jung) as follows.

Moon Type	intuition introvert	Phlegmatic temperament
Venus »	sentiment introvert	Phlegmatic/Sanguine »
Jupiter »	sentiment extrovert	Sanguine »
Sun »	intuition extrovert	Sanguine/Choleric
Mars »	sensation extrovert	Choleric »
Mercury »	thinking extrovert	Choleric/Melancholic
Saturn »	thinking introvert	Melancholic »
Earth »	sensation introvert	Melancholic/Phlegmatic»
		Melancholic »

Although it is not always as clear-cut as that, however, since there are, for instance, Moon-type people with much thinking and sentiment, and Mercury as well as Saturn with a main function of intuition, it is very rare indeed to find a Venus with a function of thinking, or a Saturn with a main function of sensation.

Maslow – Theory of Motivation

Abraham Maslow, the American humanistic psychologist, devised a theory of motivation based on a hierarchy of needs (see below). The inner nature of individuals, says Maslow, is either neutral or positively 'good'. 'What we call evil behaviour appears to be a

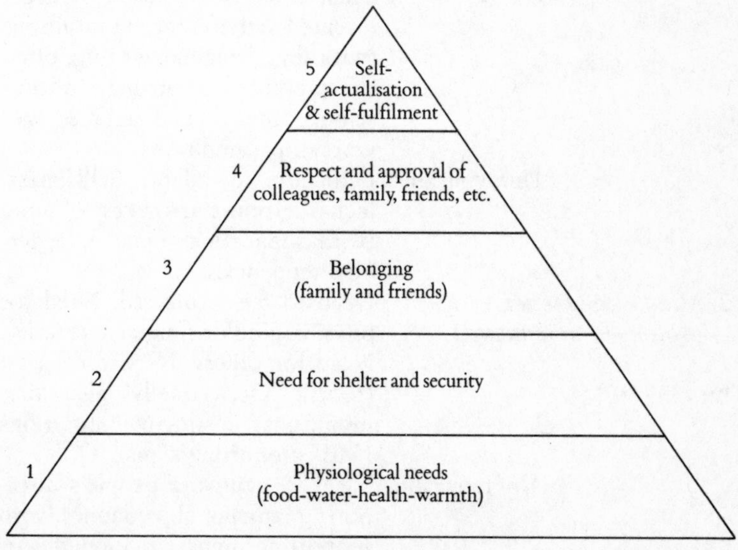

secondary reaction to frustration of this intrinsic nature.' Human beings can be loving, noble and creative and are capable of pursuing the highest values and aspirations. The constitutional differences in individuals generate personal values, i.e. he must satisfy his needs, for example, for salt or love. If deprived of satisfaction, the individual 'sickens and withers' and his growth is stunted.

All these basic needs, says Maslow, may be considered to be simply steps along the 'time path' to general self-actualization, under which all other needs can be subsumed. 'If the inner nature is permitted to guide our life we grow healthy, fruitful and happy.' For Maslow, self-actualization is a goal towards which all human beings move and is experienced as unity of personality, spontaneous expressiveness and full individual identity.

The following analysis may be seen as the graphological validation of Maslow's theory:

1. *Lower extensions prolonged*: Ex. 53, 56 (See also 'Prolonged downwards' and 'Lower extensions')	Strong instincts. Dominance of primitive forces. Need for security. Need to secure the satisfaction of basic material needs (food, warmth, reproduction). Need for territorial occupation, to establish roots. Need for possessions. Preoccupation with want. Target oriented activity. Strong intuitions (with fine, irregular writing, often sharp-pointed). Strong unconscious; unexplained agonies (gut worry), premonitions.
Unfavourable:	Difficulty to adapt. Selfishness, lack of vision, narrowness of mind (with supporting signs). Exaggerated tendencies.
2. *Middle zone letters prolonged downwards*: Ex. 23, 60	Need to feel protected. Need for physical and/or financial security. Need for others. Need for a past (roots). Occasionally also premonitions, instinctive intuitions (with supporting signs).
Unfavourable:	Need to captivate people's affections in any possible manner (with supporting signs i.e. looped garlands). Cunning selfishness (parti-

cularly if the prolongments curve to the left or end up with a small hook), possessiveness (if supported by other signs, i.e. excessively diminishing letters). Materialistic ambitions for want of security. Uncontrolled tendencies and instincts. Impulsivity.

3. Dominance of middle zone : Need to belong and to be accepted by friends and family, to be integrated within a circle. Preoccupation with everyday life and with matters of the heart. The writer's actions, thoughts and aims are directed towards this target.

Ex. 13, 47

Unfavourable: Narcissism, selfishness, egocentricity (if supported by other signs). Emotionality not always well adapted. Possible hypocrisy.

4. Supperelevations : Need to be recognized and approved by society, friends and colleagues. Need to achieve a status among one's peers. Creativity. Intelligence. Ambition. Indepedence. Activity (with supporting signs).

Ex. 25, 54
(See also 'Supperelevated')

Unfavourable: Egocentrism. Exaltation. Overestimation of self. Importance of own capacities. Inflated self. Pride not always justified or deserved. Touchiness.

5. Upper extensions prolonged : Need for self-fulfilment. Need to achieve, to make a mark, usually motivated by idealism. Rich imagination, active intellect, aspirations, ideas, projects. Enthusiasm. Mystical tendencies. Need for independence.

Ex. 26, 37
(See also 'Prolonged upwards' and 'Upper extensions')

Unfavourable: Illusions. Chimaera (fanciful). Lack of order. Lack of judgement. Possible paranoiac tendencies (with supporting signs).

9

A SUMMARY OF SYSTEMS

The following list contains some of the more common systems currently used in graphology. In alphabetical order, these are:

Gabrielle Beauchataud	The four functions and the two attitudes (Jung) The four temperaments (Hippocrates, Carton) The eight characters (Le Senne, Caille)
Emil Caille	The eight characters (Le Senne)
Dr Paul Carton	The four temperaments (Hippocrates)
Jean Crépieux-Jamin	The laws of writing Harmony The categories Characterology: intelligence morality will
Gobineau and Peron	Graphometry The four components: infantile adult personality indications of abnormality – positive or negative
Walter Hegar	The stroke: speed, pressure, form (Crépieux-Jamin) Symbolism of Space (Pulver) Harmony (Crépieux-Jamin) Rhythm (Klages)
Dr R. Heiss	The three rhythms: movement (C. Gross) space form
Dr Ludwig Klages	Formlevel Polarity The unconscious (Jung)
Hélène Koechlin St Morand	The four temperaments (Hippocrates, Carton) The eight mythological types

Thea Stein Lewinson	Dynamic (introversion–extroversion: Jung) Symbolic (Pulver) Form (written flow)
Jean-Hippolyte Michon	Relationship between thought and handwriting Anatomy of the stroke Towards a universal law of graphology Graphological and psychological signs
Dr Rudolf Pophal	Biological types of motivation: cortex subcortex striatum pallidum
Max Pulver	Symbolism of handwriting Symbolism of the written field Rhythm Ambivalence The unconscious (Jung, Klages, Teillard)
Klara Roman Staempfli	Psychogramme
Dr L. Szondi	The four bodily rhythms: sexual need for value ego contact
Ania Teillard	The unconscious (Jung) Complexes (Jung) The four Functions (Jung) The two attitudes (Jung) Animus–Anima (Jung) Persona (Jung)
R. Trillat	Letter, word, line, page Chimneys
Roda Wieser	The basic rhythm of handwriting

The above are some of the best known and most favoured systems used today. Research and experimentation is currently being carried out in many countries on new psychological theories now applicable to graphology.

There are other 'methods' than those mentioned here. Every graphologist can develop his or her own method of practising or teaching according to his skill, taste, character and temperament.

surged in me in English, in a private letter to L. Durrell and published, as a sort of joke, by him in _Personal Landscape_.

By the end of the month we are leaving for Sicily.

With much love

George Seferis

Example 1. Man 60.

-, vers huit heures du soir,

nant de la chasse suivaient

...ts, à quelque distance de

marchait un piqueur menant

[illegible]

[illegible]

[illegible]

[illegible]

[illegible]

Example 2. Man 60s
(Nobel prize winner for literature).

[illegible]

Example 3. Man 85.

vos bons voeux et
s miens, très sincères.
emercie aussi beaucoup
images!
Bien et travaille
avec toute ma
amitié – Alicia T.

Example 4. Woman 70s.

Example 5. Man 60s.

Example 6. Man 40s.

pathway and I dat think I

Of course if we would get

settle for a reasonable figure

think the time is right yet.

Example 7. Man 48.

wonder if you are free Wednesday
We should arrive back that afternoon
by Olympic — it would be such
heaven if we could all have
dinner together. Out or porridge on

Example 8. Woman 67.

Example 9. Man 65.

I hope you are well - I wish I had seen you here.
I send you my very best wishes for everything your heart may desire.
Yours
Maria

Example 10. Woman 35.

I am not certain what it
is to me ... this hand
but I feel certain I am ...
more than I should ...
presenting you with this spe...
my character.

Example 11. Man 42.

[illegible]

Example 12. Woman 70.

I really cannot wait
see you, I do need to
talk to you so much
LOVE YOU

Example 13. Woman 35.

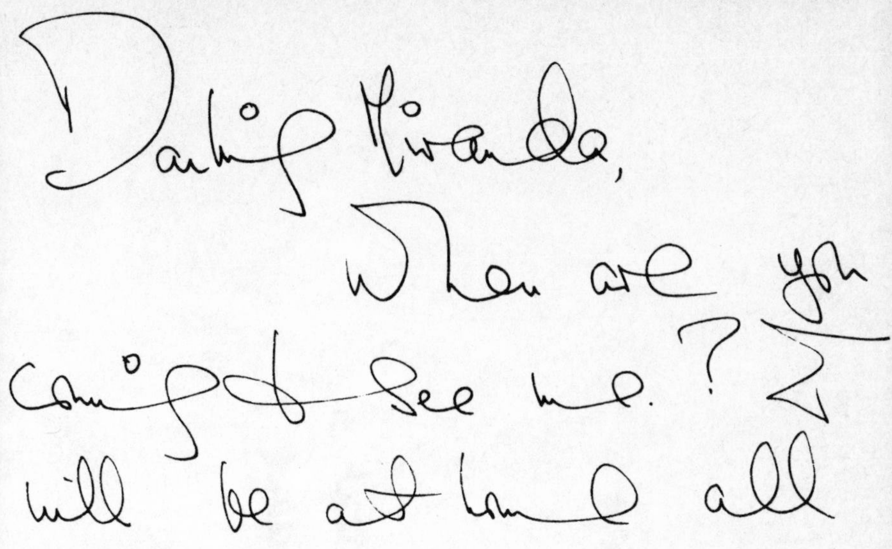
Darling Miranda,
When are you
coming to see me? I
will be at home all

Example 14. Woman 42.

To London unless there
or deliver, simply because
And I have no work
I shan't be there

Example 15. Man 50s.

cherries were you? We'll soon see
man cried; his one fearsome
.p-x. groove in his forehead.
'iend would like a cup of
mock-concern.

Example 16. Woman 22.

to as to move completely.
The other reason for
use replying is not

Example 17. Man 47.

Ekali is a lovely place to live in. We rent a
beautiful house from a kind lady called
Mrs Jatrou.

Example 18. Woman 30.

es nie mehr und Leute, d
helfen könnten findet ma
mehr. Alle Mädchen gehen
Fabrik weil nur da die L
gelt ist.
Ich schreibe lauter Dir
nicht interessieren. Die P.

Example 19. Woman 46.

Example 20. Woman 30.

Example 21. Man 60.

on the 15th then down to
Memphis for Christmas and
back here for a New Years
Eve party. I trust your
holidays will be giddy & gay,
mine will be dull.

Example 22. Man 80.

when I re...
Mother swallow, had
pur tosse sur la fenetre
s, but happily is still
in the nest, so hope
under her little shape
do not understand

Example 23. Man 44.

offered a lot of money by an American
but he would not sell it to him
because the American wanted to take

Example 24. Man 45.

Miranda
Your example of
hand writing
with my
Love
Lynn

Example 25. Woman 45.

Example 26. Man 67.

g to meet you soon
discuss those problems
ed you, dear Count-
my best regards
wishes, with which I
is, yours faithfully

Example 27. Man 40s.

all very beautiful but
at the moment extremely
noisy, Athens dinner
as before! Hope you are
OK. All Love

Example 28. Man 50s.

a heart attack. The Seminar
was a great success, and am
now free to enjoy myself, but
am not sure when I shall be

Example 29. Man 30s.

Florence is beautiful, though
time to leave for Rome
enjoying the novelty of a
first time in Italy.
take care —

Example 30. Man 21.

My Dear
Actually I miss yo
I'm having a really
time and all that
thing. At the G.B

Example 31. Man 30s.

Example 32. Woman 42.

Examples 33 and 33a. Woman 38.

Please find enclosed the invoice for the restoration which has now been completed. Also the estimates for

Example 34. Woman 36.

I hope you enjoy your stay in London. The weather is really nice at present.

Example 35. Woman 55.

20-10-

TO WHOM IT MAY CONCERN

Miss

I have been employer the past one year.
She has proved heself to be ble, hardworking, intelligent, ible and polite.
is competent and ident in her work. She is ys cheerful, and well liked everyone.
She has a gentle, caring e, and an excellent manner with ren. I can highly recommend as a nanny. Yours Truly

[T]elephone no.   Sussex

02   ..h March

Dear Miss

Thank you very much for your [l]etter which I received this morning.

I am very pleased to accept the post [as] nanny with Mr & Mrs. George S. Andreadis [in] Greece.

I look forward to hearing from you regarding the date I shall be joining the family in Athens.

Yours sincerely,

Examples 36 and 36a. Woman 22.

Example 37. Man 50.

recall having a dinner or anything
specific like that, but I do remember
Yann stopping by. He was the tall
16 year old son of another friend who

Example 38. Man 45.

telegram which touched me greatly.
As you will see, I am now living in

Example 39. Man 54.

No Christmas cards this year – So thanks

for yours & have a happy holiday. Do keep in

touch with me – at least let's have that contact.

The rest of my life & I'm 77 will be spent writing.

I'm in the midst of a book on my trips around

the world in 1925 – having a copy when finished.

Fondly,

Example 40. Woman 77.

height to the one which I purloined from you
so very long ago. Please ring my bell and I
shall use it to replace the light bulb for you.

Above: Example 41. Man 30.

een a good day. Despite the fact
orise, and that it ought not
e truth and not being believed.
to see it. Alternatively, perhaps
eding to be liked by all and sundry.
hat as it may, I had given
omething today and it was
as not a good day.

Left: Example 42. Man 20.

o the booklet of
lorries, and also
that I am going
to be away next
weekend o the week-

Example 43. Man 40.

as your mother asked us to

the rest from the time we

s, as well as the first few

ie. It has been nice here, and

Example 44. Man 30.

beautifully penned letter, addressed to Joan
and myself, telling us about the famous
fig tree and enclosing two irrefutable
photographs, and even the proverbial leaf.
The tree, I reckon, would fill most of
our lawn. It must be a delight to see,

Example 45. Man 55.

Cher Monsieur,

Nous devons partir un peu plus tôt que prévu et c'est demain 10 h que nous partons non par le Train, mais par route. Il m'est donc impossible de me rendre à votre aimable invitation et je le regrette. Après les examens des 28 et 29 Janvier, peut être trouverons nous un jour pour goûter la musique Sud Americaine.

Bonnes fêtes de Noël et de Nouvel An.

Respectueusement.

Example 46. Man 17.

Je t'en prie écris-moi quelques
mots. Dis-moi ce que tu fais et
surtout la suite de Michel -
As-tu fini complètement avec les

ez m'a im
; dit-il je proc

Above: Example 47. Woman 70s.

Life in England is
fun but freezing
cold at times.

Left: Example 48. Woman 30s.

Hôpital Dr. Schweitzer

Lambaréné 31. März 1955

Lambaréné

Liebe Madame

Welche Überraschung für Doktor Schweitzer, aus Lambarene einen deutsch geschriebenen Brief zu erhalten! Ihre freundlichen Worte freuen ihn sehr.

Sie finden anbei sein französisches Exemplar des Werk über Johann Sebastian Bach. Wir haben dieses gewählt in dem Gedanken an Mr. Baquet, der vielleicht die deutsche Sprache nicht beherrscht.

Example 49. Albert Schweitzer.

ly appreciate your hos-
lity.
If ever your travel plans
uld include West Texas,
se let us know — we
uld love to welcome and

Left: Example 50. Woman 40s.

May I suggest dinner next week — on
Friday evening 24th perhaps? If you like, ring me on
evening — or I shall ring you on Monday. I do hope
other next week! I so look forward to talking to you.

Example 51. Man 40s.

words long, is a fantasy, but one which has its

es from the real world.

Left: Example 52. Man 40s.

your company and hospitality last night

the evening enormously and really did

Left: Example 53. Man 27.

Below: Example 54. Woman 30s.

alle otto del mattino per

dirmi: se lo passavo a

prendere. E poi, mi ha

detto che anche domani...,

have 3 weeks in
quietly recuperat
It was enormously kind
of you to invite u
on for lunch with
what hospitality

Example 55. Woman 30s.

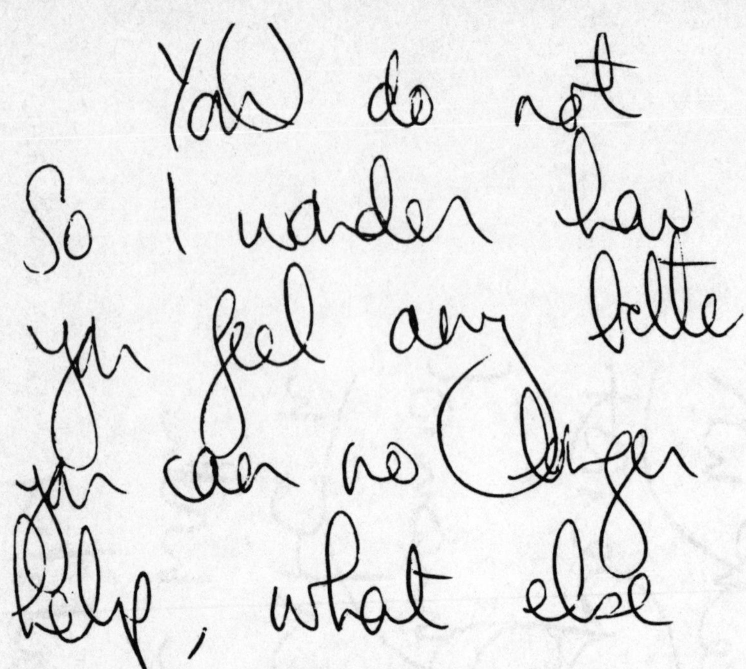

Example 56. Woman 22.

Example 57. Natalia Makarova.

She once wrote a little
excellent prose but many have
forgotten it. + she might
like to(o) know that —

Example 58. Man 50.

also. Sitting outside a
small cafe 9.30pm by
The sea. Explored the
old city today walked
round the walls took

Example 59. Woman 5.

I've got a nervous temperament
some kinda maybe

Example 60. Woman 45.

politici. Io sono convinta che alle
prossime elezioni tutto tornerà come
prima, cioè che si tratti più di
voti di protesta che di cambiate
convinzioni politiche e quindi per
paura di radicali mutamenti tutto

Example 61. 61. Woman nE.nA.P..

P.S. Voulez vous me faire cette petite copie en triple s.v.p.

Lundi soir –

Mon Cher Ami.

Ci joint mes deux petites feuilles
Voulez vous bien détacher chaque
explication avec chaque no
Merci de tout mon cœur
mon ami – j'abuse de votre
complaisance, mais si je puis

Above: Example 62.
Woman 40s.

every day to show everyone his 'new suit of clothes'. Let me say, from my personal experience, a naked Emperor looks bloody ~~sed~~ ridiculous. Most people have no choice but to accept his delusions about himself. He feels uncomfortable when certain people look at him.
I will have to send this letter without a stamp as I have not been given my canteen order today.
Its amazing how these little misfortunes happen when you talk to the Governor about your rights.

Yours ever
[signature].

P.S. SEND
STAMPS.

Left: Example 63.
Denis Nilsson.

There is sand and then
there is rock but what
about the very best of

Example 64. Man 50.

Productivity in the coal industry this year
has been the best since nationalisation
in 1947. As a result the National
Coal Board may start to break
even substantially before the target
date of the start of the 1987–88
financial year.

Example 65. Man 53.

Ma très Chère Renna,

Alors Chère Annie vous êtes
à Londres à quelques heures de Paris par
avion. Quelle joie de vous savoir si près.
Quelle joie de savoir que dans quelques jours
(le 17 exactement) vous serez à Paris et que
nous nous retrouverons.

Merci mille fois de

Example 66. Man 67.

Some presage of an act which our
eyes are compelled to witness has
forced our feet toward the Cathedral.
We are forced to bear witness

M.-T. Iatrou.

Example 67. Woman 20.

rang - wanted lunch -
you must have known!!
O tells me U R off 2
B'kok - Maggie & Don will
adore it - the incredible filth
somehow seems only to

Example 68. Woman 30s.

However, inharmonious implies a very negative personality to which not all people without harmony in their writing fit.

Example 69. Woman 54.

of some people. I am tired now so
I am going to go to bed plus I have
got a Latin Test in the morning first
thing I hate Latin so I am not going
to revise. I don't like SIRB either so I
am not going to do anything for that.
GOOD NIGHT.

Example 70. Woman 17.

BIBLIOGRAPHY

Beauchataud, G., *Apprenez la Graphologie*, J. Oliven, Paris, 1959.
Boons, P., *Le Psychologue devant l'Écriture*, Electa, Brussels, 1977.
Borie, S. *Graphologie: Introduction à la Typologie Planétaire*, EMN, 1973.
Bourdel, L., *Les Temperaments Psychobiologiques*, Maloine, 1961.
Bresard, S., *L'Écriture Empreinte de l'Homme*, Privat, 1976.
La Graphologie Méthode d'Exploration Psychologique, Scarabée, 1984.
Caille, E., *Caractères et Écritures*, PUF, 1963.
Intelligences et Écritures, Mont-Blanc, 1974.
Carton, P., *Diagnostic de la Mentalité par l'Écriture*, Librairie Le François, 1973.
Diagnostic et Conduite des Tempéraments, Librairie Le François, 1961.
Cobbaert, A.-M., *Decouvrez la Graphologie*, Ariston-Tchou, 1978.
Le Guide Marabout de la Graphologie, Le Guide Marabout, 1975.
Corman, L., *Manuel de Morphopsychologie*, Stock, 1958.
Crépieux-Jamin, J., *ABC de la Graphologie*, PUF, 1976.
L'Ecriture et le Caractère, Presse Universitaire de France, 1960.
Les Elements de l'Écriture des Canailles, Flammarion, 1976.
Crépy, R., *L'Interprétation des Lettres de l'Alphabet dans l'Écriture: Les Minuscules*, Delachaux-Niêstlé, 1968;
Les Majuscules, Delachaux-Niêstlé, 1974;
Les Signes, Delachaux-Niêstlé, 1980;
La Signature, L'Ordonnance, Delachaux-Niêstlé, 1983.
Delamain, M. and M., *Decouvrir la Graphologie*, Le Signe, 1980.
Delpech de Freyssinet, *Memento de Graphologie*, Payot, 1955.
Dubouchet, J., *L'Analyse des Phenomènes Physiques et Psychiques et l'Écriture*, Parthenon, 1960.
Faideau, P., *et al., La Graphologie*, MA Editions, 1983.
Foix, P., *La Graphologie*, Payot, 1939.
Methode de Graphologie, Albin Michel, 1972.
Freud, S., *Psychologie Collective*, Payot, 1962.
Gaillat, G. *La Graphologie*, Retz, 1973.
Gille, J.–C., *Introduction à la Psychologie de Moi*, Mont-Blanc, 1976.
Psychologie de l'Écriture, Payot, 1969.
Gonon, M., 'Les 4 Tempéraments,' *La Graphologie*, 178.

Hegar, W., *Graphologie par le Trait*, Vigot Frères, 1962.
Hughes, A., *What Your Handwriting Reveals*, Neville Spearman, 1970.
IIRG, *Cours de Pratique Graphologique*, 1963.
Jung, C. G., *Analytical Psychology*, Routledge & Kegan Paul, 1968.
Jung, C. G. Psychological Types, Routledge & Kegan Paul, 1981.
Dialectic du Moi et de l'Inconscient, Gallimard, 1966.
L'Homme a la Découverte de son Âme, Mont-Blanc, 1970.
Psychologie de l'Inconscient, Georg, 1978.
Types Psychologiques, Georg, 1958.
Present et Avenir, Buchet/Chastel, 1962.
Klages, L., *Expression du Caractère dans l'Écriture*, Delachaux-Niêstlé, 1953.
Graphologie, Stock, 1975.
Les Principes de la Caractérologie, Delachaux-Niêstlé, 1950.
Knobloch, H., *Graphologie*, Econ Verlag, 1971.
Lecerf, A., *Abrégé de Graphologie*', Stock, 1949.
Cours Pratique de Graphologie, H. Dangles, 1968.
Le Gall, A., *Caractérologie des Enfants et des Adolescents*, Presse Universitaire de France 1961.
Le Senne, R., *Traité de Caractérologie*, PUF, 1960.
Maslow, A., *Towards a Psychology of Being*, Van Nostrand Reinhold, 1968.
Michon, J.-H., *Systême de Graphologie*, Payot, 1970.
Mounier, E., *Traité du Caractère*, Seuil, 1947.
Olivaux, R., *De l'Observation de l'écriture à la Compréhension de la Personnalité*, ESF, 1969.
Periot, M., *Hippocrate avait Raison. Synthèse de la Personnalité Humaine pour le Temperament*, Leconte, 1941.
Peugeot, J., *La Connaissance de l'Enfant par l'Écriture*, Privat, 1979.
Pfanne, H., *Lehrbuch der Graphologie*, Walter de Gruyter, 1961.
Pophal, R., *Kimetische Graphologie*, Fischer Verlag, 1968.
Pulver, M., *Le Symbolisme de l'Écriture*, Stock, 1953.
Trieb und Verbrechen in der Handschrift, Orell Fussli Verlag Zurich, 1948.
Resten, R., *Le Diagnostic du Caractère*, l'Arche, 1953.
Méthode de Graphologie, Gallimard, 1952.
Rivere, J., *Graphologie du Caractère*, Mont-Blanc, 1972.
Roman, K. G., *Handwriting – a Key to Personality*, Routledge & Kegan Paul, 1949.
Rougemont, E. de, *Cours Gradué de Graphologie*, Marcel Rivière, 1950.
Saudek, R., *Experiments with Handwriting*, Books for Professionals, 1978.
The Psychology of Handwriting, Books for Professionals, 1978.
Singer, E., *Personality in Handwriting*, Gerald Duckworth, 1954.

St. Morand, H., *Les Tempéraments*, l'Art dans la Circulaire, 1972.
Graphologie. L'Écriture et la Typologie Planétaire, EMN, 1974.
Storr, A., *Jung: Selected Writings*, Fontana, 1983.
Tajan, A. and Delage, G., *Ecriture et Structure*, Payot, 1981.
L'Analyse des Écritures, Seuil, 1972.
Teillard, A., *L'Ame et l'Écriture*, Villain et Belhomme, 1966.
Toulemonde, J., *La Caractérologie*, Payot, 1961.
Vannier, L., *La Typologie et ses Applications Thérapeutiques*, G. Doin, 1955.
Vels, A., *L'Écriture Reflet de la Personnalité*, Mont-Blanc, 1966.
Vernon, M. D., *the Psychology of Perception*, Penguin Books, 1970.
Viaud, G., *Intelligence: Its Evolution and Forms*, Hutchinson, 1968.
Wechsler, D., *La Mesure de l'Intelligence de l'Adulte*, Presses Universitaires, 1973.

INDEX